CRITICAL LANGUAGE AND LITER/

M000190635

Race and Ethnicity in English Language Teaching

Korea in Focus

Christopher Joseph Jenks

MULTILINGUAL MATTERS
Bristol • Blue Ridge Summit

DOI 10.21832/JENKS8422
Library of Congress Cataloging in Publication Data
A catalog record for this book is available from the Library of Congress.
Names: Jenks, Christopher Joseph, author.
Title: Race and Ethnicity in English Language Teaching: Korea in Focus/
Christopher Joseph Jenks.
Description: Bristol, England; Blue Ridge Summit, PA: Multilingual Matters, [2017] |
Series: Critical Language and Literacy Studies: 22|
Includes bibliographical references and index.
Identifiers: LCCN 2017013358 | ISBN 9781783098422 (hardcover: acid-free paper) |
ISBN 9781783098415 (softcover: acid-free paper) | ISBN 9781783098439 (pdf) |
ISBN 9781783098446 (epub) | ISBN 9781783098453 (kindle)
Subjects: LCSH: English language–Study and teaching–Korea (South). | English
language–Study and teaching–Korean speakers. | Second language acquisition–
Social aspects. | Racism in education.
Classification: LCC PE1068.K6 J46 2017 | DDC 428.0071/05195–dc23 LC record
available at https://lccn.loc.gov/2017013358

British Library Cataloguing in Publication Data
A catalogue entry for this book is available from the British Library.

ISBN-13: 978-1-78309-842-2 (hbk)
ISBN-13: 978-1-78309-841-5 (pbk)

Multilingual Matters
UK: St Nicholas House, 31-34 High Street, Bristol BS1 2AW, UK.
USA: NBN, Blue Ridge Summit, PA, USA.

Website: www.multilingual-matters.com
Twitter: Multi_Ling_Mat
Facebook: https://www.facebook.com/multilingualmatters
Blog: www.channelviewpublications.wordpress.com

The policy of Multilingual Matters/Channel View Publications is to use papers that
are natural, renewable and recyclable products, made from wood grown in sustainable
forests. In the manufacturing process of our books, and to further support our policy,
preference is given to printers that have FSC and PEFC Chain of Custody certification.
The FSC and/or PEFC logos will appear on those books where full certification has been
granted to the printer concerned.

Typeset by Deanta Global Publishing Services Limited.
Printed and bound in the UK by the CPI Books Group.
Printed and bound in the US by Edwards Brothers Malloy, Inc.

Race and Ethnicity in English Language Teaching

CRITICAL LANGUAGE AND LITERACY STUDIES

Series Editors: **Professor Alastair Pennycook** (*University of Technology, Sydney, Australia*) and **Professor Brian Morgan** (*Glendon College/York University, Toronto, Canada*) and **Professor Ryuko Kubota** (*University of British Columbia, Vancouver, Canada*)

Critical Language and Literacy Studies is an international series that encourages monographs directly addressing issues of power (its flows, inequities, distributions, trajectories) in a variety of language- and literacy-related realms. The aim with this series is twofold: (1) to cultivate scholarship that openly engages with social, political, and historical dimensions in language and literacy studies, and (2) to widen disciplinary horizons by encouraging new work on topics that have received little focus (see below for partial list of subject areas) and that use innovative theoretical frameworks.

Full details of all the books in this series and of all our other publications can be found on http://www.multilingual-matters.com, or by writing to Multilingual Matters, St Nicholas House, 31-34 High Street, Bristol BS1 2AW, UK.

Other books in the series

Contents

Series Editors' Preface

For racial minorities, racialization and racism affect their everyday life. In many parts of world, there are growing incidents of racist harassment and violence, as seen for instance in the United States after the presidential election of 2016 (Okeowo, 2016). These incidents cause long-lasting psychological and emotional damage and at times physical harm to the victims. This does not necessarily mean that all minorities suffer daily from overt bigotry, hate speech or discrimination. Yet, the visible and sensational nature of this type of racism makes people believe that racism is mainly about such cases. For liberal majoritarian people, racism in this form is outrageous and intolerable. Nonetheless, it also seems far removed from their conscience – 'I have friends from all racial backgrounds and I work with students from all backgrounds. I don't see colour, and clearly, I am not racist'.

However, this understanding of racism is misleading. Racism is not just about overt discrimination. It is also about subtle forms of microaggression, which are often unintentional verbal or behavioral indignities that subtly communicate racial insults, disparagement and hostility (Sue *et al.*, 2007). Moreover, racism is deeply ingrained in our social structures, producing institutional inequalities. This institutional or structural racism, together with the colorblind consciousness as seen in the above claim, is characterized as 'racism without racists' (Bonilla-Silva, 2013). The existence of institutional racism will become evident once we scrutinize the following questions: What racial background do most native English-speaking teachers have? Who are likely to be hired, promoted and retained in schools and universities? Who often receive distinguished recognitions, such as awards, honors and rewards? It is clear that in many instances, racially majoritarian people predominate these privileged spaces. Because these practices and structures are so normalized, people do not usually notice the unequal power balance, until it is pointed out.

Here, we might draw a parallel between education and entertainment. In 2015, an outcry erupted against the White predominance of Oscar nominations, which was circulated on Twitter with the hashtag #OscarSoWhite. The massive antiracist campaign for more diversity on social media during 2015 and 2016 resulted in small improvements in the 2017 Oscar nominations.

#EnglishTeachingSoWhite is what Chris Jenks problematizes in this book. He writes from a positionality of a biracial Korean-American scholar, having grown up in the United States and Korea, studied in a doctoral program in England and taught at a university in South Korea. These experiences have led him to critically reflect on how racialization and racism shape and reflect institutional practices of English language teaching (ELT), which has increasingly become a profitable global business. His analysis illuminates the normativity, privilege and commodification of Whiteness within the ELT profession in South Korea and beyond.

The idea of the native and nonnative speaker is deeply bound up with questions of race: 'Both race and nativeness are elements of "the idealized native speaker"' (Romney, 2010: 19). People of color may not be accepted as native speakers (who are assumed to be White): 'The problem lies in the tendency to equate the native speaker with white and the nonnative speaker with nonwhite. These equations certainly explain discrimination against nonnative professionals, many of whom are people of colour' (Kubota & Lin, 2009: 8). Claiming native speakerhood is regulated by all those external judgments that have nothing to do with language, and everything to do with skin color. This is why people of color who consider themselves native speakers may be denied access to this category (or denied access to teaching jobs) while White nonnative speakers (especially if blond) may be given honorary access. The discussion of what counts as a native speaker cannot be abstracted from these prior racial categorizations (Pennycook, 2012).

Issues of race, racialization and racism cannot be understood or discussed in simple terms. As noted above, racism is not only about individual bigotry, but it is also rooted in institutional systems as well as the ways we understand our history, society and culture (Kubota & Lin, 2009). This is why we also have to interrogate such questions historically. Indeed, we might ask, given that the vast majority of teachers of English around the world are people of color, how is it that we are living in and perpetuating an #EnglishTeachingSoWhite world? How do we understand the complex relations between colonial and neoliberal expansion, the spread of English and racism, the role of textbooks and ELT ideologies (Chun, 2016)? How do we understand why today's White settler teachers in Canada and elsewhere still stigmatize children's 'indigenous ways of performing English' (Sterzuk, 2009: 56)? It is for these reasons that Motha (2014: 129) argues for an understanding of 'provincialized English' so that 'inherent in the learning of English would be an intense awareness of the effects of English's colonial and racial history on current-day language, economic, political and social practices'.

Race intersects with other categories, such as gender, language, nationality and social class, requiring us to be cautious of solely focusing on racism in understanding social injustices: It's not just racially majoritarian people who predominate in privileged positions but White, middle-class men. Furthermore, people's social positioning in a particular context is also shaped by their socioeconomic standing, elevating the perceived power of wealthy immigrants of color over the White working class (Kubota, 2015). In addition, each of these social categories is neither uniform nor fixed – the boundaries are often blurred and permeable. Thus, for instance, mixed race identity, as in the case of Jenks, often creates a double-edged status of both privilege and marginalization. As an earlier book in this series *Hybrid Identities and Adolescent Girls: Being 'Half' in Japan* (Kamada, 2010) showed, the hybridity celebrated from some perspectives cannot be worn quite so lightly. While on the one hand the adolescent girls in her study were able to take up positions that traded on their novel status as children of mixed background, they had to deal on the other hand with the notion of being 'half', the idea that they were less than whole, part of a mixture that renders them half Japanese and half something else.

Racialization and racism are also manifested in contextual and complex ways. Although ELT in various parts of the world perpetuates the superiority of Whiteness as various scholars have critically examined (Appleby, 2014; Lee, 2011; Motha, 2014; Stanley, 2013; Takahashi, 2013), the way in which racial and linguistic relations of power manifest in social contexts is never linear across all situations. For instance, the power imbalance could be tilted toward the opposite direction as nonwhite nonnative professionals enact resistance and become oppressors instead (Houghton, 2013).

As Jenks points out, race can be discussed or understood through multiple conceptual threads, including colonialism, linguistic imperialism, ideology, discourse, global capitalism, political economy, critical race theory, critical Whiteness studies and more. Race in ELT is indeed embedded in broader ideologies and social mechanisms. Ideologies of colonialism, imperialism and West-centrism especially in today's global marketing of ELT are promoted by academic, governmental and commercial entities, and they reinforce the superiority of Whiteness, native speakerism and standardized language.

As Jenks illuminates, these ideologies are shaped and sustained through historical, political, legal and economic forces. In particular, capitalist neoliberal ideology supporting the ELT industry commodifies English, English proficiency and English speakers, while simultaneously promoting White normativity. The critiques offered by Jenks invite us to notice and critically understand taken-for-granted assumptions about racialized English and English speakers, which undergird institutional and epistemological racism as seen in employment, pedagogy and semiotic representations in teaching materials.

A critique of #EnglishTeachingSoWhite may arouse uncomfortable feelings among those who have benefited from this system. Even though the critique is intended to problematize structural and ideological injuries of racism, those beneficiaries might interpret it as a personal attack that they do not deserve. This often creates defensive reactions, which further reinforce the colorblind denial of 'we are not racists' or 'we should not call them racists'. This problem was already debated in the field of teaching English to speakers of another language (TESOL) 15 years ago (Atkinson, 2002; Kubota, 2002), and yet it continues to resurface even today. It is indeed an ongoing struggle. In order to establish social justice and equity in our profession, it is essential to make persistent efforts to address structural and ideological problems of racism. To this end, Jenks provides us with valuable insight into how White normativity is ingrained in South Korea's capitalist industry of ELT as well as an important reminder to apply the insight to broader contexts.

Ryuko Kubota
Alastair Pennycook
Brian Morgan

References

Appleby, R. (2014) *Men and Masculinities in Global English Language Teaching.* Basingstoke: Palgrave McMillan.

Atkinson, D. (2002) Comments on Ryuko Kubota's 'Discursive construction of the images of U.S. classrooms': A reader reacts. *TESOL Quarterly* 36, 79–84.

Bonilla-Silva, E. (2013) *Racism without Racists: Color-Blind Racism and the Persistence of Racial Inequalities in the United States* (4th edn). Lanham, MD: Rowman & Littlefield.

Chun, C. (2015) *Power and Meaning Making in an EAP Classroom: Engaging with the Everyday.* Bristol: Multilingual Matters.

Houghton, S.A. (2013) The overthrow of the foreign lecturer position and its aftermath. In S.A. Houghton and D.J. Rivers (eds) *Native-Speakerism in Japan: Intergroup Dynamics in Foreign Language Education* (pp. 60–74). Bristol: Multilingual Matters.

Kamada, L.D. (2010) *Hybrid Identities and Adolescent Girls: Being 'Half' in Japan*. Bristol: Multilingual Matters.

Kubota, R. (2002) The author responds: (Un)raveling racism in a nice field like TESOL. *TESOL Quarterly* 36, 84–92.

Kubota, R. (2015) Race and language learning in multicultural Canada: Toward critical antiracism. *Journal of Multilingual and Multicultural Development* 36, 3–12.

Kubota, R. and Lin, A. (eds) (2009) *Race, Culture, and Identity in Second Language Education: Exploring Critically Engaged Practice*. New York: Routledge.

Lee, E. (2011) Ethical issues in addressing inequality in/through ESL research. *TESL Canada Journal* 5, 31–52.

Motha, S. (2014) *Race, Empire, and English Language Teaching: Creating Responsible and Ethical Anti-Racist Practice*. New York: Teachers College Press.

Okeowo, A. (2016) Hate on the rise after Trump's election. *The New Yorker*. See http://www.newyorker.com/news/news-desk/hate-on-the-rise-after-trumps-election (accessed 1 June 2017).

Pennycook, A. (2012) *Language and Mobility: Unexpected Places*. Bristol: Multilingual Matters.

Romney, M. (2010) The colour of English. In A. Mahboob (ed.) *The NNEST Lens: Non Native English Speakers in TESOL* (pp. 18–34). Newcastle: Cambridge Scholars Publishing.

Stanley, P. (2013) *A Critical Ethnography of 'Westerners' Teaching English in China: Shanghaied in Shanghai*. New York: Routledge.

Sterzuk, A. (2011) *The Struggle for Legitimacy: Indigenized Englishes in Settler Schools*. Bristol: Multilingual Matters.

Sue, D.W., Capodilupo, C.M., Torino, G.C., Bucceri, J.M., Holder, A.M.B., Nadal, K.L. and Esquilin, M. (2007) Racial microaggressions in everyday life. *American Psychologist* 62 (4), 271–286.

Takahashi, K. (2013) *Language Learning, Gender and Desire: Japanese Women on the Move*. Bristol: Multilingual Matters.

1 Introduction: Overview and Objectives

Investigating Race and Ethnicity

This book examines racism and racialized discourses in the English language teaching (ELT) profession in South Korea (henceforth, Korea). The book is informed by a number of different critical approaches to race and discourse, and the discussion below offers one way of exploring how the ELT profession can be understood from such perspectives. Observations made in subsequent chapters are based on the understanding that racism should not be viewed as individual acts of discrimination, but rather as a system of social structures. While the book is principally concerned with language teaching and learning in Korea, the findings are situated in a wider discussion of race and ethnicity in the global ELT profession. The book makes the following argument: White normativity is an ideological commitment and a form of racialized discourse that comes from the social actions of those involved in the ELT profession; this normative model or ideal standard constructs a system of racial discrimination that is founded on White privilege, saviorism and neoliberalism.

Although several investigations of race and ethnicity have been published in recent years (e.g. Curtis & Romney, 2006; Kubota & Lin, 2009a; Motha, 2014; for a seminal collection of journal articles, see also the editorial introduction by Kubota & Lin, 2006), this book is one of the first to focus on how racism props up the ELT profession in one country. A book of this kind is timely because race and ethnicity are complex issues that continue to significantly impact many individuals and communities. The book comes at a time when recent police brutality incidents in the United States have resulted in widespread media coverage of, and debates on, race, racism and racialized discourses. Such issues have coincided with growing racial tensions in Europe regarding immigrants and refugees from Muslim countries. While race and racism are complex issues rooted in a history of oppression and privilege, recent examples of racial discrimination in the United States and Europe have provided both the impetus and discursive means to investigate discrimination in other countries and contexts, such as the ELT profession in Korea that adopts the racial hierarchies from other regions to shape understandings of language proficiency and pedagogy.

Despite the pressing need to understand the ways in which race and ethnicity circulate within nations and are used as tools of oppression and privilege, ELT scholarship has, by and large, failed to address how such issues shape language teaching and learning. Indeed, the comparatively small number of studies conducted on race and ethnicity suggests either that scholars do not know how to address racism in the profession or that this particular area of study is a somewhat low priority issue in the ELT literature. Consequently, many questions remain with regard to how race and ethnicity operate within the ELT profession, and much scholarly attention is needed in order to understand what forms of racialized discourses contribute to the commonsense understandings of language teaching and learning.

The need to study racism, racialized discourses and linguistic discrimination in the ELT profession is especially urgent in a country like Korea. The country is experiencing rapid social, economic and political change and growth. These changes were set into motion by a number of factors leading up to, and during, the Korean War. Accordingly, the United States has an important role in how English language ideologies are constructed in Korea. One outcome of the country's rapidly changing cultural landscape and unique relationship with the United States is an evolving understanding of what it means to be a speaker of English in Korea and who is qualified to teach this language. In addition to understanding how skin color, nationality, ethnicity and language proficiency inform ELT practices, a discussion of race and racism in Korea contributes to larger efforts to eradicate discriminatory practices in language teaching and learning.

While a book of this kind is immediately relevant to scholars concerned with the ELT profession in Korea, the observations made in subsequent chapters contribute to a number of areas of study. For example, the observations made of language teaching and learning in Korea can also advance an understanding of critical approaches to racism in particular, as well as empirical and pedagogical issues pertaining to the ELT profession in general. For instance, a discussion of racism in Korea can be used to critique the extent to which teacher training programs adequately address critical issues in language teaching and learning. Such an exercise can be helpful in advancing teacher training programs in so-called 'inner-circle' countries like the United States and Canada, as universities in this 'concentric region' are responsible for educating large numbers of teachers from around the world (for a discussion of the concentric circles model of Englishes, see Kachru, 1985). Further, a discussion of racism in Korea, and in particular an exploration of how neoliberalism shapes hiring practices in ELT, can provide a framework for understanding how free market principles in education systems in other countries establish the conditions for racial discrimination. To this end, the discussions contained in this book use an understanding of White normativity, saviorism and neoliberalism to identify themes and issues that scholarship must address in future work (e.g. White public spaces in teacher training programs) and explore the extent to which the global ELT profession is complicit in racial and linguistic discrimination (e.g. the promotion of native speakerism).

Before laying out the foundation for this book, it is important to provide a critical reflective account of how my lived experiences shaped the conceptualization and writing of this project. Such narratives are foundational to critical discussions of race and racism, and are underpinned by the belief that the subjectivities of the observer shape how the observed is studied and understood. This reflective account is both an exercise in exploring how my life is related to the issues discussed in this book and an opportunity for readers to examine my positionality in relation to race and racism.

Critical Reflexivity

The present book is the result of several years of teaching in the ELT profession in Korea, as well as over a decade of living in the country. In this sense, this book is based on numerous years of experience in, and participant observations of, language teaching in Korea. These professional and life experiences have shaped who I am as a researcher and explain why the present investigation has been conducted. Furthermore, in preparing this book I have reflected extensively on my own experiences with racism and how these unfortunate situations may have guided me in understanding the issues investigated in subsequent chapters.

I am aware of the highly subjective nature of empirical studies (Woolgar, 1988); that is, I understand that research is based on the subjective realities of the researcher and that objectivity is only achieved through the lens of these subjectivities; therefore, I subscribe to the notion that what we produce in our research is a reflection of who we are as researchers. This reflection extends beyond research interests and disciplinary commitments. The observations that I present in this book, for example, not only reflect my interest in critical issues in ELT, but are also a projection of who I am as a father, husband, biracial Korean American and heritage language learner.

This section represents my attempt to provide a critical reflexive account of the book. That is, how have my subjectivities influenced the observations made in subsequent chapters?

In order to answer this question, an understanding of reflexivity must first be established. Reflexivity 'expresses researchers' awareness of their necessary connection to the research situation and hence their effects upon it' (Davies, 1999: 7). Reflexivity is an investigatory practice; it can be carried out in a number of ways, which may include keeping a journal during ethnographic fieldwork or writing a public account of the potential effects of different research subjectivities (Davies, 1999), such as the discussion contained within this section. My purpose in writing a critical reflection is not to achieve some level of objectivity as understood within academic circles that are guided by positivism, though an argument can be made that a connection between researcher and researched is necessary for *all* ELT scholarship (e.g. Shacklock & Smyth, 1998). Rather, the goal here is to provide an autobiographical account of how I evolved as a person and scholar interested in writing a book of this kind (cf. Okely, 1996). The autobiographical approach to reflexivity is a form of self-analysis, which demonstrates that not only are researcher subjectivities always present in empirical studies, but also that the research process is, in and of itself, a life experience.

Reflexivity is part of a larger investigatory principle that assumes researchers possess multiple identities (and thus subjectivities) that potentially shape the knowledge produced in studies (for an excellent discussion of how an author struggles to manage multiple identities, see Du Bois [2007] and his use of the term *double consciousness*). This principle is often referred to as positionality, which 'recognizes research spaces as sites of struggle, in which researchers risk reinscribing dominant discourses of research participants through their practice' (Crumpler *et al.*, 2011: 57). As Milner (2007: 388) argues, positionality is an important issue to address in critical race scholarship because 'dangers seen, unseen, and unforeseen can emerge for researchers when they do not pay careful attention to their own and others' racialized and cultural systems of coming to know, knowing, and experiencing the world'. In other words, a researcher's position within the process of engaging in investigatory work is a form of knowledge production. Such knowledge, when left unattended to, can create a lens through which the cultural Other is misinterpreted and misrepresented (Milner, 2007). In the most basic form, positionality statements allow the public to know (and appreciate) where the researcher is coming from and how this may have shaped the knowledge produced in an investigation. Low (1999: 297) takes this a step further by stating that positionality statements challenge 'the assumption that fixed standpoints of truth exist'. More importantly, addressing the issue of positionality permits 'those in more advantageous positions to speak in solidarity with (and not on behalf of) oppressed minorities' (E. Lee & Simon-Maeda, 2006: 576). Reflexivity, then, is an investigatory tool that allows researchers to assess their influence on, or positionality within, the research process.

Reflexivity, also commonly practiced in critical race scholarship where researchers employ personal narratives, is a central part of how individuals address and dispel oppressive narratives, discourses and ideologies. In this sense, critical race scholarship uses reflexivity as an investigatory tool to make connections between the individual and wider societal issues. Pennycook (2001) also discusses the importance of questioning the researcher's role in applied linguistics scholarship, what he refers to as self-reflexivity, when providing a critical account of issues central to knowledge production in the profession.

The notion that researcher positionality is bound to the research process suggests a power dynamic. Researchers are in positions of power, and therefore must be aware of, and reflect on, their positionality when engaging in investigatory work, especially studies that analyze marginalized or oppressed individuals or groups. While investigating race and racism in the ELT profession, for example, I must be cognizant of my own participation in knowledge production and how this may create other forms of racialized discourses (for a discussion of what can be done to address the oppressive discourses in the ELT profession, see Chapter 7). That is, scholars should not only engage in a discussion of social rights and injustice, but they must also consider how being in positions of power and privilege influence their research (cf. Kubota, 2015b). In other words, the critical ELT scholar addresses the issue of positionality by engaging in reflexive practices (for an excellent book-length study that includes an extended autoethnographic discussion, see Phan, 2008: 14).

My story: A brief critical self-narrative

Experiencing racism forever changes the way you see the world. When I was a very young child in the 1980s, I remember vividly my first encounter with racism. I was just outside of Seattle in a small town with my family visiting relatives. My brother and I, along with a White cousin, were strolling along the town's quiet sidewalks. It was early in the afternoon. We were not causing any trouble, nor did we do anything to draw attention to ourselves. We were simply walking.

A few rocks rolled in front of us. I looked down to see if I had kicked them. Strange, I thought. A few more rocks came our way. I looked up and noticed two older kids about half a football field away from us. They looked angry and were yelling something. I could not make out what they were saying, but it was clear that the rocks were coming from their direction. I remember to this day the feeling of complete bewilderment. Why were they throwing rocks? As they continued to yell and throw rocks, my cousin said that they were talking about us. I only realized after leaving the situation and having time to take in what had happened that the two kids were yelling Asian slurs. 'Chink' was one of the words thrown in our direction. This defining moment taught me, for the first time, that my racial and ethnic background may upset people, be used against me and represent an object of ridicule. Wu (2002: 7), in his book on the Asian American experience in the United States, talks about how similar experiences taught him that 'The lives of people of color are materially different than the lives of whites, but in the abiding American spirit we all prefer to believe that our individualism is most important'. Experiencing racism early in and throughout my life, coupled with being a biracial Korean American in the United States, I, like Frank Wu (2002: 8), 'alternate between being conspicuous and vanishing, being stared at or looked through'. This complex and complicated alternating life view is one of several reasons why I decided to work in Korea later in my life.

Was my first experience of racism a catalyst for writing this book? Most likely not, but I am aware that having rocks thrown at you while being called racial epithets creates a heightened awareness of the emotional and psychological damage of racism. So while my initial decision to write a book on racial discrimination in the ELT profession was not overtly guided by my unfortunate experience outside of Seattle, my treatment of racial issues in this book is aided by an awareness that racism is not merely an analytic topic that should be exploited for empirical goals. Racism has real-life consequences for individuals. Thus, researchers should make some effort in reflecting on how the responsibilities of conducting research hinder or facilitate their ability to be both an investigator with empirical interests and a 'vulnerable observer' (Behar, 1996).

While it is important to treat victims of racism as individuals with unique experiences, I am also aware that racial discrimination extends beyond individual acts of oppression or exploitation (Delgado & Stefancic, 2012). That is to say, racism is a projection of wider societal issues. I understand, for example, that the two kids in the small town outside of Seattle were not simply throwing rocks, but were also projecting many years of racialized socialization. As a critical race scholar, I am committed to understanding how individual acts of discrimination are connected to larger socialization processes. As a victim of racism, I select topics that reflect the questions that I am personally invested in, such as how a privileging of Whiteness in society compels individuals to feel threatened by, for example in my situation, Asian Americans. I am particularly interested in understanding how White normativity – like the discourses and ideologies that circulate within society that tell children that it is acceptable to throw rocks and hurl racial epithets at ethnic minorities – shapes our understanding of what it means to be a speaker of English. As a vulnerable observer, however, I would be careless not to acknowledge that while White privilege exists in language teaching and learning, Korean Americans are above many ethnic groups in a global ELT racial hierarchy that oppresses many professional communities. That is, being a biracial Korean American is a form of racial privilege. My ethnic status affords me occupational rights that are not available to other instructors of different ethnicities (see Chapter 4). One of the goals of this book is to identify and explore what discourses and ideologies drive such privilege.

My decision to focus on White normative discourses (e.g. privilege and saviorism) in subsequent analytic chapters was not made during the early stages of writing this book. The analytic chapters are an expression of my interests evolving over time as I reviewed critical race scholarship and reflected on my own experiences with racism. I initially envisioned a book that focused on racism from the perspectives of instructors of color, which would have allowed me to demonstrate that their experiences should not be viewed through a single lens. However, my focus shifted as I noticed that White normativity is an underexplored issue in ELT scholarship (many studies are based on examining the cultural Other, a historical artifact of language teaching and learning). This new focus also allowed me to better understand the root cause of racial discrimination in the ELT profession. That is to say, I wanted to know more about the discourses and ideologies that individuals rely on to carry out racial discrimination, rather than, or in addition to, understanding the lived experiences of teachers of color.

Through my reading of the literature (see Chapter 2), I have come to view racism as a system of racial hierarchies that ascribes identities and social categories to the oppressed, such as novice, incompetent, learner, non-native and foreigner. These categories allow dominant groups to maintain their positions of power. In my many years of experiencing various forms of racism, I have learned that my racial and ethnic identities are bound to similar hierarchies and are used to maintain the same power dynamics. I have come to learn, for example, that the many slurs used to emasculate me as an Asian American when I was younger are simply efforts by White Americans to maintain their positions of power and privilege. Again, I am also aware that being a biracial Korean American can afford me certain privileges in other contexts, such as the ELT profession in Korea. Therefore, when I examine how racialized discourses disadvantage teachers of color, I cannot detach myself from their plight; we all belong to the same racial hierarchy that privileges and oppresses. My analytic observations may allow me to maintain an observer position in their world, but my life experiences are forever connected to theirs. I will always be connected to the participants that I examine in this book because of our shared participation in, and resistance to, racialized discourses. In this respect, the observations and suggestions that I make in this book are an extension of my life experiences.

Although I would not wish racism on anyone, my experiences with racial discrimination have been valuable learning events. For example, being a victim of racism has forced me to think on many occasions about how racialized discourses come into being. This critical reflection does not simply happen, however. Racism first leads to an emotional response (e.g. anger), which then gives way to a more cerebral state that asks questions and seeks answers. I will use a more recent example of racism to illustrate this point.

Much later in my life when I was living in England and pursuing a doctoral degree, I was told by an acquaintance from a Western European country that I was not a 'proper American'. This label stemmed from a discussion the said acquaintance was having with my roommate at the time about his 'White friend' who *was* a 'proper American'. The conversation led to an emotional response that was not too dissimilar to my feelings after having rocks thrown at me. I believe he meant no harm, but I was left speechless, confused and somewhat angry. Why would someone believe that the United States is a racially homogenous country? I have experienced racism many times before, but like my encounter outside of Seattle, the conversation was a defining moment. Being labeled an illegitimate American in England by a Western European made me realize that racialized discourses commonly circulated in the United States exist in other regions of the world. The perpetrator in this instance had been conditioned to view the United States as a White nation, where the authenticity of an individual's nationality is bound to race (for a similar critical reflexive account in the Canadian context, see Kubota, 2015b). This limited and racialized view of nationality is based on a discourse that privileges the predominantly White institutions that control the United States while forgetting the minorities and peoples of color who contribute to the country in significant ways. As a Korean American, I have intimate knowledge of how being a person of color in the United States, especially one of Asian heritage, means being viewed at times as an outsider or foreigner (cf. Wu, 2002). Just this past year, for instance, I was asked 'my country of origin' by a White American academic at a conference in the United States because I apparently have 'a bit of an accent'. Microaggressions like this are not uncommon. Indeed, I knew from previous experiences that the Asian-equals-foreigner assumption is widespread in the United States, even among educated academics who are ostensibly 'trained' in dealing with multicultural and multilingual issues. Nevertheless, my encounter in England was especially revealing because I did not realize at the time that the racial hierarchies that I grew accustomed to in the United States existed in other countries and were available to anyone exposed to 'American culture' (e.g. popular music, political systems and Hollywood movies). In other words, I learned that racialized discourses, such as the many images that present the United States as a racially homogenous country, get circulated from one region to another (for a collection of studies that examine racism in different contexts, see Hall, 2008). For many people, these racialized discourses may be the only exposure to 'American culture' they have. For example, the racial hierarchy that existed in the US military before and during the Korean War, and more specifically the differences in how Black and White soldiers were treated, is a form of racism that helps perpetuate certain stereotypes and ideologies in other countries.

My memory of having my nationality questioned because of my race stayed with me after I completed my doctoral program, and was particularly relevant when I applied for university teaching positions in Korea. During my time searching for work, and through my 18 months of teaching at a Korean university, I internalized the possibility that my biracial background would hinder me professionally in some way. I was particularly concerned that prospective employers would not hire me because of my racial background. Although I have no evidence to suggest that I was discriminated against during (and after) my job search, the impact of my previous experiences with racism, including unconnected episodes in Korea when I was yelled at in a subway and harassed by a security guard in a bookstore, had real emotional and psychological consequences. This was exacerbated by the common assumption within the ELT profession in Korea that employers prefer White teachers. Prior to leaving England, for example, I remember preparing myself for a professional life in Korea. Immediately before and during my job search, I spent many hours making sense of the Korean ELT profession by reading experiences of past and current language instructors in Korea posted on different online forums and blogs. My conclusion was that racial discrimination in the ELT profession in Korea is real. Consequently, rarely did I initiate discussions of my racial background, despite my physical appearance that may suggest to some people that I am neither 'Korean' nor 'American'. Furthermore, there were very few situations in Korea where I thought I would be able to use my race to my advantage despite being in a position of privilege as a citizen of the United States (see Chapter 4). I am not suggesting that I was in any way a victim of institutionalized racism while working in the ELT profession, nor do I want to give the impression that I had a horrific time while teaching in Korea. The larger point that I would like to make is that racism transcends contexts because victims of racial discrimination carry with them such experiences from one place to another (e.g. Wu, 2002). Even so, possessing a heightened awareness of race and racism while teaching in Korea did not compel me to engage in the type of critical scholarship that I present to you in this book.

Korea and Koreanness, as well as race and racism, were not research interests until long after my marriage in 2007, and more specifically shortly after the birth of our daughter in 2013. The evolution of my research interests is discussed briefly in a recent autoethnographic study on learning Korean as a heritage language (see Jenks, in press). I discuss in this book growing up in the United States and Korea, speaking Korean as a primary language as a toddler, and questioning my racial and ethnic identities as I got older and moved between the two countries. I reflect on, among other cultural issues, how living in the United States as a teenager with little access to Korean-speaking peers led to the attrition of my Korean language and identity. The autoethnographic study of the semiotics of Korean language learning obliged me to make connections between my new family role as a father and evolving research interests.

Caring for my daughter involved, in part, thinking about how I would like her to grow up and considering the environment that would be most conducive to ensuring a happy childhood. As a person of color, I naturally thought about issues of diversity and inclusion. We wanted our daughter to grow up in the United States, but were concerned that multilingualism and multiculturalism are not widely celebrated in that country. As a father of a Korean American daughter, my parental responsibility naturally brought about a new sense of pride in my own racial and ethnic identities. My Korean wife and I knew that our daughter must learn Korean and have a strong sense of pride in her cultural heritage. This required creating a home environment where Koreanness is not seen as a foreign object. Although the goal was to construct an environment where our daughter would be socialized in the Korean language, creating a bilingual setting at home was exceptionally transformative for my own personal and professional growth. It allowed me to be more comfortable referring to myself as a Korean American, but more importantly, it compelled me to learn and use Korean at home much more than I had in the past. This renewed sense of ownership of the Korean language stemmed partly from my fear that my daughter would question her identity if put in challenging situations similar to those of my own childhood. Perhaps more importantly, I did not want her to experience the same trajectory of language and culture loss. My desire to learn Korean and be more participatory at home in the language led to many moments thinking about the significance of my previous scholarship. The conversation analytic work that I had devoted much of my attention to in previous years was no longer rewarding after the birth of our daughter. I realized that the issues critical to raising a bilingual child in the United States, and matters related to dealing with my own racial and ethnic identities in a country run by predominantly White institutions, would lead to a more productive and enriching body of scholarly work.

In this sense, my new parental responsibility led to the conceptualization and completion of this book. Specifically, my experiences with racism projected onto the typical concerns parents have for their children's welfare. I felt that I had a professional responsibility to engage in research that was potentially more impactful and reflected the concerns that I have as a father. The racism that I have experienced throughout my life allows me to better appreciate the significance of racial discrimination while applying a critical lens to the investigation of the topic, although my life history certainly does not preclude me from reinforcing problematic narratives and misinterpreting the topics and people investigated in this (or any) book.

I am aware, for example, that working in a US university while investigating racial discrimination in Korea can be interpreted as a form of academic colonialism. Mignolo (2009: 1) uses the term *locus of enunciation* to denounce the common belief within academia, and in particular disciplines that examine the cultural Other, that researchers are in neutral positions: specifically, he questions the assumption 'that the knowing subject in the disciplines is transparent, disincorporated from the known and untouched by the geo-political configuration of the world in which people are racially ranked and regions are racially configured'. Uncritically examining the widespread belief that scholars like myself have something to offer the cultural Other because we possess 'Western scientific knowledge' may potentially reinforce oppressive discourses by maintaining control of knowledge production. In other words, without any attempts to engage in critical reflexivity, my book could be interpreted as a form of academic colonization. That is, I am potentially creating a lens through which the cultural Other views their own world. Mignolo (2009: 4) suggests that 'in order to call into question the modern/colonial foundation of the control of knowledge, it is necessary to focus on the knower rather than on the known. It means to go to the very assumptions that sustain locus enunciations'.

Following the logic of this quote, my reflections thus far have attempted to 'focus on the knower' by exploring how my multiple social identities, including researcher, father, husband and Korean American, simultaneously fit within and shape the current book. My aim is to demonstrate that the current investigation is not only a product of observing the cultural Other, but it is also a dialogic process between my own subjectivities or life experiences and the scholarly goals that I have set out for this book. That is to say, I am not simply reporting on what I have observed. My reporting has been significantly influenced by who I am as a person and what I have encountered socially and professionally over the past three decades (for a lengthy exploration of how personal subjectivities shape research practices, see Burke, 2007). Sharing my experiences of racism, for example, has hopefully demonstrated that research, even the most ostensibly empirical and 'objective', is always situated within larger narratives and influenced by subjectivities (for a study based on a detailed positionality statement, see McClure, 2007).

In addition to the importance of engaging in discussions that treat research as a highly subjective endeavor, researchers should also address the extent to which their investigatory ambitions exploit the very issues, people or phenomena they seek to examine. For example, I have benefited, both financially and professionally, from working in the ELT profession in Korea. I understand that my employment in Korea was based on the erroneous assumption that speakers from the United States are superior teachers with the best command of the English language. Although I did not read the works of Pennycook (2001), Phillipson (1992) and other critical ELT scholars at the time of my employment in Korea, I am now aware that Korean immigration laws discriminate against millions of qualified teachers who speak English as an additional language. In this sense, my employment in Korea was based on linguistic discrimination. Although I was not aware of it at the time, I exploited the ELT market at the expense of teachers who cannot work in Korea because of their citizenship.

This book represents one way of confronting these issues; my university teaching is also committed to addressing the power dynamics in, and racial hierarchies of, the ELT profession. This book is my attempt to bring further attention to the racial and linguistic discrimination that exists in the ELT profession in Korea (and beyond). It is hoped that my observations here, and in subsequent chapters, will encourage ELT scholars to do the same. Investigating race and racism in the ELT profession without reflexively addressing researcher positionality can potentially reinforce oppressive narratives, as mentioned previously. While individual efforts cannot stop systemic racism and linguistic discrimination, the profession can collectively disseminate counter-narratives by drawing more from critical race scholarship. The next chapter provides an overview of this scholarship, and explores how it can be applied to the study of race and racism in the ELT profession.

Prefatory Remarks on Korea

The Korean War had just ended, and the wretchedness of Korea at that time beggars description: the hills were brown and stripped for firewood; sick and injured people were everywhere; entire city blocks lay in rubble. Everywhere one looked there was meagerness and suffering. Clark (2003: ix)

The quote above describes the state of despair in Korea during the period immediately after, and following, the Korean War. The three-year war, which began in 1950 and ended in 1953, resulted in hundreds of thousands of casualties. Although many were involved in the fighting, including the United Nations, the United States had, and continues to have, a significant military role in the region. At the time of writing, the two Koreas are still effectively at war.

Younger generations of Koreans, as well as many people outside of Korea, do not know or perhaps do not fully appreciate the events and impact of the Korean War. The Korean people – including their attitudes and perceptions about themselves and the world around them – have been shaped by decades of exceptional political and economic turbulence leading up to, and following the war. Examples inadequately capture such precarious times, but do provide a simple contrast to what most see today as a thriving country. Korea lost much of its economy after World War II (Japan owned 94% of businesses in Korea in 1940); the Korean War resulted in damages to major industries that almost equaled national production for a two-year period prior (US$3.0 billion); and political volatility led to financial instability leading up to, and following, the 1961 military coup (Frank *et al.*, 1975). Interestingly, and somewhat ironically, North Korea was ostensibly the more prosperous region prior to the Korean War partly because of its control of mineral resources, power generation and chemical production (Frank *et al.*, 1975). Simply put, a divided, post-Japanese colonial Korea was a poor nation with few resources.

The image of a country stricken with poverty is particularly salient to the topics and issues discussed in this book because, as many readers familiar with the nation's current prosperity will be aware, Korea today possesses one of the largest global economies. What socioeconomic and political developments led to this accelerated rise? While this question may not seem directly relevant to a discussion of race and ethnicity, it nonetheless underpins some of the key issues discussed in subsequent chapters. The six decades of development since the Korean War, and the rate at which this has occurred, must not be overlooked in sociological and anthropological discussions of contemporary Korea. In other words, discussions of contemporary Korea that do not account for, or consider, the historical forces that shaped the region into the nation that it is (and is becoming) only provide a partial, conceivably skewed, interpretation of social issues and events. It must not be forgotten that Korea, while ostensibly modern, industrious and socially and politically progressive, did not achieve its current state in a vacuum. It is a country that has been relatively isolated from the rest of the world, though it has experienced invasions (Turnbull, 2008), colonialism (H. Lee *et al.*, 2013), military 'occupation' (Seth, 2010) and coups d'état (B. Kim & Vogel, 2011). It is a country that takes great pride in notions of nationhood and ethnicity (G. Shin, 2006a, 2006b), though some would argue that concerns for education and career advancement are more important to individual Koreans (see, for example, Seth, 2002). It is a country that is indeed complex and complicated. Although Korea is not unique in this sense, it is important to highlight these social events at the start of the book. It is a reminder for both the author and the reader that race, racism and racialized discourses in the ELT profession in Korea are interconnected with a host of social issues, events and phenomena, and that these issues, events and phenomena are central to an understanding of the ELT profession in Korea.

Why Study Race and ELT in Korea?

The need to study race and ethnicity in the ELT profession is justified in the answer to one, simple question. Does racial and ethnic discrimination exist in the ELT profession in Korea (and beyond)? The short and simple answer to this question, as numerous studies have demonstrated in contexts outside of Korea (e.g. Kubota & Lin, 2006; Motha, 2014; Ruecker, 2011), is a resounding yes. Mahboob (2009: 38) takes this impetus to study race and ethnicity a step further when he argues 'that if ELT wants to develop into a profession rather than remaining a largely unlegislated industry, then it should aim to eradicate all forms of discrimination'. Although the semantic distinction made in this quote is important, especially in discussions of race and ethnicity, it can be said with certainty that English language teaching and learning is indeed a profession that is guided by workplace principles: codes of conduct, notions of compulsory qualifications and ethical guidelines, to name a few (see, for example, TESOL, 2012). Mahboob is correct, however, in arguing that the profession is responsible for eliminating discrimination in ELT. Despite ongoing advancements in professionalism, racial and linguistic discrimination is omnipresent in ELT. What evidence exists, then, to suggest that racial and linguistic discrimination shapes the ELT profession in Korea? Why should the profession care about such injustices and social inequalities, and what can scholarship glean from an investigation of race and ethnicity in ELT? These questions represent a few of the many issues addressed in this book.

According to Mutuma Ruteere, special rapporteur on racism for the United Nations, widespread racial discrimination exists in Korea (OHCHR, 2014). Ruteere's observation stems from a recent trip to Korea where he reported wage disparities between migrant workers and Korean citizens, verbal and physical abuses in the workplace, and marriage laws that discriminate against multicultural families (Lee, C., 2014a). While Ruteere did not observe racism at the institutional level (for evidence that suggests otherwise, see Chapters 4 and 6), he recommended that Korea pass an anti-discrimination act and revise employment legislation to protect foreign and migrant workers (OHCHR, 2014). At the time of writing, Korea is working on implementing an anti-discrimination act that prevents egregious acts in the workplace; however, immigration laws, especially as they pertain to the ELT profession, still privilege Western or inner-circle countries. For example, immigration laws for language instructors only recognize a small group of countries as English speaking, a central legal requirement for teachers seeking employment in Korea (see Chapter 4). Thus, there are thousands of qualified teachers from so-called non-English-speaking countries who, because of their passports, cannot obtain legal work in Korea.

While some of the reports identified in the paragraph above relate to discriminatory practices in non-teaching workplace environments, numerous media reports suggest that a preference for White teachers in the ELT profession is widespread (e.g. Strother, 2007). Discriminatory practices against teachers of color, including Korean citizens, in recruiting and in the workplace, have also been reported (e.g. Hyams, 2015). For example, a teacher from the United States was recently turned down for two different jobs in one week for being Black, as his recruiter and prospective employers disclosed. The Facebook message sent from the recruiter to the teacher reads (T. Lee, 2014a):

> I'm sorry, I just found out today that my school is one of ones that won't hire black people.

Such examples provide a window into the racial climate of the country in general and the ELT profession in particular (for a study that reports on Korean students' negative attitudes toward vernacular Englishes, see Yook & Lindemann, 2013), but do not explain why race-based discrimination and privilege exist and how they are historically situated; the ways in which language, identity and culture are used to construct discourses and ideologies of the 'ideal' teacher; or the role political forces, including neoliberal policies, have in shaping the ways in which language teaching and learning are managed in Korea. These issues and themes are the central focus of the investigation presented in the following chapters.

An exploration of these issues and themes is important because, in many parts of the world, employers engage in hiring and occupational practices that do not reflect current scholarship in critical race studies, global Englishes and multiculturalism. Such practices are based on racial and linguistic hierarchies that originate from Western scientific knowledge (cf. Chapter 7). White supremacy and privilege are unspoken realities in language teaching and learning, but little is being done to explore what this means for the ELT profession. Furthermore, extensive discrimination continues to oppress under-represented professionals, including instructors of color, and superficial notions of what a native speaker is and can thus do in the classroom continue to close off markets to otherwise competent teachers and speakers of English.

Accordingly, colonial and imperial mentalities are alive and well in various parts of the ELT profession. These discriminatory and oppressive practices deserve much more attention in the ELT literature than they have been given in previous years. All language scholars and practitioners are otherwise, in some ways, complicit in racial and linguistic discrimination. The profession as a whole is to blame if race and racism continue to be treated as taboo topics and/or empirical issues not worthy of investigation.

Addressing racism and race-based privilege requires journals, publishers and professional organizations to actively seek out work done on racial and linguistic discrimination in ELT (cf. Kubota & Lin, 2006, 2009a), and teacher training programs to incorporate mandatory coursework on race and ethnicity. Oppressed, under-represented and disadvantaged teachers in ELT must also be given a voice (cf. Chapter 7); action needs to be taken to change the status quo. Racial and linguistic discrimination in ELT must be exposed, investigated and eradicated.

Critical ELT

The present investigation is concerned primarily with providing a critical understanding of how the ELT profession operates and what can be done to address the challenges facing language teaching and learning in the years to come. This book does this, in part, by advancing a social justice agenda. But before discussing what social justice means in and for the profession, it is important to briefly address what is meant by ELT. In this book, ELT refers to the profession that is concerned with all aspects of teaching and learning English as an additional language, including teacher training programs, the scholarly work done by applied linguists, small private language academies and large testing organizations that administer standardized tests, among others. ELT educators and scholars possess a wide range of pedagogical and empirical interests, including understanding how some of the issues identified in the preceding section shape language teaching and learning. The ELT profession has many organizations around the world that take part in knowledge creation, including Teachers of English to Speakers of Other Languages (TESOL). ELT should not, however, be confused with TESOL. Although ELT and TESOL are often used synonymously in the literature, the latter term is also associated with the remarkably large, American-conceived international association with the same name. Because of the terminological confusion that comes with using TESOL, ELT will be employed throughout this book.

ELT educators and scholars have a long history of promoting social justice and educational equity. For example, as early as 1966 (for a comprehensive treatment of the historical developments of ELT, starting from the 14th century, see Howatt & Widdowson, 2004), teaching projects were funded to provide English language support for disadvantaged students from Spanish-speaking communities or who spoke a Native American language (Light, 1967). The ELT profession has since been an advocate for laws that promote bilingualism and fairness in education (e.g. Cummins, 2000). In many parts of the world, teacher training programs encourage instructors to be cognizant of, and employ learning materials that are pedagogically sensitive to, the political, social and cultural issues and conditions that shape, and sometimes hinder, students' ability to learn. Less often, though equally if not more important, ELT professionals discuss critical issues in classrooms, like class, religion and race, with the transformative goal of equipping students with the knowledge to better understand the world's many social inequalities, power imbalances and hegemonic and neoliberal forces.

The political, social and cultural issues and conditions that shape ELT practices represent a growth area in language teaching and learning research, and are commonly and collectively referred to as critical pedagogy. While critical pedagogy has been defined and operationalized in many ways (cf. Norton & Toohey, 2004), the approach can be traced back to Freire (2000), whose pioneering and seminal work addressed the social mechanisms that shape (and distort) humanity, the existence of oppression and the roles the oppressed and the oppressor play in humanizing (and dehumanizing) each other. Critical pedagogy is more than just an approach to teaching, however; it is a struggle to achieve humanization: 'emancipation of labor', 'overcoming of alienation' and 'affirmation of men and women as persons' (Freire, 2000: 44). According to Freire (2000: 54), critical pedagogy is about the oppressed fighting 'for their own liberation' by engaging in a dialectical practice, what he calls praxis, that uncovers 'the world of oppression' and transforms existing social structures (e.g. racial and linguistic hierarchies). Critical pedagogy is underpinned by the idea that oppression can be overcome, but it requires the oppressed and the oppressor to co-facilitate a middle ground where both groups are aware, and in some way a part, of each other's humanity.

ELT educators and scholars have, to varying degrees, used Freire's (2000) 'pedagogy of the oppressed' to understand the critical issues surrounding the teaching and learning of additional languages (for an edited collection of such studies, see Norton & Toohey, 2004). Specifically, critical approaches to ELT seek to uncover the ways in which language is used to configure (and reconfigure) social inequalities, and to identify methods to bring about change through mediation, advocacy and reform (e.g. Crookes & Lehner, 1998; Gebhard, 2004). In some cases, attempts have been made to set out parameters that determine the core features of critical approaches to ELT. For example, Pennycook (1999: 331) argues that critical approaches to ELT comprise three facets: connecting the micro everyday to the macro sociopolitical, transforming lives through education, and self-reflexive practice. While many scholars do not explicitly address how their work builds on and/or borrows from Freire's (2000) observations, critical pedagogy is an underlying issue for most ELT scholarship concerned with improving student learning. This calls attention to another important point regarding critical pedagogy. Critical approaches to ELT have, will and should always be appropriated to fit unique pedagogical circumstances and investigatory goals. In other words, critical pedagogy should not be discussed as a monolithic idea.

Drawing from Pennycook's (1999) work, the critical elements of this book can be found in the examination of how race and ethnicity are used as symbolic, occupational and political resources to benefit, exploit and disadvantage ELT teachers working and/or seeking employment in Korea. Thus, this book contributes to scholarship that can be broadly defined as critical ELT, which is an investigatory branch of, but is not limited to, critical pedagogy. That is to say, although this book uncovers many social processes that can help scholars come to a more critical understanding of the language teaching profession, the observations made in subsequent chapters somewhat neglect the pedagogy that readers come to expect in critical ELT work (see Pennycook, 1999: 330). This more traditional approach to critical ELT can be characterized as being primarily concerned with bringing about change from the inside out (e.g. examining what teaching approaches can be used to best equip students with the sociopolitical knowledge to make changes outside of class, in the so-called 'real world'). Pedagogy, or what happens inside the classroom, is the focus of discussion and analysis. In this book, by contrast, the 'real world' is the focus of discussion and analysis. The objective is to transform teaching and learning conditions in Korea (and beyond) by providing a better understanding of how race, racism and racialized discourses operate within, and shape, the ELT profession. Therefore, rather than explore how race should be introduced to a class of, say, Korean graduate students who will later become responsible for hiring ELT teachers in Korea, this book is concerned with, for example, how recruiting practices are interconnected with ideological and political notions of race, nationality and citizenship.

The critical work done in this book is not limited to an examination of race and ethnicity. All language, including the words on these printed pages, is political and bound to larger social structures (van Dijk, 1997). Thus, critical approaches to ELT should not only engage in a discussion of social rights and injustice; scholars ought also to consider how being in positions of power and privilege influences their research. The critical researcher must reflect on how professional obligations and identities determine all aspects of carrying out research and explore how personal life experiences determine what data to collect and how to analyze it. This self-reflexive component of doing research is a key feature of critical applied linguistics, a domain of study that subsumes critical approaches to ELT (for a brief discussion of the relation between critical pedagogy in ELT and critical applied linguistics, see Pennycook, 2001: 14–16). Critical self-reflexivity is needed in such work, as it demonstrates that the knowledge created in and through studies of the cultural Other is connected not only to what is going on with the observed, but also to the lived stories, professional and personal identities and institutional constraints of the observer. The present study has fulfilled the self-reflexive aspect of doing critical work by exploring how often-undisclosed matters, like the author's ethnic identity, professional history and personal life experiences, have shaped the observations made in the following chapters.

Although this book builds on the critical work done in ELT, the observations made in subsequent chapters are interdisciplinary in nature. Theories from sociology, anthropology, political science and legal studies are borrowed to understand racialized discourses in language teaching and learning. The themes that are examined include, but are not limited to, social (in)justice, activism, racism, Whiteness, identities, neoliberalism and professional practice. Finally, it must be briefly mentioned again that while there is a growing body of work on race and ethnicity in critical language scholarship, few studies (and indeed even fewer book-length investigations) have examined how race, racism and racialized discourses shape commonsense understandings of teaching and learning in a particular country, and what such observations say about the global ELT profession.

Some Key Terms: Race, Ethnicity, Racialized Discourse and Racism

Many terms and theoretical constructs are used in the observations made in subsequent chapters. None are perhaps more important than the four descriptors discussed in this section: race, ethnicity, racialized discourse and racism. It is important to explore what is meant by these terms at this particular juncture because race, ethnicity, racialized discourse and racism are used in varied ways for different purposes. Perhaps more importantly, such terms conjure up strong emotional states that result in debate and ignorance in their usage and description.

Race is a contested term used to assign individuals into distinct groups, like Black, White and Asian. The term has evolved over the years to include a number of cultural and ethnic variables, including language and ancestry, though it is often reduced to physical features, such as facial morphology and skin color. While scholarship in several disciplines has done much to promote a social view of race (see, for example, Fought, 2006), many laypeople view the term as a biological descriptor and use this understanding to organize their worldview. As a result of this limited and essentialized, yet widely adopted, application of the term, it is not difficult to find scholarship that rejects the notion that race is a legitimate category or unit of identification (see Goldberg & Solomos, 2002). Researchers have for many years argued that race, when used to categorize individuals or groups based on biological differences, has little genetic validity. Critical race theorist Haney López (1994: 12), for example, observes that 'greater genetic variation exists *within* the populations typically labeled Black and White than *between* these populations' [original emphasis]. In an early and seminal paper on genetic variation, Lewontin (1972: 397) argues that 'Human racial classification is of no social value and is positively destructive of social and human relations. Since such racial classification is now seen to be of virtually no genetic or taxonomic significance either, no justification can be offered for its continuance'. Despite continued efforts to abandon or problematize biological notions of race, however, the term is a social reality for many. The practice of racial classification has, unfortunately, reduced large groups of people to single bodily features, such as the stereotype that Asians have 'slanted' eyes; or worse, a negative behavior or trait, like the belief that all African Americans are violent. Racial classification has, as a result, created an overall simplified understanding of culture and cultural groups (for an excellent critique of the term *race*, see Appiah, 1985).

Attempts to move away from using race as a tool for classification have led to an increase in the use of ethnicity. For some scholars, this term is devoid of the cultural and political baggage that comes with using the term *race*. Although race and ethnicity are often used synonymously, and indeed the distinction between the two words is fuzzy, the latter term has a history of being understood from the observation that shared beliefs and practices (e.g. religious affiliation), as opposed to physical features (e.g. skin color and hair type), lead to group formation. It should be noted, however, that ethnicity can also be used to categorize communities based on physical characteristics or traits, and thus has the potential to provide an equally narrow lens through which to understand cultural groups. For both terms, therefore, there is a need to move discussions of cultural groups away from biological differences.

A simple, albeit superficial, way of appreciating the difference between race and ethnicity is to think of the different ethnic groups that fall under a racial category like Asian: Koreans, Japanese and Chinese, and so on. Specifically, an ethnic group is like a community of practice in that its members have ways of distinguishing between insiders and outsiders, between people who abide by its cultural norms and those who do not, and between actions that reflect valued beliefs and actions that violate them (for a critical discussion of communities of practice, see Barton & Tusting, 2005). Again, while there is some overlap between race and ethnicity, the latter term is somewhat more fluid. Take, for example, a region like Hong Kong, where a number of different ethnic groups complicate notions of nationhood, Chineseness and Asianness. In Hong Kong, the term *Chinese* can be associated with a number of ethnic groups, including, but not limited to, Hakka, Cantonese, Shanghainese and Filipino.

Ethnicity clearly provides a more nuanced way of understanding cultural groups, but the term should not be seen as an alternative to race for a number of reasons: (1) race is not devoid of theoretical and practical validity and application despite the Lewontin quote above; (2) meanings of race are not limited to biological differences, as mentioned previously; (3) some researchers believe that ethnicity subsumes race while others think the two terms are fundamentally the same (see Fought, 2006); (4) if ethnicity does in fact subsume race, then the two terms must be examined together; and (5) scholars using either term are equally challenged in identifying and eradicating bigotry, prejudice and discrimination.

Race and ethnicity are socially constructed terms in that they are both used to manage social encounters and therefore shape how people self-identify. For example, individuals belonging to more than one ethnicity, say French and Canadian, will often self-identify with the group that best meets their immediate communicative goals and/or exigent social pressures. As a side note, this phenomenon can occur with race, but for obvious reasons is much less common (cf. racial passing; see Hobbs, 2014). In addition to highlighting the role others have in shaping social identities, the example of 'passing' highlights another important issue with regard to race and ethnicity. Both categories can be used as a resource to accomplish a number of different social actions and practices (see Hansen, 2005). Race and ethnicity are used to affiliate with communities, ridicule people and provide a compliment, for example. In institutional encounters, race and ethnicity can be used to marginalize and dominate individuals who are in less powerful positions (e.g. immigrants in therapy sessions; cf. Lee & Bhuyan, 2013). Race and ethnicity are co-constructed, discursively situated categories that, when used as a resource, reveal how people make sense of themselves, each other and the world around them (e.g. Day, 1998).

Although the discussion above suggests that ethnicity offers a nuanced understanding of culture and cultural groups (cf. Waters, 1990), the term is not immune to criticism. Ethnicity is somewhat problematic, methodologically speaking, in that it is associated with the idea of a 'shared culture'. It is not only difficult to establish what constitutes a shared culture, but researchers must also consider how ethnic groups can be divided (and categorized together) according to cultural knowledge and practices. More importantly, grouping people according to knowledge and practices can also create stereotypical images, and result in the same essentialized notions of communities that come from racialized observations of the cultural Other. Despite these theoretical and methodological problems and challenges, ethnicity is used throughout this book, as it encompasses cultural groups that may not fit within traditional notions of race (e.g. Koreans). At times, however, it is used as a metonym for race for stylistic and rhetorical purposes, and more importantly, to demonstrate that racial and linguistic discrimination operate at the 'ethnic level' (e.g. racism against Korean Americans in Korea). Furthermore, race and ethnicity, as well as religious affiliation, sexuality and gender, among other categorizations, are all interconnected and operate with varying degrees of saliency (Stryker & Serpe, 1982; see also Chapter 2).

Although ethnicity may provide a more nuanced understanding of cultural groups and reflect the different communities living within and across defined geopolitical spaces, it is important to continue using race in discussions of discrimination in language teaching and learning. Take, as a starting point, the belief that race should not be used to discuss cultural groups because the term maintains an erroneous biological basis and provides a means for continued racism (cf. Appiah, 1985). While this is a compelling argument, and indeed race is frequently used problematically, simply abandoning the term does not change the color of one's skin. That is to say, racism will exist regardless of the terminology used to differentiate people. Further, abandoning the term race does not move scholarship any closer to an understanding of how racism operates at various levels of sociality and in different domains of life. As Haney López (1994: 20) clearly expresses: 'To cease speaking of races in order to hide from the racists would hinder our understanding of the way people think about their daily lives and obfuscate the very real connection between who we are and what we look like'.

While identifying peoples based solely on features like shades of skin color is deemed highly problematic, many researchers continue to use the term *race* in various word forms because it is useful for the examination of racial inequalities and prejudices in societies (e.g. racism, critical race theory). For example, *racialized discourse* is a term that is used widely in the literature to capture the many ways in which discrimination and bigotry are perpetuated and advanced in text (e.g. law, media, the internet), talk (e.g. insults) and social interaction (e.g. gestures and body language). 'Non-native English speaker' (NNES) and 'native English speaker' (NES) are prototypical examples of racialized discourse; NNES and NES become racialized when ELT professionals use language proficiency to mask the desire to exclude instructors of color (e.g. Mahboob, 2009). In this example, the term *racialized discourse* is not used to distinguish between peoples, but rather to discriminate on the basis of race. It allows scholars to better demonstrate that discriminatory practices exist, and are put into motion in and through social actions and practices, such as hiring policy.

Racism is defined in this book as a belief, manifesting in a discursive act or social action, that privileges or disadvantages one ethnic or racial group; it creates essentialized images, often negative, of an entire population of peoples and produces an asymmetrical distribution of power between two cultural groups. Although racism is a serious topic that warrants attention in all academic circles, it is important to note that this book is not chiefly about the general cultural attitudes and perceptions of Koreans in relation to their ethnic identities and those of others (for an interesting discussion of stereotypical images of Black males in the Korean media, see VanVolkenburg, 2012), a topic that no doubt requires a separate book-length examination. It is true, however, that a knowledge of the attitudinal and perceptual climate in which racialized discourses play out at the national level (cf. 'racial discourse'; see Doane, 2006) is helpful in understanding why racial discrimination exists in the ELT profession. For example, it is worth noting that for many Koreans, 'racial purity' and ethnic nationalism are central to how Korean identity is constructed (see, for example, G. Shin, 2006b).

While racial purity and ethnic nationalism are interesting areas of investigation, the teaching and learning of English in Korea is not entirely shaped by the cultural attitudes and perceptions of Koreans in general. Indeed, a spectrum of sociocultural variables, including racial and linguistic commodification and objectification, complicates the relation between, say, 'what Koreans think about White people in general' and 'what Koreans think about White teachers specifically'. Put differently, 'what Koreans think about White people in general' does not necessarily correlate with 'how ELT professionals in Korea recruit and hire language instructors'. These issues are addressed later in this book during the analysis chapters.

Deeper examination of these juxtaposing statements also establishes that racism is context specific, context dependent and context shaping. It is context specific, as the discriminatory acts or actions of one group of people are not necessarily representative of another. For example, the ELT profession in Korea does not epitomize the attitudes and perceptions of an entire nation – that is, the existence of discriminatory practices in the ELT profession does not mean that Korea, as a nation, is racist, nor does it follow that other professions in the country see the world through a race-based prism. Racism is also context dependent in that discriminatory acts or actions are shaped by unique sociocultural affordances and constraints. In the ELT profession in Korea, discriminatory practices are shaped by economic, linguistic and social forces; for example, the perceived need to learn English in Korea creates social barriers and structures in the ELT profession that may not exist in, say, international business, commodity trading and even the factory industry that employs a large number of migrant workers from Southeast Asia. Racism is context shaping because discriminatory acts or actions have the power to reconfigure existing social structures (e.g. racial hierarchies and language ideologies) within particular situations (e.g. online recruiting spaces). Specifically, discriminatory practices in the ELT profession can reconfigure existing belief systems by perpetuating stereotypical beliefs, such as the misconception that ethnic groups from inner-circle countries are superior teachers, or worse, better speakers of English (for a discussion of different types of racism in ELT, see Kubota & Lin, 2009a).

The descriptors outlined above are crucial to the investigation conducted in subsequent chapters. While this section has provided a brief theoretical foundation for race, ethnicity, racialized discourse and racism, it will be necessary throughout this book to revisit the discussion above in order to understand how such descriptors are used in the context of the ELT profession.

The Aim of this Book

The central aim of this book is to examine how race, racism and racialized discourses shape the ELT profession in Korea, but the observations made in subsequent chapters are situated in, and are relevant to, wider discussions of global Englishes, neoliberalism, linguistic imperialism and critical race theory.

In addition to establishing a critical, reflexive account of how my racial and ethnic background, as well as professional experience, shaped the writing of this book, discussions in subsequent chapters apply critical race scholarship to an understanding of language teaching and learning. The book also identifies the social architecture of White normativity in the ELT profession; uncovers how race and ethnicity are used as symbolic resources to recruit and hire language instructors; and scrutinizes the interface between linguistic competence, race and citizenship. Observations made throughout the book contribute to a better understanding of the ways in which White saviorism shapes notions of good and bad language teaching, the role White neoliberalism has in commodifying race, and the consequences of racial capitalism and the economic exploitation of language teachers. In so doing, the book addresses, and thus contributes to the eradication of, discrimination in the ELT profession. These discussions help identify ways ELT scholarship can move forward in addressing racism in language teaching and learning.

While several related phenomena are explored in this book, a discussion of race and racism in language teaching and learning requires taking into consideration a number of different contextual issues and aspects of social life. This is particularly true for investigations that seek to uncover how language ideologies are bound to racial and linguistic hierarchies. The study of race and ethnicity in the ELT profession is further complicated by the fact that Korea has a complex relationship with the English language (J.S. Park, 2009). That is to say, the book objectives identified above are all interconnected at some social and/or discursive level, and merely identifying them does not mean that they will be investigated as separate topics or research questions. Again, the thesis of this book is that White normativity is an ideological commitment and a form of racialized discourse that comes from the social actions of those involved in the ELT profession; this ideal standard constructs a system of racial discrimination that is founded on White privilege, saviorism and neoliberalism (for a reminder that racism in the ELT profession is not always based on White epistemologies, see Kubota, 2013).

The data used to address this central focus are immigration documents, government reports, interviews with ELT teachers, historical records, online discussion board conversations and news media texts. These sources are discussed in greater detail in subsequent analytic chapters. Although a number of different analytic lenses are used to understand this data set, much of the analysis draws from critical discourse and race studies.

The role that critical race scholarship can play in moving the ELT profession closer to a better understanding of racial discrimination and privilege cannot be overstated. Race, racism and racialized discourses have been the subject of some publications in the ELT literature, but the scholarship of critical race theory has failed to play a significant role in shaping language teaching and learning research. Since the days following slavery, critical race scholars in the United States have created new ways of understanding how race and racism are central to different domains of social life (e.g. W.E.B. Du Bois); their work has informed scholarship in a number of disciplines, transformed notions of race, uncovered how oppression is tied to racial hierarchies and changed living and working conditions for marginalized communities. Despite these interdisciplinary contributions, however, ELT scholarship appears to be somewhat agnostic on the utility of applying critical race theory to investigations of language teaching and learning.

Accordingly, a considerable amount of attention is given in the next chapter to exploring the scholarship of critical race theorists. Moreover, the peripheral role that critical race theory plays in ELT scholarship is why this chapter has dealt at length with race, racism and racialized discourses in relation to language teaching and learning. In addition to serving as a backdrop for the book, it was also important to provide a critical reflexive account of how my identity as a biracial Korean American, including personal experiences with racism in the United States and Korea, informed the contents of subsequent chapters because storytelling is a central aspect of critical race theory. In so doing, this chapter argued for the importance of researcher positionality in investigations of language teaching and learning in general, and in discussions of race and racism in particular. Such introductory and reflexive discussions are crucial to the observations made of race, racism and racialized discourses in language teaching and learning in subsequent analytic chapters. These analytic chapters will argue that in order to create disciplinary and pedagogical spaces where language scholars and practitioners can better interrogate race-based discrimination and privilege, the ELT profession must prioritize critical race scholarship in its work to train teachers, teach languages and create scientific knowledge.

Outline of the Book

Chapter 2 presents an overview of key themes and issues in critical race scholarship, reviews the literature on race and ethnicity in ELT and explores how linguistic imperialism can inform a discussion of racism in language teaching and learning. Topics reviewed in this chapter include, but are not limited to, what can be learned from legal studies about institutional racism, personal accounts of racial discrimination in the profession reported by applied linguists and language teaching practitioners and how the social construction of Whiteness shapes racialized discourses and ideologies. This chapter identifies research gaps and briefly considers how the present book builds on current discussions of race, ethnicity and ELT.

Chapter 3 provides background information that contextualizes the racialized discourses that exist in the ELT profession in Korea. The discussion is concerned primarily with notions of Korean ethnicity and the significance of (English language) education in Korea. In addition to examining what it means to be 'Korean' according to a collective imagination, the chapter explores how multicultural families and 'foreigners' are portrayed in the media. This chapter also explores the degree to which education is inextricably connected to many aspects of daily life; scrutinizes the amount of time spent on English language instruction; and explores the stress experienced by families, especially children, because of the staggering pressure to get admitted into one of the few 'good' universities in Seoul, a situation that is partly responsible for creating a climate commonly referred to as 'education fever' (see Seth, 2002). In short, Chapter 3 identifies and explicates the 'macro' sociological issues that shape the discursive construction of race and ethnicity in the ELT profession in Korea.

Chapter 4 applies critical race scholarship to an examination of how immigration laws, racialized discourses in the ELT profession and the ideological commitments of teachers create and prop up White normativity. It does this, in part, by examining the jurisprudence of ELT in Korea. This discussion of the legal aspects of ELT employment identifies the countries that are recognized as English speaking; explores the different working visas that are issued to language teachers; and uncovers whether certain ethnicities, including Korean American, are privileged as a result of immigration laws. The chapter draws from global Englishes scholarship and makes use of critical White studies to uncover the historical reasons for creating – and the social and educational implications of employing – immigration laws that prevent a large population of the ELT profession from working in Korea. The chapter also looks at how African American language teachers construct their professional and linguistic identities in general and, in particular, it explores how race and ethnicity shape their experiences in and outside of the classroom. Chapter 4 addresses these issues by building on the macro sociological issues discussed in Chapter 3, and by analyzing interview data, media texts and discussion board conversations. The chapter also investigates whether White privilege exists in the ELT profession and traces the historical and cultural forces that help construct White normative discourses in Korea.

Chapter 5 examines White saviorism in the ELT profession. The analysis demonstrates that social events and phenomena that challenge instructors' sense of contribution to the ELT profession provide a window into, or trigger the discursive construction of, racialized ideologies and linguistic hierarchies. Specifically, the chapter examines how recent budget cuts to education spending have ostensibly undermined the omnipresent White normative discourses that currently exist in language teaching and learning. The chapter analyzes how ELT instructors have responded to budget cuts, and what their discourses and ideologies say about race relations and linguistic hierarchies in language teaching and learning in Korea. The analysis demonstrates that White saviorism is a projection of White normativity, and that NES instructors who construct saviorist discourses do so in order to maintain their dominant positions in the ELT profession. In other words, the chapter argues that White saviorism represents one of possibly many discursive tools used to oppress teachers of color, including Korean ELT instructors. That is, saviorist discourses prop up power imbalances in the profession by maintaining racial and linguistic hierarchies.

Chapter 6 uses sociolinguistic theories, global Englishes research and critical race scholarship to examine how racialized discourses (e.g. the belief that ELT leads to professional success) are used as symbolic resources to objectify and commodify the teaching and learning of English in Korea, namely that of White teachers. The analysis builds on the commonsense understanding that White normativity in language teaching and learning is a result of an ideology that regards speakers of inner-circle varieties of English as superior teachers. The chapter argues that while this privileging of 'inner-circle' speakers may partly explain White normativity in the profession, a more nuanced account of these racialized discourses must also include the possibility that free market principles (or neoliberalism) are central to how ELT instructors are imagined and recruited. To this end, Chapter 6 analyzes how neoliberal forces shape many aspects of professional life in Korea, including notions of who is considered an 'ideal' language teacher and the belief that 'White' is good for business.

Chapter 7 situates the study of Korea within a larger discussion of the global ELT profession. Specifically, the analyses conducted in previous chapters are used to investigate racial capitalism and White public spaces in the ELT profession. The aim is to develop a more critical understanding of how race-based discrimination and privilege can be addressed at the 'global' level. The chapter examines whether the lack of racial diversity in teacher training programs in places like the United States, including the curricular materials used to train student teachers, is part of the reason why racial discrimination exists in language teaching and learning. Chapter 7 considers what can be done to reform education practices in light of racial capitalism in language teaching and learning. This effort may entail investigating how critical pedagogy can provide a framework for a more politically and culturally sensitive curriculum that prepares language professionals to address racial and linguistic discrimination.

Chapter 8 concludes by summarizing key findings and identifying what can be done in future critical race scholarship to promote a more racially harmonious profession.

2 Critical Approaches to Race

Discussing racism is often uncomfortable, particularly in TESOL and applied linguistics. The field of L2 education by nature attracts professionals who are willing to work with people across racial boundaries, and thus it is considered to be a 'nice' field.... However, this does not make the field devoid of the responsibility to examine how racism or any other injustices influence its knowledge and practice.
Kubota (2002: 86)

Introduction

Studies that seek to understand how race and ethnicity circulate within, and shape various aspects of, the ELT profession face a number of challenges, as highlighted in the quote above. Kubota's (2002) remarks are a reminder that although the ELT profession is in the business of helping the cultural Other (for a discussion of the problematic nature of the 'Other' in the teaching English to speakers of other languages [TESOL] acronym, see H. Shin, 2006), it is not protected from racism. Furthermore, the practice of helping the cultural Other is inherently problematic, as it has the potential to mask the power and privilege that shape such practices, thus reinforcing racial and linguistic hierarchies. In other words, language teaching is inherently good, but this does not mean that scholars should ignore the discrimination, oppression and chauvinism that exist in the ELT profession.

Kubota's (2002) remarks stem from an earlier critique that views knowledge creation in the ELT profession as being partly connected to a 'legacy of colonial discourse' (Kubota, 2001: 31). Despite recent attempts to address the legacy of colonialism and linguistic imperialism in the ELT profession, and using the counter-narratives that result from such studies to historically reframe 'English language teaching to acknowledge its rootedness in racialization, globalization, and empire' (Motha, 2014: 16), scholarship appears to be collectively reluctant to tackle racism. For example, Atkinson's (2002) response to Kubota's (2001) paper demonstrates that the profession fails to appreciate the extent to which language teaching and learning, like many aspects of life, are rooted in, and intertwined with, historical race-based struggles, linguistic hierarchies and racialized ideologies. By simply cautioning researchers to avoid 'branding whole fields (TESOL and applied linguistics, in this case) as racist', Atkinson (2002: 83) perpetuates the familiar discourse that race-based discrimination and privilege are individual acts, and not 'woven into the very fabric of our institutions' (Kubota, 2002: 90). The main challenge, it seems, is moving researchers away from the belief that racism is limited to exceptional, as well as historical, moments of discrimination, including slavery and Jim Crow laws (cf. Kubota, 2013). While the racism of the 1960s in the United States in particular is a vivid reminder of what discrimination can look like, race-based struggles not only continue as contemporary problems, but can also manifest in more subtle ways than formerly understood and experienced.

For many decades, both explicit and covert forms of racialized discourses have been topics of investigation in a number of disciplines, including critical race scholarship; nevertheless, responses and reactions like Atkinson (2002) and others (see Kubota & Lin, 2009b: viii) suggest that some areas of study, including ELT scholarship, hold nescient positions regarding structural racism. Yet, all that is needed to acquire a better understanding of how structural racism shapes many aspects of life is a brief and superficial review of some key texts in critical race scholarship. Such a reading will quickly reveal that most, if not all, scholars now insist that discussions of race must move beyond the individual act, or a debate on who is or who is not racist, to a broader exploration of the historical forces and systemic mechanisms that create the conditions for racial and linguistic discrimination.

Although the Kubota–Atkinson debate took place over a decade ago, it establishes that race and racism are potentially contentious and uncomfortable topics in the ELT profession. In order to understand whether the ELT profession has indeed moved beyond the assumption that language teaching and learning are immune to racial and linguistic discrimination because the profession is in the service of advancing multiculturalism and translingualism, it is important to seek answers to many questions. Are teacher training programs in countries responsible for preparing large numbers of instructors requiring students to take courses on race and racism? What steps are being taken within the ELT profession to confront immigration laws that promote discrimination? Are students of color in teacher training classrooms given opportunities to express how their experiences may differ from what is typically experienced by White instructors? To what extent does the ELT profession address the racial and linguistic biases present in course materials? These sample questions provide a window into what must be done to better address racism in the

ELT profession; and while the present book investigates a different set of issues, what is clear is that much more work is needed to confront racial discrimination in language teaching and learning.

One of the first steps that must be taken to address racism in the ELT profession is to accept that race shapes notions of language teaching and learning in different and sometimes profound ways. Simply rejecting race as a useful construct to examine structural inequalities in the ELT profession is a form of colorblindness (see below for a more extensive discussion of colorblind ideologies). Colorblind ideologies maintain racial hierarchies within the profession by masking prejudice and bigotry with overt attempts to help the cultural Other. The ELT profession, though helpful in promoting cultural diversity and inclusiveness, must continue asking difficult questions. Language scholars and practitioners must seek to uncover how ELT instruction is built on a system of racial and linguistic discrimination. The eradication of racial and linguistic discrimination within the profession requires knowledge of the vast array of work done in critical race theory (CRT). This chapter introduces such work.

Critical race theorists have been foundational in promoting an understanding of how race and racism are woven into the social fabric of society; such work is thus integral to examining how race and racism operate within the ELT profession, and what this may mean for notions of 'good' language teaching and learning. The review of critical race scholarship below functions as the theoretical framework for the main analytic chapters of this book. The sections that follow are organized into three main topics: CRT; race in ELT; and colonialism, imperialism and globalism. Each section provides a different way of understanding how race and ethnicity circulate within, and shape various aspects of, the ELT profession.

Critical Race Theory

The conceptualization of this book, and the analysis conducted in subsequent chapters, are broadly informed by CRT, an assemblage of analytical and theoretical positions that seeks to understand how racial discrimination and privilege operate within different domains of life (Delgado & Stefancic, 2012). CRT aims to understand how race informs individual attitudes, shapes societal expectations of communities and creates and maintains social structures, but is chiefly interested in understanding how individual acts of racial discrimination or privilege are situated within a broader social and historical context. CRT scholars maintain that racism exists partly because individuals from the dominant (elite) class, such as government officials, maintain racial hierarchies in and through colorblind ideologies (Taylor *et al.*, 2009). Despite a strong emphasis on scholarship, empirical studies and theorization, CRT is informed and led by activists who seek to eradicate racial discrimination (Delgado & Stefancic, 2012).

CRT emerged from a '1970s movement' that wished to uncover how an ostensibly fair and balanced US legal system privileges certain ethnic communities while disadvantaging others. Led initially by legal professionals, CRT came into being from a concern that the civil rights movement was not adequately producing social reform. Derrick Bell, an established civil rights lawyer and early proponent of CRT, 'argued that U.S. jurisprudence on racial issues, even when seemingly liberal in thrust, serves to entrench racism and that in the post-civil rights era, although legal segregation and institutional discrimination have been struck down, formally neutral laws continue to uphold White racial domination' (Schaefer, 2008: 344). Other notable academics, or indeed founding CRT scholars, include Alan Freeman, Richard Delgado and Mari Matsuda (see also the influential work of Kimberlé Crenshaw and Patricia Williams; Delgado & Stefancic, 2012). CRT is now adopted in a number of disciplines, and several intellectual offshoots, such as critical race theories in Asian Studies (AsianCrit), have developed from calls to focus on social issues specific to ethnic communities (cf. Quach *et al.*, 2009).

Scholarship within CRT falls within one or more of the following 10 themes, as outlined in Delgado and Stefancic (1993: 462–463):

(1) Critique of liberalism

CRT is overwhelmingly dissatisfied with the ability of liberalism to address social issues pertaining to race and ethnicity, and more specifically, the failure of liberal jurisprudence to promote social equity (cf. affirmative action). Many scholarly texts view liberalism as a covert way of maintaining racial hierarchies (Bell, 1992). Liberalism in the ELT profession can be found in immigration laws that encourage language instructors to teach in Korea but at the same time maintain a system of White privilege (see Chapter 4). Zooming out from the Korean context, liberalism within the ELT profession is the common-sense assumption that being in the service of language instruction, and helping students from diverse linguistic and cultural backgrounds, contributes to the eradication of social injustices and racial discrimination. This liberal position leads to the misconception, or colorblind ideology, that racial discrimination and privilege do not exist within the profession because ELT scholars are 'nice' people (cf. Kubota, 2002) with good intentions.

(2) Storytelling

CRT scholars address and challenge racial hierarchies by providing counter-narratives to reshape dominant epistemological examples of discrimination that circulate within society. In other words, storytelling has the power to shape how members of society construct their understanding of themselves and the world around them. More storytelling and counter-narratives are needed in the ELT profession in Korea, as notions of pedagogy continue to be conceptualized through a race-based prism. Although the bulk of the race-based work done in ELT relies heavily on storytelling, such counter-narratives have not reached the professionals in Korea responsible for creating and changing education and immigration policies. Storytelling is one of several important discursive tools that can be used to change how scholars and professionals view dominant ideologies in language teaching and learning (see Curtis & Romney, 2006; Motha, 2014).

(3) Revisionist interpretations of American civil rights law and progress

The ability of antidiscrimination laws to bring about social change, including racial equality, is an issue taken up by many scholars in their CRT work. For example, in a seminal piece on antidiscrimination laws in the United States, Crenshaw (1988) provides a critical understanding of structural racism by showing how civil rights reforms continue to oppress Black communities, and offers nuanced ways of looking at concealed forms of discrimination, including material subordination (e.g. pay inequality and urban zoning). In a similar vein, applied linguists claim that educational reform laws that are meant to help students from diverse linguistic backgrounds, such as the No Child Left Behind (NCLB) Act, do not adequately provide the resources necessary to bring about change (cf. Liggett, 2014: 115). ELT scholarship is similarly concerned with how English-only laws disadvantage immigrants by limiting the resources needed for them to make a successful transition into their new home country (e.g. McKay, 1997). Thus, language scholars and practitioners have, to some extent, provided their own revisionist interpretation of language education laws and immigration reform. Chapter 4 continues this line of inquiry by uncovering how elite discourses in the ELT profession in Korea, such as immigration laws, are founded on an ideology that sees Whiteness as an indispensable facet of the English language.

(4) A greater understanding of the underpinnings of race and racism

Examining different conceptualizations of race, and uncovering the social mechanisms that facilitate racism, represents a large part of CRT scholarship. These efforts are accomplished by drawing from a number of different areas of study, including literature (e.g. Appiah, 1985) and anthropology (Hill, 1999). An exemplary, interdisciplinary example is provided by Haney López (1994: 61), who draws from a number of theories to argue that while biological notions of race are an 'illusion', they are nonetheless a 'fabrication' that has 'vigorous strength in the realm of social beliefs'. ELT scholars have added to this body of work by uncovering how language intersects with race and racism (cf. Theme 6 below), though such research represents a very small percentage of scholarship in language teaching and learning. In the Korean ELT context, the interface between race and language manifests in many domains of the profession, including immigration laws, education policies, the professional identities of language instructors and recruiting practices. A central argument of this book is that language discrimination in the ELT profession in Korea is propped up by racial hierarchies.

(5) Structural determinism

CRT scholarship aims to uncover how social structures (e.g. laws, institutional rules, standardized tests) and symbols (e.g. language, racialized discourse, embodied actions) shape behaviors toward, and the belief systems of, racial and ethnic groups. A number of structures and symbols have been investigated in the study of structural determinism. For example, Delgado and Stefancic (1989: 216) uncover how structures within scholarship, namely databases and indexing systems, while helpful in streamlining research production, bring about 'the false impression that law is exact and deterministic – a science – with only one correct answer to a legal question'. The authors consequently urge researchers to transform notions of civil rights by using non-conventional methods of scholarship, such as employing Derrick Bell's 'parables of racial injustice' to 'reexamine long-held [race-based] assumptions' (Delgado & Stefancic, 1989: 223). In ELT scholarship, researchers have examined how widely used 'empirical' terms create static, racialized images of the profession. The term NES, for example, limits notions of who is a legitimate speaker of English while disadvantaging many other teaching professionals (Leung et al., 1997). The ELT profession in Korea is largely organized according to the belief that being an NES is not only a professional 'qualification', but also a privilege that guarantees an ability to teach effectively in classrooms. This belief comes from a history of colonialism and linguistic imperialism, as demonstrated in the next chapter, and is circulated in and through the many elite discourses that exist in the ELT profession in Korea, as highlighted in the previous theme.

(6) Race, sex, class and their intersections

Race, while central to CRT scholarship, is only one of many social categories that collectively shape how societies are structured. CRT scholarship is aware of, and actively seeks out to understand, the intersections of race, gender, sexual orientation, class and religion. For many CRT scholars, race cannot be fully understood without understanding these other social categories (cf. Crenshaw, 1991). For example, in the case of Asian American identities in the United States, research has shown that racialized discourses are connected not only to gender, but also to the different sexual imaginations that are constructed of Asian men and women (Sheffer, 2014). Applied linguists have added to the body of intersectionality work by uncovering how race interfaces with language (e.g. Amin, 1997), a focus that has not seen a great deal of attention within traditional CRT scholarship. LangCrit is the name that attempts to formalize the empirical relation between race and language (see Crump, 2014). The analytic chapters presented later in this book show how racism in the ELT profession in Korea is built on notions of language proficiency and pedagogy and woven into discourses of nationality and citizenship.

(7) Essentialism and anti-essentialism

Intersectionality is an important aspect of conducting race-based studies because it reveals the rich and complex ways in which racial discrimination and privilege operate within society. However, it is just as important to understand, and be critical of, the very social categories that are under investigation. For example, should researchers continue to use race as a descriptor and unit of analysis or is ethnicity a more culturally sensitive term? Haney López (1994) argues that while race has no biological significance, CRT scholars must continue to use the term because it acknowledges how people make sense of each other. Other empirical issues that may be examined under this theme include, but are not limited to, the cultural and linguistic significance of using terms like Asian American, Black American and indeed simply American. ELT scholars, particularly those who work in intercultural studies, have done much to critique outdated, essentialized notions of big C culture, such as the notion that China is a collectivist society while countries like the United States are not (for a collection of studies that move away from essentialized notions of culture, see Jenks et al., 2013). In a similar vein, ELT scholarship is critical of how researchers essentialize notions of linguistic expertise when dichotomizing native and non-native speakers, and has additionally unpacked the sociopolitical baggage, including covert racism, associated with using such terms (Holliday & Aboshiha, 2009; Mahboob, 2009). The ELT profession in Korea similarly imports essentialized notions of race and language from the United States, which creates the conditions for a privileging of White instructors from a small group of English-speaking countries.

(8) Cultural nationalism/separatism
Some CRT scholars believe that racial equality can only be fully achieved in and through the creation of laws (and community efforts) that are designed to address the needs of specific ethnic groups. What this involves specifically is open to debate, but it is clear within this critical theme that national interests, as identified and implemented by government institutions, are not aligned with minority communities. Williams (1985: 397), for example, acknowledges that the US government has made some efforts to advance the cause of American Indians (cf. the Indian Tribal Governmental Tax Status Act of 1982), but such attempts fall short of 'empower[ing] Indian Nations with the means to begin constructing their own vision of economic and social self-sufficiency'. Although insular approaches to social advancement may lead to separatism, it is believed that this is a necessary first step in establishing and preserving minority causes. Similar caucuses in the ELT profession have also been formed, and while such groups have special interest causes that may not be shared by 'mainstream' language professionals and practitioners, it should not be assumed that these efforts have led to divides within the field. Within the Korean ELT context, language scholars use their scholarship to advance the causes of instructors of color, including ethnic Koreans, by addressing the cultural hegemony of English and the racial discrimination that arises from the teaching of this language. However, attempts to formalize the professional groups in Korea that are marginalized for racial, ethnic and linguistic reasons have not been made in any significant way.

(9) Legal institutions, critical pedagogy and minorities in the Bar
An important issue for CRT scholars is the promotion of wider representation of gender and social class in government institutions, schools and professional industries. Traditionally, CRT proponents have been concerned with diversity in law schools and the legal profession, but scholars from other fields and areas of study have embraced this cause (e.g. popular culture writers and their critique of a racially homogenous Hollywood). An urgent need for racial diversity exists in teacher training programs in places like North America, where an immense number of student teachers from post-colonial nations are exposed to a largely

racially homogenous group of faculty who are responsible for knowledge creation within the profession (cf. Chapter 7). To this end, scholars must create teacher training materials that encourage difficult questions regarding race, racism and racialized discourses. This may entail using CRT principles to promote the benefits of exposing students and student teachers to instructors and professors who come from a wide range of cultural backgrounds. Such materials are especially needed for student teachers from Korea who are often asked to use textbooks that are based on the cultural norms of Western societies.

(10) Criticism and self-criticism

The last theme identified in Delgado and Stefancic (1993: 463) is the 'criticism[s] addressed at CRT', as well as responses to such critiques (cf. West, 1988). Underpinning this theme is the notion that ways of knowing can only evolve if there is room within fields of study for critical discussions of differing viewpoints. The impediment to such growth in ELT scholarship is the ostensible reluctance to apply critical studies of race to language teaching and learning. As a result, there are very few debates within ELT scholarship that address critical race issues (for an excellent overview of CRT, including some of its criticism, see Kubota, 2013). This does not mean, however, that criticisms of, and resistance to, critical race work in language teaching and learning do not exist. Although Atkinson's (2002) response to Kubota's (2001) study is a remarkable example, the dearth of ELT studies utilizing critical self-reflection, as well as the promotion of theoretical constructs based on ethnocentrism, suggests that there is some resistance to pointing the critical eye toward the very principles and constructs that shape the field.

Moving forward, it is important for scholars to seek ways of understanding how decisions made in the ELT profession today are built on a history of cultural hegemony, linguistic imperialism and colonialism. Criticisms of, and resistance to, such work can provide a springboard for a more meaningful discussion of race and racism in the ELT profession. To this end, the ELT profession in Korea can benefit from extending the empirical and theoretical purview beyond traditional language teaching and learning matters to include critical social issues, such as an understanding of how a history of Japanese colonialism, modern-day American imperialism and social class, shape understandings of who is a legitimate speaker of English.

CRT scholars draw from, and place varying degrees of emphasis on, the 10 themes discussed previously. All 10 themes are, however, fundamental to advancing critical race scholarship. Further, these different foci, while examined for several decades now, are all relevant in contemporary society and germane to current race relations. With that said, however, racism today does not come in the same radical form as slavery and Jim Crow laws, despite many extreme cases of criminal acts in modern society. The challenge now, as a result, is understanding how racism is carried out in veiled, undisclosed and indirect ways. At the core of this concern is identifying racism that maintains racial hierarchies and power imbalances.

This line of work has been carried out by a small, but growing group of scholars in the ELT profession. These contributions will be discussed in greater detail later in this book, including, but not limited to, the works of Kubota, Motha, Ruecker, Liggett and Mahboob. Although such work uncovers how discrimination in the ELT profession is often based on racial hierarchies, scholars must also be cognizant of how inequalities are maintained by 'doing nothing'. Ignoring racism, and engaging in colorblindness, is the main focus of the next section. Following this discussion is a review of White studies, Marxism and neoliberalism.

Colorblindness

The United States elected a Black president in 2009, so the logical conclusion for many is that racial discrimination is now in the proverbial rearview mirror. However, despite advances in civil rights in many regions of the world, as well as a growing multicultural demographic in numerous countries marked traditionally as racially homogenous, CRT scholars are quick to point out that racism is still as relevant today as it was many decades ago. Namely, of significance in contemporary society is how individuals, often people belonging to the dominant class, maintain racial hierarchies by rejecting race as a valid lens through which to see the world. Such people reject the need to create systems and laws that are aimed at helping communities of color because doing so, they claim, would be tantamount to racism. In other words, colorblind proponents use the call to eradicate discrimination to reject the need to employ race as a lens through which to understand social structures. In so doing, such individuals can portray themselves or be seen as proponents of equality (i.e. calling for the eradication of discrimination) while preserving racial hierarchies that disadvantage minority groups (i.e. rejecting race as a valid way of addressing inequities). This contradiction is what defines colorblindness. Haney López (2006), a CRT scholar who has written extensively about how racial subordination is achieved in and through such contradictions, describes colorblindness as an ideology that self-righteously wraps itself in the raiment of the civil rights movement and that, while proclaiming a deep fealty to eliminating racism, perversely defines discrimination strictly in terms of explicit references to race. Thus, it is 'racism' when society uses affirmative race-conscious means to respond to gross inequalities, but there is no racial harm no matter how strongly disparities in health care, education, residential segregation, or incarceration correlate to race, so long as no one has uttered a racial word. Colorblindness wears its antiracist pretensions boldly but acts overwhelmingly to condemn affirmative action and to condone structural racial inequality. (Haney López, 2006: xviii)

Underpinning the observations made of colorblindness by CRT scholars is the need to continue seeing the world through a race-based prism. This may entail, for example, remembering that the hardship experienced by peoples of color in contemporary society is deeply rooted in, and inextricably connected to, historical race-based struggles and discrimination. Race, even with its widespread terminological misuse and tenuous connection with biology, is a reminder that there are equal rights issues that must be identified and addressed. As alluded to in the quote above, for example, access to affordable housing and quality education is a problem facing many societies, and often these equality issues are divided along racial lines. In ELT, it is also important to see the profession through a race-based prism. Simply rejecting the use of race as a marker of physical characteristics does nothing to help the many teachers of color who face discrimination because of some outdated notion of who is considered a speaker of English, nor does it contribute to understanding why such beliefs exist in the first place. The current book is informed by the belief that colorblind ideologies are not only broadly circulated within the ELT profession, and in teacher training programs in the United States and England in particular, but that they also frame professional expectations and pedagogical goals. These observations will be returned to later in this book.

Critical White studies

A person from any ethnic background can espouse colorblind ideologies, though it is more commonly adopted by White individuals with little to no understanding of, and/or personal experience of, racial discrimination. Ignorance exists because such people often belong to, and/or are associated with, the dominant class in their society or profession. Members of the dominant class are sheltered from discrimination and intolerance because they represent and reflect the norms of the majority (in the United States, these are White Americans), and thus their daily actions and cultural practices are rarely questioned or seen as problematic. This is one of several examples of White privilege: the dominant class is widely represented in most domains of public life, and thus their imagined culture shapes notions of what is normal. Being part of the dominant class thus leads to a situation where such individuals need not concern themselves with issues of race, a characteristic that Haney López (2006: 109) refers to as 'transparency'. A life free of the need to worry about society creating essentialized discourses and images that, at the same time can function as an oppressive and repressive tool, is fundamental to what is meant by racial privilege.

White privilege, and the ideologies and social conditions that manifest as a result of being on the receiving end of such entitlement (e.g. colorblindness), is a topic of interest in critical White studies (CWS). In the United States and other regions with similar racial hierarchies, White privilege is an 'invisible' power that allows 'Whites ... to ignore and neutralize race when race benefits Whites' (Case, 2012: 79). This area of concern stems from a larger interest in understanding Whiteness, which includes, but is not limited to, the examination of how the state of being White creates norms and expectations within a society (see the early works of W.E.B. Du Bois for foundational accounts of Whiteness). Also of great interest is how the social construction of Whiteness came into being and what this has meant to different communities and domains of life (e.g. Whiteness in the ELT profession). CWS has emerged as a key empirical strand within CRT scholarship because uncovering what it means, socially and legally, to be White helps address other important racial equality issues, such as how American popular culture continues to define good/bad, beautiful/ugly, hardworking/lazy, hero/villain and normal/deviant according to notions of Whiteness (Delgado & Stefancic, 2012). Herein lies a critical observation made by CWS scholars: the state of being White 'exerts its power as an invisible and unmarked norm against which all Others are racially and culturally defined, marked, and made inferior' (Kubota & Lin, 2009c). CWS scholarship attempts to understand how such invisible and unmarked norms, which are not limited to popular culture but indeed exist in legal discourse (Delgado & Stefancic, 2012), produce the conditions necessary for racial discrimination, colorblindness and White supremacy.

Also of great importance to CWS scholarship, including the present investigation, is how White normativity transforms attitudes and behaviors. For example, CWS scholars attempt to understand how White privilege informs an individual's ability to be cognizant of, and sensitive to, the existence of racism, the harm it does to people and the benefits received as a result of possessing the 'right' skin tone (cf. transparency). CWS scholars are further concerned with uncovering the social conditions that are created as a result of living an insular life. In the United States and other regions with similar racial equality issues, for example, 'White people ... live in a social environment that protects and insulates them from race-based stress. This insulated environment of racial protection builds white expectations for racial comfort while at the same time lowering the ability to tolerate racial stress, leading to what I refer to as White Fragility' (DiAngelo, 2011: 54). White Fragility prevents people from having serious and objective discussions of race, and in doing so, maintains racial hierarchies. It is not uncommon to hear individuals with White Fragility use the term, for instance, 'race baiter' to shut down any possibility that racial equality issues may have shaped a particular social outcome or event. The use of such descriptors occurs frequently with a reaction or emotional state, often anger or indignation.

Bonilla-Silva *et al.* (2006) examine how such emotional states, reactions and attitudes come into being; they use the term *White habitus* to describe the lack of racial empathy that exists when communities insulate themselves from Other, ethnic groups. Living an insular, White life creates 'a racialized, uninterrupted socialization process that conditions and creates whites' racial taste, perceptions, feelings, and emotions and their views on racial matters' (Bonilla-Silva, 2006: 104), which in turn 'leads to the creation of positive self-views ("We are nice, normal people") and negative other views ("They are lazy")' (Bonilla-Silva, 2006: 124). However, the social psychological effects of a White habitus are not limited to in-group members; forming communities that shut out individuals from other ethnic groups also shapes the perceptions and attitudes of so-called out-group members. Being excluded from social and professional networks and activities because of the psychological and spatial barriers that are created as a result of a White habitus can lead to hostility, anger, frustration, sadness and fear. Thus, discussions of a White habitus must be located in a larger understanding that racialized group formation has social and psychological effects on both in- and out-group members.

A White habitus can be applied to the ELT profession in similar ways. Hiring practices that favor 'white' features not only lead to a racially homogenous workforce (i.e. a White habitus), but they also socialize language professionals and laypeople into thinking that English speakers should possess certain phenotypic characteristics, such as blond hair and blue eyes. Participating in a profession that impedes the development of a multicultural workforce can result in members of the in-group (i.e. White instructors) believing that they possess a superior language ability and teaching acumen. This can lead to a sense of entitlement, which manifests itself in several ways. For example, it is not uncommon to hear instructors justify their membership in a White habitus by stating that they are doing their students a favor by teaching English. This ideology prevents students from taking ownership of their English, and indeed alienates them from the 'target' language by creating social, linguistic, racial and psychological barriers between the teacher and themselves. The implication for teachers of color is equally problematic. Being excluded from a workforce because of certain phenotypic characteristics tells teachers of color (as well as students) that English is a White language, and thus does not belong to them.

The underpinning idea of a White habitus is the belief that 'ethnic identity and boundaries … can be explained in terms of lived experiences, habitual practices that produce the codes and inscribe meanings onto the body and psyche of the individual' (Spencer, 2006: 102). Useful to this discussion is Bourdieu's (1977: 82) understanding of habitus, which he describes as 'a system of lasting, transposable dispositions which, integrating past experiences, functions at every moment as a *matrix of perceptions, appreciations, and action*' [original emphasis]. While people are capable of being individuals – that is to say, they can sometimes think for themselves – their practices and actions are 'steeped in the specific traditions of a group, embodying all its social codes' (Spencer, 2006: 103).

CRT scholars argue that efforts to eradicate racial discrimination must move beyond the investigation of the disadvantaged and disenfranchised minority (i.e. the tradition in ELT and applied linguistic scholarship). Scholars must also examine how the dominant class discursively constructs its position and role in society, and the ways in which this understanding manifests in various domains of life. In other words, efforts to understand and eradicate racism must include an examination of both discrimination and privilege. The latter focus of investigation is particularly important in CRT scholarship, as Whiteness is not only a resource that is used to oppress and repress minority and less powerful communities, but it is also a valuable commodity that skews notions of what is normal. In the ELT market, for example, the promotion and recruitment of, and preference for, White teachers define what is a valuable 'teaching' commodity (see Chapter 6).

Marxism: Exploitation, alienation and oppression

Marxism is understood to be a theory of society that is principally concerned with class exploitation (e.g. Marx, 1976), and as such, is often not associated with, or applied to, critical race issues. However, according to Bakan and Dua (2014: 95), this disassociation is a fallacy because Marxism 'provides insights into alienation and oppression', two areas of scholarship taken up by critical race theorists. Spencer (2006) similarly adds:

> Although Marx made little mention of 'race', the legacy of his conception of society as a struggle between the exploited and the exploiters has remained an influential discourse and one that many social commentators see as increasingly more relevant as the global forces of capitalism expand, as they consolidate their grip on resources and as divisions between economic classes reach unprecedented distances. (Spencer, 2006: 82)

Despite some doubt cast upon the connection between (classical) Marxism and critical race scholarship (see, for example, Rex, 1986), globalization processes in modern society, including migratory trends and international trade agreements, have a central role in class exploitation, which for many centuries has been inextricably connected to race, ethnicity, nationality and citizenship. For example, slavery is a vivid reminder that race and ethnicity are part and parcel of class exploitation, the production and consumption of material wealth, and commodity trading. As Spencer (2006) observes:

> The roots of racism could be argued to always have been grounded in labour relations. Race was a constructed concept which, as we have seen, enabled colonialists to justify an expendable workforce of slaves. In contemporary society, it could equally be argued that the focus on difference (ethnicisation or racialisation) between workers is still maintained and serves a similar function ... Race is fundamental to the formation of the working classes in general and to the experience of black labour in particular. (Spencer, 2006: 86)

Globalization similarly generates economic value in and through the exploitation of race and ethnicity. Such practices often feed into, and draw from, extant racial hierarchies, widespread minority discrimination and oppression, and persistent forms of White supremacy. In (international) education, for example, diversity has become a commodity that predominantly White institutions in English-speaking countries seek to acquire for their cultural and economic value. Thus, the issue is not whether Marxism is relevant to studies of racism, but rather how race intersects with class exploitation and the distribution of power and material wealth.

Although Marxists assume that race is a 'false consciousness' (e.g. Marcuse, 1964), racial categories have always been seen under Marxism as resources that are used for the organization and often exploitation of labor (i.e. the commodification of race or what is referred to in this book as White neoliberalism). In other words, Marxists believe that race, though delusive and illusional, is used to create class divisions. By exploiting racial hierarchies (e.g. colorblind ideologies), individuals from the dominant class can use race to, among many things, profit from communities in less powerful positions in society. In the ELT profession, this means using White instructors as a resource to sell an 'authentic', 'Western' experience (see Chapter 6). Profiting from the widespread, though erroneous, assumption that English is best taught by White instructors preserves the very discourses and images that circulate and maintain racial hierarchies in the ELT profession.

Marxist perspectives on class exploitation are relevant to discussions of race, and help to inform the present investigation, because the teaching and learning of English are tied to oppressive market forces, especially those guided by neoliberalism (for a general discussion of Marxism, race and education, see M. Cole, 2009, 2012). For example, students from countries where English is associated with material wealth and possesses cultural capital are socialized into thinking that they must spend enormous amounts of time and money learning the 'global' language. This ideological commitment to the English language is profoundly shaped by the free market principles that exist in most, if not all, developed countries. Because the ELT profession is propped up by such ideological commitments, Marxism is a logical response to the exercise in understanding a number of critical issues in language teaching and learning, including those related to race and ethnicity. In addition to understanding the class exploitation, oppressive power dynamics and professional alienation that exist in the ELT profession, Marxist perspectives may provide the means to understanding how government officials, university departments and school owners commodify race, exploit the neoliberal logic and oppress teachers by perverting what is and what is not deemed valuable in the ELT profession.

Neoliberalism

Several definitions or conceptualizations of neoliberalism exist. While scholars are informed by different schools of philosophical thought and possess varying empirical goals (cf. Saad-Filho & Johnston, 2005), neoliberalism is most often defined as an economic theory (Chomsky, 1999). A number of researchers also discuss neoliberalism as a set of mechanisms that produce a free market economy (Doogan, 2009). Further, scholars from a range of disciplines are particularly interested in understanding neoliberalism as a powerful discursive construction (Krinsky, 2007; Springer, 2012) and/or an ideology (Holborow, 2007). These four different, often overlapping conceptualizations of neoliberalism are considered in Block *et al.* (2012) and will be similarly discussed in this section. To summarize, neoliberalism can be viewed as (1) an economic theory, (2) a new form of capitalism, (3) a discourse and/or (4) an ideology. An understanding of the discursive formation of neoliberalism, including the ideologies that drive such constructions, has been approached using a number of methodological tools, including Foucauldian discourse analysis (e.g. critical discourse analysis; cf. van Dijk, 2007: 160) and Russian Marxist approaches to language study (cf. Vološinov, 1973).

First, neoliberalism is an economic theory that, as Harvey (2005: 2) states, 'proposes that human well-being can best be advanced by liberating individual entrepreneurial freedoms and skills within an institutional framework characterized by strong private property rights, free markets, and free trade'. He goes on to observe that under neoliberalism the prime role of the state is to ensure the financial health of the free market, which includes governing monetary policies, using force if necessary to protect private property, and creating and enforcing laws that ensure 'good' business practice. Despite the doctrine of deregulation and privatization, a policy adopted by many countries as they transitioned from one economic and/or political situation to another (e.g. Chile, South Africa, China), neoliberalism requires, at least in actual governing practice, more state involvement than economists and politicians would have people believe (cf. the 2008 financial crisis). This contradiction, however, has not stopped neoliberalism from becoming so pervasive that it is now, as Harvey (2005: 3) puts it, part of the 'common-sense way' of understanding the world. In other words, the idea that deregulation and privatization benefit all members of society, a type of trickle-down economics (cf. Aghion & Bolton, 1997), has become so widely promulgated that even the poor and disadvantaged espouse the immeasurable potential of living in a system that privileges the elite and wealthy. In the United States in particular, this warped view of the world has been partly shaped by the notion that freedom, a common marker of national identity, is made possible in and through neoliberal policies and practices.

Second, neoliberalism is a form of new capitalism, an economic system that places greater emphasis, even after the 2008 financial crisis, on deregulation and privatization. For instance, new capitalism honors neoliberalism by simultaneously placing the blame for the 2008 events on a few bad corporations and highlighting the great economic prosperity that was achieved by people of all socioeconomic classes around the world prior to the financial crisis (Doogan, 2009). The latter assertion is curious given the expanding wealth gap between rich and poor witnessed in many countries that embrace new capitalism. Neoliberal policies and practices – fueled by, and also used under the guise of, globalization – have created a new capitalistic mentality that exploits the blurring of boundaries between time and space by technological advancements. Industries, like call centers, and companies, such as Apple, can now more easily than ever move entire operational or manufacturing units from one country or region to another, exploiting cheap labor and tax incentives that ultimately hurt the very individuals that neoliberalism purports to help. Under new capitalism, where global networks facilitate precipitous business transactions, an advanced 'knowledge-based economy' has emerged that necessitates the use of English for multinational negotiation and transnational communication (for a study that examines the effects of globalization on English language use in Korea, see Piller & Cho, 2013). In this respect, the English language has become a commodity in a knowledge-based economy that places great value on the ability to communicate across national boundaries (for a study that examines linguistic capital in the Korean job market, see J.S. Park, 2011).

Third, neoliberalism is a discourse, or rather neoliberal policies become discursive constructions when they are used in business practices and transactions. Put differently, neoliberalism is not simply an abstract system of beliefs that operates on a different social plane from business practices and transactions. For example, aligning with 'free market' principles requires as a minimum constructing a discourse that justifies this particular worldview. The ostensibly simple construction 'I believe in free market principles' is, in and of itself, a discursive construction. In this sense, ideology and discourse are inextricably tied to each other (see the next paragraph for how ideology and discourse are different). The discourse of neoliberalism accomplishes many social actions, including establishing and ratifying the worldview that 'free trade' is in the best interests of individuals and society. Neoliberal discourses also become part of an individual's sense of national identity; a way of understanding social systems and structures; and indeed a form of representing economic policies, countries and business practices as either good, bad or evil.

Furthermore, the discourse of neoliberalism is more than an ideology in that it can encourage language choice. For example, the ostensible need to maximize corporate profits through transnational agreements elevates the role and status of English in business practices and negotiation. This means that neoliberalism is not only associated with a core set of discursive constructions (e.g. small government, increased privatization, free market, globalization, individualism), but that these neoliberal symbols are often associated with, and require the use of, English. As noted at the end of the previous section, one consequence of the elevated need to use the English language is the commodification of race, which is the topic of analysis in Chapter 6 that deals with White neoliberalism.

Fourth, neoliberalism is an ideology; it is a system of beliefs that promotes the maximization of corporate wealth and the elimination of regulation. Although neoliberalism represents an ideological commitment to an abstract set of economic values, what is important in investigations is not understanding what individuals believe, but rather uncovering the social actions and practices of neoliberal proponents. This is because in some (if not many) situations, neoliberal ideologies and discourses diverge. For example, free market principles are often incommensurate with what governments ultimately do to cultivate economic growth. In other words, neoliberalism is an ideological contradiction. This was evidenced again most vividly during the 2008 financial crisis that demonstrated the level of state involvement that is needed in order to prop up and sustain neoliberalism. Thus, discussing neoliberalism strictly as a discourse or as an ideology belies the complex interplay between what proponents of neoliberalism call 'free market' and how the notion of 'privatization' is handled, or enacted, in the real world. This contradiction reveals the true nature of ideologies (cf. Marx & Engels, 1998); they are not only 'distortions that suit the interests of its promoters' (Holborow, 2007: 52–53), but a system of beliefs that also reflects class struggles, political oppression and financial inequality. To avoid what Marx and Engels (1998: 36) describe as 'combating solely the phrases of this world', it is necessary to recognize 'the interaction between the material and the representational … between what happens in society and what appears to be common sense' (Block et al., 2012: 23). Neoliberalism is indeed an ideology, or a set of common-sense assumptions, but beliefs must be set into motion by real people, concerned with real things.

Neoliberalism is most often associated with abstract discourses and ideologies, but as alluded to in this section, one outcome of the neoliberal logic is a racialized economic system that transforms the English language, and thus ELT instructors (see Holborow, 2012), into a commodity. This market process not only distorts notions of what it means to be an ELT professional, but it also exploits and oppresses language instructors by commodifying race and ethnicity (see Chapter 6). Although many of the studies cited in the following section are not situated in a larger discussion of neoliberalism, and neglect how 'free market' principles racialize discourse and commodify race, the ELT profession is bound to exploitative and oppressive market forces, as demonstrated in subsequent analytic chapters.

Race in ELT

Studies that explore the role of race in language teaching and learning play a minor role in the production of knowledge in ELT scholarship. A search on Linguistics and Language Behavior Abstracts using the keyword 'race' with either 'TESOL', 'language teaching' or 'ELT' yields 24 peer-reviewed articles from 1974 to 2014. Although this number does not include several notable studies, including articles published in 2015 and a handful of books on these issues, the search provides a clear, albeit crude, understanding of where critical race issues stand in the ELT literature. For example, searching the same database with the keywords 'culture' and 'language teaching' produces over 1100 peer-reviewed articles from 1974 to 2014, which amounts to approximately 27 articles per year over the last four decades. It can be said, therefore, that the dearth of ELT scholarship that examines race is not an issue of whether there is an interest in understanding how social and cultural factors and issues impact language teaching and learning. The observation that ELT scholarship has a long tradition of investigating the cultural facets of language teaching and learning becomes even more apparent when searching the same database with other keywords, such as 'identity' or 'community'. Although it is difficult to identify why ELT scholars have not taken up the study of race to the same extent as other cultural facets of language teaching and learning, it is possible that researchers find the topic to be too contentious. Whatever the reasons may be, the lack of race studies in ELT scholarship is astonishing given the great body of work being done on such issues in education studies.

Despite the lack of ELT research on race, several researchers have taken seriously the importance and utility of seeing language teaching and learning through a race-based prism. For example, Crump (2014: 207) attempts to formalize the investigation of race and racism in ELT by suggesting a new critical strand that examines, among other things, the 'propagation of Whiteness as a norm associated with native English speakers' (cf. CRT Theme 6). This critical strand is referred to as LangCrit, and related work is concerned primarily with how subjects are 'seen and heard', or how physical characteristics and speech particularities are racialized in and through social actions and practices. Simply put, LangCrit attempts to understand the intersection of race and language. LangCrit studies that examine ELT issues have made important contributions to the literature and provide an important foundation for the investigation carried out in this book. These contributions are reviewed below and organized into four, overlapping subsections (or themes): positionality and identity, racialized discourses, ideologies and critical pedagogy. Although many of the studies reviewed below belong to two or more themes, in the interest of clarity the review will limit the discussion of each investigation to one subsection. The review is organized in such a way because the overarching goal is to establish a general understanding of what has been done in relation to race in the ELT literature.

Positionality and identity

The bulk of ELT scholarship that examines race is concerned with language instructors discussing – either in interviews or in reflective journals – how their professional identities and pedagogical practices are shaped by race, racism and White privilege. Many of the studies cited in this section also demonstrate that race, in addition to functioning as a resource to guide understandings of linguistic proficiency and teaching ability, also shapes how individuals construct notions of character and intelligence.

Curtis and Romney (2006) make a significant contribution to this body of work; their collection of 13 papers uses storytelling (see CRT Theme 2) to explore what it means to be an ELT professional of color. Contributors to the volume reflect on how their racial status shaped certain life experiences and explore what they have learned from such events. For example, Stephan (2006) considers the ways in which his status as an educated Black male transforms from an ostensibly inconsequential aspect of his life in his homeland of Suriname to a salient identity in the United States with real professional consequences. The transformation occurred when the author realized that some of his Asian students had adopted the same racial hierarchies circulated in the United States in their understanding of what it means to be a good language instructor. While space does not permit a review of the entire collection of narratives, it can be said that the contributors to the Curtis and Romney (2006) volume all critically examine the ways in which racial positionality and identity have influenced their understanding of pedagogy, relationships with colleagues, sense of self-worth in relation to the profession and interactions with students in the classroom. These topics are also examined by some of the contributors to a special issue edited by Kubota and Lin (2006) of *TESOL Quarterly*. Motha's (2006) longitudinal study, for instance, investigates how four language instructors attempt to understand how their professional and racial positionalities are situated in an inherently racialized ELT profession:

> The three White women … constructed themselves as working against layers of colonialism embedded in the ELT enterprise, and they were conscious of the potential hegemony to which they could contribute. The Korean-born woman … sensed that her authority was in question because of her racial identity, and she was influenced by her own history of shame about her race. (Motha, 2006: 504)

Motha (2006: 504) goes on to argue that language instructors must learn 'how to position themselves within an institutional culture [i.e. the ELT profession] whose dominant ideology' supports White supremacy and privileges native speakers. Work on positionality and identity is not, however, limited to the examination of personal experiences. Many researchers within this empirical strand use autoethnographic reports to examine larger, macro issues in the profession. For example, Motha (2014: 77), building on her earlier critical race work, uses the voices of the four teachers to argue that the 'inequitable power dynamics' in ELT have created a profession where 'the mere act of teaching ESOL reproduces racism'.

Although investigations of positionality and identity are dedicated to uncovering individual, lived experiences, it is not uncommon for researchers to use narratives to critique larger theoretical issues. Take, for example, the study conducted by Lee and Simon-Maeda (2006); the researchers analyze how their racialized identities color the ways in which they carry out ELT research. Speaking of the challenges of investigating race and racism in the ELT profession, Lee and Simon-Maeda (2006: 589) assert that researchers who do not question their positionality in the research process help 'proliferate hegemonic representations of participants' experiences'. In other words, researchers actively engage in discursive constructions of race when conducting ELT research; thus, the issue of positionality is crucial to the examination of race in language teaching and learning. Reflexive methods that force researchers to answer difficult questions pertaining to how the lived experiences and privileged status of the 'observer' co-produce racialized spaces help bridge 'the gulf between emancipatory intentions and actual steps toward progressive reform in the ESL/EFL field' (Lee & Simon-Maeda, 2006: 590).

Such reflexive methods are adopted by Lin *et al.* (2004: 488), who collectively examine how their experiences working in ELT exposed 'consistent hierarchical patterns across different institutional contexts', which in turn 'require ... attend[ing] to issues of not only gender but also of race and social class'. The authors make an important contribution to the literature by showing that disparate narratives or experiences, when viewed collectively, can act as a powerful tool to identify and remove policies and practices that discriminate and privilege individuals from certain racial and ethnic backgrounds. In addition to investigating the racial positionality of different teachers (see also Ajayi, 2011; G. Park, 2009), the paper by Lin *et al.* (2004) demonstrates how race intersects with other important social categories, like gender. In the same vein, Appleby (2013) examines White racial positionalities in relation to masculine and heterosexual identities. Her study of 11 White Australian male teachers shows that, although race and gender offer certain occupational privileges, the participants struggled to negotiate their professional identities because their workplace blurred the boundaries between 'teacher and student, male and female, customer and product, agent and object, [and] prey and victim' (Appleby, 2013: 144).

The collection edited by Kubota and Lin (2009a) builds on the body of work concerned with racial positionalities and identities, though many of the contributors, unlike the studies cited previously in this section, analyze student learning experiences. Ibrahim (2009) considers how immigrants and refugees in the United States position their English language identities in relation to notions of 'Blackness' and hip-hop culture (for a similar study, see also Bashir-Ali, 2006; Shapiro, 2014). Quach *et al.* (2009) examine how the learning experiences of Asian students in North Carolina are formed by the tensions that exist in, and are a result of, living in a largely monoracial and monocultural community. Like the teachers in the preceding paragraphs, the racial identities of these Asian students intersect with a number of different social phenomena, including marginalization, pedagogical needs and relations with peers. Other notable studies include Katz and DaSilva Iddings (2009), who analyze the positionalities of young children from two different social and educational contexts; their findings demonstrate that narratives and storytelling help uncover how racial and linguistic identities change according to social roles and contexts (e.g. identities that are relevant when helping a parent with limited English at home versus participating in class).

The strength of the research discussed in this section is the use of storytelling as an instrument to provide spaces for marginalized voices to be heard, explore how individuals position themselves in different educational contexts and uncover the many ways in which race intersects with other social categories. In so doing, these studies establish the utility of using race as a theoretical tool to uncover how language teaching and learning converges with a host of other cultural issues, including ethnicity, class and nationality. While the research discussed in this section makes up a large part of the ELT scholarship concerned with race, most positionality and identity work examines teachers and students of color. Indeed, very little is known about how White instructors and students construct their racial positionalities and identities, and even fewer studies have been conducted on male teachers (cf. Appleby, 2013). A considerable amount of research has, however, analyzed how notions of linguistic expertise are used to racialize the ELT profession.

Racialized discourses

Racialization is a process of using race as a discursive tool to categorize, identify and understand both the Self and the Other (Miles & Brown, 2003: 100). Racialized discourse is a term that simply highlights this discursive process in a more explicit way. Attempts to use race to categorize, identify and understand people from diverse backgrounds stem from years of colonialism and linguistic imperialism (Kubota & Lin, 2009c) and have over subsequent decades manifested in the conceptualization and delivery of ELT policies and practices (Motha, 2014).

The body of work devoted to understanding race and ethnicity in the ELT literature has done much to understand how racialized discourses operate within, and define, the profession. A key concern within this line of investigation is the examination of the NES–non-native English speaker (NNES) dichotomy, which has been criticized for being overly simplistic and essentialist (for alternative descriptors, see Rampton, 1990). Although NES and NNES are contested terms in the ELT literature, research has only recently attempted to explore how this dichotomy frames racial hierarchies (for an earlier study that examines how NES–NNES intersects with ethnicity, see Leung et al., 1997).

Lindemann (2002) examines university students collaborating on a task-based activity and demonstrates that ethnicity can negatively shape perceptions of communication ability; her investigation is one of the first papers to empirically validate the observation that notions of native speaker status are not only associated with linguistic competence, but are also inextricably connected to race and ethnicity. That is to say, notions of linguistic expertise are bound to racialized beliefs and discourses (for an even earlier study that examines how ethnicity shapes perceptions of NNES teaching assistants, see Rubin & Smith, 1990). Studies that use experimental methods (e.g. Lindemann, 2002) and examine international teaching assistants (e.g. Rubin, 1992) help bring attention to racialized discourses, but these earlier papers do not specifically critique the NES–NNES dichotomy nor do they investigate why Asian speakers of English are often believed to have poor English skills (for an investigation that examines negative attitudes toward Korean-accented English, see Butler, 2007).

In recent years, however, researchers have criticized the NES–NNES dichotomy for perpetuating racial hierarchies in the ELT profession. A frequent criticism is that the NES descriptor racializes hiring practices because the term is often associated with Whiteness (Holliday, 2008). This association stems from decades of colonialism and linguistic imperialism and is thus historically situated, but nonetheless has real-world consequences for ELT professionals. Mahboob (2009), for example, argues that the term NES is used to mask a preference for White teachers from the United States, Canada and other inner-circle countries (Kachru, 1985); racial bias materializes in many ways, including in the language used to seek and hire ELT instructors (e.g. Mahboob & Golden, 2013; Ruecker & Ives, 2015).

Ruecker (2011) uses C. Harris' (1993) argument that racial identity intersects with property rights to further establish how ELT professionals racialize the NES descriptor in, and through, legal discourse. Drawing from a small data set of job advertisements posted on popular ELT websites, Ruecker (2011) argues that draconian work visa laws in East Asia allow recruiters to engage in racial discrimination by hiding behind immigration policies that narrowly define native speaker status. Although such findings are of great importance to ELT scholarship (see also Ruecker & Ives, 2015), few researchers have yet to fully examine why White and NES privilege exists in places like Korea in the first place (cf. Chapter 6). For example, what role do American popular culture and politics have in shaping the English language imagination?

The contributions made to the ELT literature by examining native speaker beliefs have been significant, but not all studies of racialized discourses are concerned with notions of Whiteness (e.g. Ellwood, 2009). Attention is also paid to how racism against, and the racial identities of, students of color are discursively constructed. Talmy (2010), for instance, conducted a longitudinal ethnography of high school students in Hawai'i; his findings show how racial hierarchies are co-constructed in classroom interactions between Micronesians and East/South East Asians. Talmy's (2010) study uncovers the complex ways in which language competence, regional family heritage (e.g. FOB or 'fresh off the boat' versus non-FOB) and course enrollment (ESL versus mainstream) are used as resources to construct racialized discourses (for a theoretical discussion of the importance of ethnicity in language learning, see Trofimovich & Turuševa, 2015). Thomas (2013) takes an equally important look at how racialized discourses transcend the meanings that words convey. Her study of US study-abroad scholarships demonstrates that oversimplified notions of race and ethnicity exist in the literature, and that such discourses are not only circulated within and beyond the academic community, but that they also shape how higher education institutions provide educational support for students of color.

The studies cited in this section contribute to the ELT literature by establishing how race interfaces with language (e.g. Haque & Patrick, 2015). Race, it has been shown, is discursively constructed. As such, racial identities are embedded in, and are transmitted through, talk and interaction (e.g. Kobayashi, 2006). Further, race is a discursive tool or interactional resource that is used to discriminate, privilege and oppress. Race, in other words, is used to carry out discursive actions and social practices. The discussion presented in subsequent chapters builds on these observations by showing that racialized discourses, in addition to interfacing with linguistic expertise and cultural heritage (see above), are bound to economic and political factors and processes, such as neoliberalization, commodification and imperialism.

Ideologies

Racial ideologies, a set of beliefs that include attitudes and feelings, have been investigated from several perspectives (e.g. White instructors, parents, native speakers). Investigations that examine racial ideologies overlap a great deal with the studies cited in the previous section in that belief systems based on race are expressed in, and through, discourse. That is to say, studies that examine racialized discourses often at least tangentially discuss racial ideologies. Despite the important connection between ideology and discourse (e.g. H. Shin, 2015), a section devoted to the former is necessary because, in addition to needing to know the ways in which racial identities are discursively constructed (cf. the previous section), it is important to examine what people are thinking and how this may inform and define the ELT profession. Further, ideologies circulate within the profession and shape norms and expectations regarding language and race.

Within this line investigation, Amin (1997) provides a revelatory account of the perspectives of five ELT instructors of color when asked to nominate who their students would regard as the ideal language teacher. The study reveals that the interviewees believed their students would assume only White individuals could be considered NESs and Canadians, and that belonging to the former category meant speaking proper English. As the investigation presented in subsequent chapters will reveal, these ideological commitments are not uncommon, and unfortunately shape hiring practices in many regions and professional contexts. Sung (2011) reports on similar ideologies in his observations of, and experiences working at, a private language academy in Hong Kong where the marketing approach was to highlight the 'foreign' teachers employed at the school. Despite recruiting very few NNESs from the local pool of competent Hong Kong teachers, the school hired an unqualified teacher with limited English proficiency because of her, as Sung (2011: 27) notes, European features. Such marketing and hiring practices exist partly because many parents believe English is a White language, an ideology that also problematically equates race with language expertise. Of course, parents are not the only individuals who subscribe to such ideologies. In an experimental study conducted by Rivers and Ross (2013: 334), for instance, Japanese students were found to have a clear preference for White male instructors from the United States. The research participants were, however, partial to instructors with at least five years of teaching experience and some proficiency in the Japanese language.

Although scholars gravitate toward peoples of color in investigations of racial ideologies (e.g. Aneja, 2014), White instructors and students (as well as notions of Whiteness) have been the focal point of analysis in some empirical work. Shuck (2006) examines the ideologies of first-year undergraduates in a US university who speak English monolingually and self-identify as White. Her interview-based study describes how students discursively construct essentialized notions of nationality, language and race, thus revealing ideological commitments to racial and linguistic hierarchies that maintain Whiteness and monolingualism as privileged statuses in the United States. As Pennycook (1999) observes (see also Phillipson, 2008), these ideologies adopt a colonial mindset that circulates within places like the United States (for colonial discourses in Canada, see

Sterzuk, 2015), but are also more problematically disseminated to different regions of the world through popular culture and media.

Liggett (2008) establishes how such ideologies shape the ways in which White instructors manage classrooms with students of color. The teachers in her study were committed to a belief system that downplayed racism (cf. colorblindness) because their membership to the dominant social class did not require them to reflect on the importance of race in shaping world views (see also Herrera & Morales, 2009). This ideological commitment meant that the teachers often mismanaged and misinterpreted students' race-based contributions to classroom discussions. Liggett's (2008) study is a stark reminder that teacher training programs must take seriously the importance of race and ethnicity in preparing future instructors for a profession that is increasingly multicultural and multilingual. To this end, the ELT literature has made significant contributions to critical pedagogy. The following section ends the larger discussion of race in ELT by exploring this important body of work.

Critical pedagogy

Critical pedagogy in ELT is primarily concerned with bringing about change from within the classroom. Operating from within the classroom, or working from the inside out, often means having an overt pedagogical outcome for the participants involved in a research project. This approach may entail addressing discrimination by designing teaching materials that equip language learners with knowledge to understand how racism operates within different domains of life (cf. Taylor, 2006). While many of the studies cited above inform critical approaches to pedagogy, in that such research is often carried out because there is an underlying aim to bring about change by better understanding how race and racism operate within the profession, the scholarship included in this section uses educational practices and policies to create immediate transformative experiences for teachers and students.

Hammond (2006), for example, uses a racial inequality exercise to explore how her Japanese students deal with race and racism in society. Although her class demonstrated some empathy in reflecting on inequality, the exercise failed to create an awareness of the implicit ways that language is used to engage in racism. The failure to prepare her students to participate in a multicultural world did not, however, prevent Hammond (2006) from identifying several ways in which the exercise could be revised to transform students into more critically aware participants in society. In so doing, the study demonstrates how critical pedagogy operates within a classroom setting.

In the same vein, Chun (2016) examines how an instructor manages classroom discussions around racialized multicultural discourses in an English-language textbook (for a similar study of early childhood education, see Michael-Luna, 2009). His study uncovers how the level of critical engagement with racialized discourses adopted by an instructor can promote (or hinder) opportunities for students to develop linguistically and grow as socially aware and responsible citizens. Ferreira (2007) provides similar observations in her study of Brazilian teachers of English; she argues that curriculum design efforts will always fall short in multicultural regions like Brazil if teachers and administrators are not adequately trained in theories of race and racism (for similar observations of White instructors in the United States, see McCann, 2012; for Venezuela, see Chacón, 2009).

Designing instructional materials for language learners or teacher trainees is a core area of investigation for critical pedagogy scholars. The investigation conducted by Charlebois (2008) to understand how film can be used to promote racial awareness among students is one such example. His study establishes that classroom discussions based on a film can encourage students to think about how life experiences are shaped by not one, but many, social categories (e.g. race and gender). Charlebois' (2008) instructional materials allowed his students to work simultaneously on their target language skills and their ability to critically reflect on the intersection of race and gender. Bangou and Wong (2009) similarly uncover the ways in which pedagogy can be used to provide immediate transformative experiences. In their study, the researchers explore how online technologies help two pre-service teachers of color fight racism in the classroom. The researchers argue that educators must approach discussions of technology use in teacher training and language teaching with the understanding that access to such tools is tied to race and ethnicity. Other researchers who argue for the need to incorporate discussions of race and ethnicity in teacher education and language teaching include, but are not limited to, Austin (2009), Haque and Morgan (2009) and Luke (2009).

Studies that seek to critique the theoretical and pedagogical principles that are adopted in language teaching and learning research also contribute to critical pedagogy by shaping how instructors approach, and deal with, issues of racial and linguistic discrimination and equity (e.g. Ibrahim, 2015; Kubota, 2003a; Kubota & Chiang, 2012). The seminal piece by Leung et al. (1997) is a reminder that careful analysis of contemporary social issues, such as the linguistic implications of living in a multilingual urban environment, can have a profound impact on how teachers view their students. Their study brought to light the overt ways in which idealized notions of native speakers, which continue to dominate thinking in the ELT profession, discriminate against multilingual and multi-ethnic students and oversimplify the relations between language, ethnicity, citizenship and nationality (for a study that complicates notions of citizenship and race, see Fleming, 2015). Liggett (2014) takes the efforts of Leung *et al.* (1997) a step further by proposing a more formal dialogue between ELT researchers and critical race scholars. She identifies three areas of critical scholarship that must be taken up by researchers in order to create a more equitable ELT profession: linguicism, European colonialism and storytelling. The first two critical areas are discussed in the next section. Kubota (2001) makes similar points in her discussion of the discursive constructions of students in the United States. She argues that 'colonialism did not merely exist in the past – its legacy has continued to the present' (Kubota, 2001: 25). Colonial discourses manifest in many ways; in the ELT profession, such discourses create false dichotomies (Self versus Other) that view students as, for example, culturally strange (for similar observations in a Canadian context, see E. Lee, 2015).

A considerable amount of work in critical pedagogy is also devoted to multicultural education. Unfortunately, space does not permit a review of such work. With that said, scholarship in this area, though revelatory in its treatment of racism in education (e.g. Ebonics and English-only debates), is not strictly concerned with ELT issues. Many exceptions to this observation exist, of course, including Kubota's (2004) piece on liberalism in education that argues that multicultural scholarship promotes tolerance but does so through essentialized notions of cultural differences (see also Kubota 2003b). Such work will be referred to at times in subsequent chapters (see, for example, Kubota, 2015a, 2015b).

Colonialism, Linguistic Imperialism and Globalism

Race intersects with language in many ways. The studies cited in the previous section demonstrate that language is not only a vehicle for discrimination and privilege, but it is also symbolically tied to racial ideologies. Language, in other words, is a resource to carry out, and a symbol of, race-based social actions and practices. For example, an individual who uses language to construct essentialized notions of an ethnic group, say the trope that Asians speak broken English, relies on a history of struggles that obliges people to view notions of standard English in a limited, racialized way. The discussion below is concerned with exploring the latter process. Put differently, while the previous section dealt with the intersection of race and language in teaching and learning, the discussion below addresses some of the historical and social processes that underpin racial and linguistic discrimination and privilege in the ELT profession. The historical and social processes discussed in the following sections are colonialism, linguistic imperialism and English globalism. The discussion that follows is not a comprehensive review of scholarship on these issues, but is concerned with establishing how historical and social processes feed into, and create the structures necessary for, a system of cultural and linguistic hierarchies that controls how individuals view the world.

Colonialism

Early British colonialism resulted in an outward migration of the English language (Pennycook, 1998). Such efforts, though not unique in that colonial ambitions existed for millennia, established contact zones that required – through political, economic, ideological and military force – individuals from colonized regions to possess some working knowledge of English (the ways in which language is used to exert power over regions is examined in the next section). Although the global spread of English continues today, and is partly a result of earlier British endeavors, this section is not concerned with extrapolating colonialism. This is because colonialism in general, and the colonial efforts by the British Empire in particular, are both rooted in a misguided sociological project that objectified and exoticized individuals from colonized regions and, in doing so, constructed images of inferior, even sub-, human beings. Therefore, the question that is pertinent to the present book is not who was colonized and for how long, but rather how the 'West' constructed images of the Other through the lens of the Self (for insightful examples, see Pennycook, 1998). This ethnocentric way of understanding the world, as demonstrated below, is crucial to how racial discrimination manifests in the teaching and learning of languages. As such, the discussion here deals with understanding how race and racism fit within a larger discussion of colonialism. Such a discussion requires a focused examination of the epistemologies that are used to justify, and are created as a result of, the occupation of a culturally 'strange' and 'exotic' country. Several theories and approaches help understand what these colonial epistemologies are and how they came into being, including observations made by postcolonial theorists like Homi Bhabha (see Chapter 7). Despite these theoretical possibilities and opportunities, this section is concerned primarily with how Orientalism, as originally put forward by Said (1979), as well as related colonial processes (e.g. linguistic imperialism), are helpful in understanding the ways in which Western colonialism – both past and present – creates structural biases and privileges in the ELT profession.

Said (1979) dates Orientalism back to the late 18th century when Europe had a voracious desire to occupy the lands that are now commonly referred to as the Near/Middle East. Orientalism has several interpretations, but is centrally about the representation of 'other cultures, societies, and histories' (Said, 1985: 89). At the most basic level, Orientalism is the study of the peoples from, and cultures of, the Orient: 'Anyone who teaches, writes about, or researches the Orient – and this applies whether the person is an anthropologist, sociologist, historian, or philologist – either in its specific or its general aspects, is an Orientalist, and what he or she does is Orientalism' (Said, 1979: 2). The Orient, though used originally in a rather limited sense to denote the Middle East, now refers to 'the East' more broadly, albeit problematically. Indeed, it can be said that Orientalism transcends the geographical spaces and places that make up the East and includes any description of the cultural Other. Orientalism is based on an epistemology that seeks knowledge production through the perceived and ostensible differences that exist between the West and East or Self and Other. This may entail making a value judgment of a cultural practice based on how 'alien' it is to the observer's point of view, lived experiences and own societal norms. Characterizing a particular grammatical construction as deviant because it does not conform to one's own view of what is standard is an epistemological observation based on differences. In this sense, many ELT scholars and practitioners are Orientalists, and indeed the profession is founded on a structure of Orientalism (see, for example, Kubota, 2001). Said (1979) notes that generating knowledge based on (cultural) differences allows the observer/colonialist to exert and maintain power over the observed/colonized. Put differently, Orientalism results in asymmetrical distributions of power by ascribing negative attributes to the cultural Other. In Said's (1979) original writing, European colonial power is a result of creating false cultural dichotomies and binaries. Simply put, Europe (and other colonial powers) created an identity of power and strength by viewing the cultural Other as weak, unintelligent, uncivilized and powerless. Like earlier colonial efforts, ELT scholars and practitioners exert and maintain power imbalances in the profession by regarding their form of English as correct or standard while viewing deviations as incorrect and non-standard.

The discourses that are created as a result of making value judgments of cultural practices based on the ostensible differences that exist between the observer and the observed provide the foundation for racism. While not all Orientalism leads to race-based observations, its epistemological project ascribes characteristics to the cultural Other that are bound to racial hierarchies. Indeed, Orientalism is inherently racist because it is rooted in the belief that the observer/colonialist is intellectually superior to, and thus able to make more accurate observations of, the cultural Other. Said (1985: 97) speaks of the inherently racist project that is Orientalism in his discussion of European settler observations of Islam: 'Here, of course, is perhaps the most familiar of Orientalism's themes – since the Orientals cannot represent themselves, they must therefore be represented by others who know more about Islam than Islam knows about itself'. It should be noted here, however, that not all forms of Orientalist discourses are based on racist assumptions. Yet, because Orientalism is rooted in asymmetrical divisions of power and histories of oppression, observations of the cultural Other must be situated in a larger discussion of how the observer's privileged status shapes the research process. Further, although critics like Atkinson (2002: 80) have argued that Said perpetuates the same essentialized discourses that he attempts to eradicate (e.g. all European discussions of Asians are essentializing), such criticisms fail to consider the fact that White institutions, societies and communities benefit from a system that has historically privileged individuals from former colonizing states and oppressed those who have been colonized, especially with regard to the English language. Such criticisms follow the same failed logic that is used by individuals who claim 'reverse racism'. That is to say, criticizing scholars who denounce systemic discrimination is immensely problematic because such criticisms silence and marginalize those very individuals who have historically been oppressed and disadvantaged. Like critical pronouncements of White privilege in the United States, the significant issue is not whether a particular analytic description is essentializing or all-encompassing, but rather to what extent an observation seeks to fight a system of discrimination. Put differently, the key issue is not whether Said is an essentialist (by definition, he is), but rather that his observations of Orientalism seek to bring into discussion the present-day significance of colonialism.

Scholars are critical of Orientalism because they seek to problematize the social dynamics involved in describing the cultural Other. However, not all descriptions of the cultural Other are negative; indeed some forms of Orientalism, and colonial discourses more broadly, are based on a White savior imagination that seeks to help, rescue or enlighten the cultural Other. Though on the surface White saviorism seeks to repair ostensible problems or advance social issues, it reinforces power imbalances, maintains racial hierarchies, neglects the local dynamics and histories that are integral to the people and culture being 'rescued' and conserves the privileged status of the 'liberator'. Such observations can be applied to the ELT profession; that is, teaching English as an additional language can be considered White saviorism if instructors view their position as one of linguistic or cultural liberator without considering how their privileged status reinforces historical biases (see Chapter 5).

Colonialism creates ideologies that have historical significance within society (cf. Orientalism and White saviorism), yet such belief systems continue to be adopted in different domains of contemporary life. Over the years, these ideologies lead to structures within society that shape the way people behave and see the world. Although such ideologies circulate within postcolonial regions, they are also adopted by countries without a colonial past. The racial hierarchies that are created in and through the use of English in postcolonial regions (e.g. the belief that English is a language spoken by White individuals), for example, can be found in countries like Korea, Japan and Thailand. The adoption of colonial discourses throughout the world is a result of many phenomena, including efforts to sell the idea that English should be used according to the norms established by one or two countries. Decontextualizing and delocalizing English so that the norms established by one or two countries do not dictate correct language use challenges linguistic imperialism, a topic that is taken up in the next section.

Linguistic imperialism

The global status of English is a remnant of British colonialism. This fact is undisputed: the quest to occupy distant lands and accumulate wealth led to English spreading from one region and country to another. What is less discussed in the ELT literature is why English continues to be the preferred language in business, academia, medicine and technology. Is it because English is the most aesthetically pleasing language, provides the most efficient way of communicating or can be acquired relatively easily? Phillipson (1992) argues in his seminal book on linguistic imperialism that in addition to a history of colonialism, the global spread of English is a result of ongoing political events, a global economy that requires transnational business negotiations, and a multi-billion dollar ELT profession. Phillipson (1992) goes to great lengths to demonstrate that the global spread of English is not, however, an accidental outcome of globalization and economic development (cf. English language spread policy; see Phillipson, 1994). English maintains its global status because it is 'owned' by countries, such as the United States, with a tremendous amount of political, economic and cultural power. The belief that places like the United States should dictate how English is used globally is partly a result of such countries being in a position of great power (Pennycook, 1994). For example, US military occupation and corporate development colonize spaces throughout the world, which symbolically informs people that English is the language of corporatism, capitalism, neoliberalism and armed occupation. The United States is thus directly and indirectly responsible for creating discourses that circulate the belief that English is required for participation in the global community, a misconception that is often promoted under the guise of social and economic advancement (for a discussion of how these aspects of globalization manifest in Korea, see Chapter 6). Linguistic imperialism is defined in this way: it is an often unspoken policy that states that English must not only be learned, but that it must be done according to the standards established by countries in power. Linguistic imperialism, as Phillipson (2009: 2) argues, 'presupposes an overarching structure of asymmetrical, unequal exchange, where language dominance dovetails with economic, political and other types of dominance. It entails unequal resource allocation and communicative rights'.

Further, linguistic imperialism requires control over how people construct their ideological commitments to the English language. For example, NNESs far outnumber NESs (Crystal, 2012), yet the latter group of speakers continue to dictate how English should be used. The economic success of the ELT profession is dependent on speakers of English as an additional language believing that their local pool of instructors is inferior, and that their variety of English is substandard (H. Shin, 2006). Countries that currently use 'standard Englishes' are politically and economically invested in maintaining the power associated with their varieties. Indeed, an exceptional amount of effort has been, and is currently being, placed on creating standardized tests and teaching materials that reflect the linguistic and cultural practices of a few countries (Phillipson, 2008). In terms of empire building, Phillipson (1992) argues that English has replaced England in the familiar effort to consolidate power, dictate notions of what is 'normal' or 'standard' and maintain a system of oppression and control. While England does not engage in the same colonial activities as before, it is perhaps more accurate to say that English has not replaced anything, but is rather used as a vehicle to maintain control and power.

Linguistic imperialism occurs in many domains of life, and its existence is not limited to countries that have historically been considered non-English speaking. In the United States, for example, efforts to create English-only laws have intensified alongside an increase in immigration. Such laws represent a collective 'Anglo-American' fear of losing power as a result of changing demographics (Barker & Giles, 2004). English-only laws are acts of oppression in that they deny important social services to linguistic minorities (who are often students of color); more problematically, such laws lead to language attrition, especially among younger generations of immigrants and refugees who already have little incentive to maintain their cultural and linguistic heritage (Ferguson, 2006). Practices that privilege English while discriminating against speakers of other languages can occur in less overt ways, such as standardized tests that do not provide multilingual support to immigrant and refugee students. For example, the NCLB Act of 2001 – a set of policies that by its very name suggests diversity and inclusion – drastically cut funding for bilingual programs while requiring language learners to complete standardized tests in English only (Liggett, 2014: 115). Denying heritage language support for immigrants, refugees and multilinguals who enter school systems with limited English proficiency maintains a system that has historically disadvantaged students of color (Wright, 2007).

The ELT profession is also guilty of such practices. In many developed regions in Asia, for example, billions of dollars are spent collectively on English language instruction (see Chapter 6). Underneath this immense financial investment is a shared belief that learning English leads to the betterment of society. This ideological commitment stems from many factors, including colonial discourses (Pennycook, 1998); the ELT profession, however, plays a significant role in circulating the belief that English must be acquired, and done so in a way that reflects the norms and standards of a few countries. The perceived need to acquire English is so strong that learners sacrifice important aspects of their personal well-being while acquiring the 'global language' (Pennycook, 1998), such as maintaining good family relations and learning other academic subjects (see, for example, Chapter 3). In this sense, English symbolizes power, and can indeed be used in positive ways, but it also acts as a powerful force over those individuals who seek its apparent economic rewards.

The economic system tied to the ELT profession is fertile ground for racialized discourses, and the power that is bound to the English language provides a means for racism to be executed. For example, racial discrimination can be carried out by creating occupational prerequisites based on false racialized dichotomies, such as NES–NNES. Linguistic discrimination of this sort is referred to as linguicism, which Skutnabb-Kangas (1990: 85) defines as '[language] ideologies, structures and practices which are used to legitimate, effectuate and reproduce an unequal division of power and resources'. Accordingly, the privileging of NES teachers from inner-circle countries is linguicism – a form of colonial discourse or a type of linguistic imperialism (Phillipson, 2007: 379) in that such practices inform all members involved in the ELT profession, from the student to the school administrator, that English is a language best spoken, and thus taught, by members of the inner circle. Indeed, an ELT model that is based on the norms and standards of, say, some generalized notion of North American English, perpetuates and maintains the necessary power imbalances for linguistic imperialism to continue. That is to say, language learners will never be North American speakers of English because each speech community possesses its own sociolinguistic histories and identities that make it unique. Asking language learners to be someone they are not creates a hierarchical system in which speakers of so-called privileged varieties are always placed on top because of the difficult, if not impossible, task of ignoring, if not eradicating, the rich first languages and heritage cultures that influence how bilinguals and multilinguals use English. In this sense, linguistic imperialism can facilitate language decay or death in multilingual societies (Fernández, 2004).

Discussions of linguistic imperialism, as noted above, cannot be detached from histories of discrimination, oppression and privilege. Linguistic imperialism is rooted in colonial discourses, and thus understanding how language can exert power over the powerless or less powerful requires examining the unique histories that countries and regions have with the English language. A small body of work, as highlighted in this section, is devoted to examining linguistic imperialism in the ELT profession; these studies provide a critical lens through which scholarship can better understand how language teaching and learning are bound to a host of social, political and historical issues and processes (see, for example, Modiano, 2001a; Mühlhäusler, 1996). Notwithstanding the work done in this area of investigation, race and racism are often only tangentially discussed in linguistic imperialism research. Thus, it is not clear how racial discrimination and privilege operate within regions that privilege English to the detriment of other important facets of life. For example, how do race and ethnicity factor into the belief that learning English is a prerequisite for a better life in Korea and beyond?

English globalism

One very real consequence of linguistic imperialism is the perceived need to communicate across significant geographical distances with business partners who may not speak the same national language, and more importantly, in a way that reflects the professional and cultural norms and standards of a few countries that control international monetary and political affairs. On the back of nearly 500 years of British colonialism, the imagined national language of the United States has become the de facto medium of communication for neoliberal policies (cf. Phillipson, 2007: 381). The efforts of the US government and military to police the world, coupled with the tremendous growth and recognition of multinational companies and popular culture, including, but of course not limited to, Apple, Boeing, Google, a racially homogenous Hollywood and an essentializing pop culture industry, have seen English come to represent the language of success, wealth, beauty, intelligence, creativity and, of course, power.

The global spread of English should not, however, be seen as an entirely organic process that is devoid of power struggles, social inequalities and economic exploitation (Phillipson, 2007). While reasons for English globalism may appear on the surface to be spontaneous or involuntary, such as the captivation with 'American culture', languages spread from one region to another because of conscious efforts to expand, economically, politically, culturally and militarily (Phillipson, 2008). Indeed, regions have experienced language evolution and movement throughout history as a result of hostile and forceful efforts (cf. the Korean War); in other conscious efforts, non-violent forces have led to the spread of language from one region to another, such as the proselytizing and language teaching that occurred in Korea before Japanese colonialism (Weems, 1962). Thus, it is important to frame discussions of race, ethnicity and the English language with an understanding and appreciation of historical and global events and phenomena. For example, the implementation of neoliberal policies in developing countries and the widespread belief in global competition are connected to corporate wealth, including the financial health of the American military–industrial complex. The global spread of English has occurred with, and is a resource for, market fundamentalism and international corporatization (Holborow, 2006). And indeed the perceived need to learn and use English will continue to grow around world, with the United States dictating international issues.

Many global forces have enabled the spread of English (cf. Crystal, 2012), including globalization, transnational business negotiation, popular culture, war, imperialism and colonialism. Within this system of linguistic imperialism there is an unmistakable benefit for individuals who possess the language of neoliberalism (J.S. Park, 2013). Proficiency in English can mean upward mobility, respect from one's peers and educational opportunities. That is, English is a form of capital. Researchers have discussed in great detail how individuals can transform capital, in this case English, into material wealth, occupational benefits and social privileges. Bourdieu (1984: 114), for example, argues that class struggles and differences exist in society because lives are defined and shaped by 'the overall volume of capital, understood as the set of actually usable resources and powers – economic capital, cultural capital, and social capital'. The ability to use English in Korea, for example, can mean admission into a top Korean university, an ostensibly less strenuous position as a draftee in the military working with the US Armed Forces, study abroad opportunities that are greatly valued by prospective employers both in and outside of the country and greater employment possibilities and financial benefits. English operates within Korea as a form of capital because of the global forces briefly mentioned above, which will be discussed in greater detail in Chapters 6 and 7.

Conclusion

A wide range of critical research contributes to an understanding of how race and ethnicity operate within the ELT profession. For example, CRT scholarship, which comprises 10 overlapping theoretical and empirical themes, has a history of uncovering the many ways in which race and ethnicity are woven into the fabric of society. CRT scholars possess varied interests and concerns, but are all inherently skeptical of liberal policies that mask structural racism. Researchers working in CRT are also committed to revisiting, revising and recasting the historical events and processes that shape contemporary race-based understandings of society. An emerging concern within CRT is an understanding of how race intersects with other social categories, including, but not limited to, gender, religion and class. Although intersectionality is an important aspect of CRT, research to date has somewhat neglected the role that language plays in facilitating racial discrimination and privilege. The analysis chapters that follow narrow this empirical gap by examining the extent to which the ELT profession is part of a larger system of, among other things, colonial mentalities, linguistic imperialism and linguicism.

Also germane to a consideration of how CRT informs the ELT profession are colorblind ideologies, theories of Whiteness and White privilege and Marxist notions of exploitation, alienation and oppression. Colorblind ideologies, Whiteness and White privilege are revisited later by drawing from the works of several critical race and discourse scholars, including most notably Haney López (cf. Chapter 4), while Marxist approaches to class exploitation are foundational to the discussion of neoliberalism in the ELT profession (cf. Chapter 6). By drawing from this scholarship, this book adds to the growing body of work that is concerned with examining how Whiteness and White normativity shape notions of language standards and good pedagogical practice.

This chapter has also established that a small, but important, group of ELT researchers are highly cognizant of the ways in which the English language is bound to essentialized notions of race and ethnicity. Such work is carried out by examining the positionalities and identities of students and teachers, how racialized discourses are embedded in the teaching and learning of English, the connection between race-based ideologies and learner identities and the extent to which critical pedagogy can be applied in the language classroom. These empirical foci, though revelatory and impactful, represent a small share of ELT scholarship. Thus, there are many investigatory opportunities to advance the state of race-based knowledge in the ELT profession, including exploring how language teaching is inextricably connected to a history of colonialism, colonial discourses, including Orientalism and White saviorism, linguistic imperialism and English globalism.

3 Korea in Context

Introduction

A study of White normativity in the ELT profession requires understanding the cultural forces that shape education, language and ethnicity in Korea. This chapter thus explores several contextual issues pertinent to an investigation of the ELT profession in Korea, including notions of Korean ethnicity, expectations of education attainment and success, ideologies pertaining to the English language and linguistic imperialism. The aim of this chapter is to discuss Korea as a nation that is shaped by social issues and phenomena that are both unique and central to how the ELT profession is managed. In ways that will be revealed below and throughout this book, ideologies and discourses regarding notions of Koreanness are closely tied to, and are indeed visible in the organization of, the ELT profession.

Although no single chapter can offer a comprehensive overview of a country, care has been taken to include references for further reading throughout the discussion below. Furthermore, additional contextual information is provided throughout the analyses of Korea in subsequent chapters.

In the interest of comprehension, many of the terms that are central to understanding the ELT profession are provided in Korean and English. For English transliterations of Korean, the *Revised Romanization of Korean* is used (Ministry of Culture, Sports and Tourism, n.d.). These English transliterations are provided in standard font and with hyphens to aid the reader in the pronunciation of Korean words; in subsequent chapters, these English transliterations are often only presented in italicized font and without hyphens.

Ethnicity in Korea

The issue of ethnicity in Korea is ostensibly simple. Korea is ethnically homogenous, a fact conveyed in many surveys and demographic accounts of the country, including the *World Factbook* (Central Intelligence Agency, 2016; see also Seth, 2011). The responses to demographic surveys can be partly understood by looking at the ubiquitous belief within the country that the nation is 'based on shared blood and ancestry', including 'an intense sense of collective oneness' (G. Shin, 2006a). Although many Koreans view Koreanness as a monolithic and fixed concept (G. Shin, 2006b: 2), the notion of a Korean ethnic group evolved from a history of contact with other groups, including the Japanese during colonial rule. Furthermore, the social construction of a Korean ethnic identity is complicated by many decades of isolationism, which has led to an uncomfortable relationship with outsiders throughout Korea's history.

Korean is overwhelmingly the first and primary language of spoken and written communication in the country (King, 2007). Proficiency in Korean is obligatory for the discursive construction of national identification and belonging, including fulfilling social and civic responsibilities. Unsurprisingly, ethnic identification among the population majority is inextricably connected to the ability to speak Korean (J. Kim, 2014). The importance of Korean language proficiency in the construction of ethnicity is neither a new nor a novel phenomenon; indeed, the country's early encounters with English-speaking missionaries, and later US military troops, continue to shape how Koreans view notions of language ownership, including who is considered a legitimate speaker of English and ideologies regarding the physical appearance of such interlocutors.

The coupling of language and ethnicity is particularly revelatory in understanding who is considered Korean in Korea. For the purpose of this introduction, understanding what it means to be Korean in Korea requires identifying individuals or groups who are not traditionally viewed as members of this ethnic group. For example, many Korean adoptees who return to Korea for short or extended periods of time know all too well the importance of speaking the 'mother tongue'. Anecdotal and academic accounts of Korean adoptees include stories of alienation and bigotry (e.g. Connolly, 2014). In a similar vein, Koreans who have experienced varying degrees of sociolinguistic attrition while living abroad and/or emigrating overseas may not fit the traditional ethnic citizen mold and are in fact routinely otherized by being labeled a 교포/gyo-po. Interestingly, the official terminology for a Korean citizen living abroad, or 재외국민/jae-oe-guk-min, while not as common and colloquial, is not used interchangeably with 교포/gyo-po. The former term evokes images of the '96% majority', while the latter designation can, among other things, be used to refer to a biracial or 'mixed blood' Korean (혼혈/heun-hyeol). This system of categorizing who is and who is not Korean represents decades of sociopolitical baggage, and indeed more recent examples of South East Asians living in Korea provide vivid examples of how fixed and monolithic the Korean ethnic identity is for many (cf. Choo, 2016). For example, a common ideology that is circulated is the belief that Korea is a nation of 'one people', or 단일민족/dan-il min-jok (Seth, 2011). This ideological construct (see J.S. Park, 2009), while historically rooted in Korean–Japanese sociopolitical relations, is central to the ways in which many Korean citizens construct narratives of national and ethnic identity and pride in contemporary times (M. Kim, 1997).

Despite what would appear to be a homogenous ethnic group with a rigorous and narrow (national) identity belief system, a growing body of writing in academic and mainstream media reveals a more complex picture. In 2011, for example, Korea abolished a law that made it illegal for biracial Koreans to serve in the armed forces (T. Lee, 2010), ending decades of institutional racism in the military. Inward migration is increasing at a steady pace, partly because of economic growth and comparatively good living standards in the region; currently, over 1.5 million 'non-Korean' citizens live and/or work in Korea, which amounts to approximately 3% of the country's population (C. Lee, 2014b). Low-paying positions are increasingly taken up by migrants from South East Asia and, to a much lesser extent, some African countries (for a somber look at the plight of migrant workers in Korea, see Denney, 2015). The ELT profession in Korea employs over 20,000 workers, mostly from countries outside of Asia, and nearly 30,000 US military troops are stationed throughout the peninsula (Capaccio & Gaouette, 2014).

Some of these so-called foreigners, or 외국인/oe-guk-in, marry Korean citizens and stay in the country for varying amounts of time, while other bicultural/biracial families leave for other countries. The offspring of such families, including children who were born and raised in Korea and those who come back for personal and/or employment purposes, add to the racial and ethnic dynamics of the country. The number of multiracial families in Korea is in fact steadily increasing: over 60,000 students, or approximately 1% of the total student population enrolled in schools throughout the country, are from multiracial families (S. Kim, 2014). At the most celebrated, though perhaps superficial level (see, for example, C. Lee, 2015), successes of professional athletes like Hines Ward, the son of an African American father and Korean mother, who won the 2006 most valuable player award in Super Bowl XL, momentarily reminded the country that Koreans come in many ethnic varieties. Other, more recent success stories of biracial peoples in television and movies, including accomplishments that occur in Korea, complicate traditional racialized discourses and create images of a more racially diverse country. For instance, Ricky Kim, who is a biracial model and actor originally from the United States, is currently portrayed on television as a caring husband of a

Korean wife and a responsible father of two children (for a different, albeit outdated, portrayal of Ricky Kim, see Lo & Kim, 2011).

Moreover, Korean citizens living abroad are exposed to diverse groups of people as well as heterogenous societal norms and expectations. The current estimate of Korean citizens living abroad is around seven million. More than half of these Koreans reside in China and the United States; other notable regions include Japan, Canada, Russia, Uzbekistan and Australia, where the combined population of Koreans is somewhere between 1–2 million. The transnational experiences that are afforded to Koreans living abroad can filter back into the racial and ethnic awareness and sensitivity of the nation, though this is an empirical issue that has not received much attention (see, however, Lie, 2014). What is clear is that racial and ethnic images, experiences and assumptions are in a state of flux because of, among other things, global economic forces, ubiquitous popular culture, international education, English as a global language and internet-based media consumption (J.S. Park, 2009, 2014). Despite the transnational experiences of many Koreans, however, the country is still largely influenced by racialized discourses and ideologies. In their study of language policy in Korea vis-à-vis racialized attitudes in the United States, Grant and Lee (2009) argue that Koreans still subscribe to outdated racial and linguistic hierarchies:

> South Koreans' prejudice against Blacks had existed long before the globalization policy [see Chapter 6]. South Koreans first became familiar with American values of democracy, Christianity, meritocracy, and individualism as South Korea underwent rapid industrialization and modernization following the Korean War. Since then, U.S. mass media, especially Hollywood movies and television shows, as well as American Forces Korea Network (AFKN) programs have been the primary tools for South Korean exposure to American values and racial attitudes. These media sources perpetuated stereotypical portrayals of Blacks, resulting in the exportation of racism. (Grant & Lee, 2009: 56)

The economic and social climate and trajectory of Korea are crucial considerations in a discussion of racialized discourses given the country's somewhat static, albeit changing, racial and ethnic belief system. Korea has experienced rapid economic, and to a lesser extent social, progress in the last six decades since the Korean War. In considering the ethnic make-up of the country and the ideologies adopted by Korean citizens, readers must not forget that Korea went from an impoverished post-war country to a nation with one of the largest economies in the world in just over 60 years (Seth, 2010, 2011). This rapid progression has created differences, sometimes significant, in the degrees to which older and younger generations subscribe to traditional notions of ethnic nationality and embrace a future of racial and linguistic diversity (cf. G. Shin, 2006a, 2006b). The success of Korea has complicated attitudes and perceptions of ethnicity, as Koreans are now more than ever required to manage their ethnic and linguistic identities in the context of globalism, neoliberalism and transnationalism.

Education in Korea

Korean education is widely championed for its success in student achievement as measured by a number of testing systems, including the Program for International Student Assessment (PISA). This success is remarkable given the state of education in Korea during Japanese colonial rule in the early 1900s and immediately after the Korean War in 1953. During these times, little money was available to create quality curricular materials and expand tuition to meet the needs of a growing population, but since then the government's evolving role in education, as well as increasing parental aspirations for student success, have led to the current situation where Korea now outperforms most other developed countries (C. Lee *et al.*, 2012). The 1980s and 1990s were particularly noteworthy times with regard to ELT education. Although after-school language academies (학원/hag-won) were, and continue to be, a key component of Korea's success in standardized tests, private education (과외/gwa-oe) was banned in the 1980s; however, this law was deemed unconstitutional in the 1990s (S. Park & Abelmann, 2004: 648).

Underneath the remarkable and rapid success of Korean education is an insatiable desire for younger generations of Koreans, often propagated by parents, to do well in school, gain entry into a top university and secure a high-paying occupation. In his seminal book on the politics of schooling in Korea, Seth (2002) refers to this yearning as 'education fever'.

Much of this fever stems from the College Scholastic Ability Test (CSAT), the national standardized examination required for admission into Korean universities. The CSAT functions as a gateway to future prosperity and success. As reported by a number of media outlets and academic publications, the country is on high alert during the examination period. Seth (2002) makes the following observation of the situation:

A great air of tension hovered throughout South Korea on 17 November 1999. A special task force had spent months planning for that day. The night before, President Dae Jung had appeared on television to announce that the nation was prepared for the event. All nonessential governmental workers would report to work only later in the morning, as would employees of major firms. Thousands of special duty police were on hand in many cities; thirteen thousand police had mobilized in Seoul alone. Flights at all the nation's airports had been restricted, and special efforts had been made to halt construction to avoid creating noise or commotion of any kind. It was the day of the national university entrance examinations. (Seth, 2002: 1)

Many scholars have attributed Korea's economic success to the extraordinary amount of time and money spent on developing, administering, preparing for and taking the CSAT. This expenditure, it has been argued, is 'the product of the diffusion of traditional Confucian attitudes toward learning and status, new egalitarian ideas introduced from the West, and the complex, often contradictory ways in which new and old ideals and formulations interacted' (Seth, 2002: 6).

The nation's commitment to examinations has propelled Korea into the global discussion of educational standards. Whether this accelerated rise in educational attainment is a result of traditional Confucian ideologies or a neoliberal logic, there have been, and continue to be, substantial costs to families, students and the country as a whole as a result of 'education fever'. These costs extend far beyond the financial expenses related to private tutoring (Seth, 2002). Families are often separated for long periods during the day, with some students rarely seeing their parents at all (Hu, 2015a; S. Lee, 2013). Furthermore, it is not uncommon for fathers to stay behind in Korea while their families live and study abroad (cf. 기러기 아빠/gi-reo-gi a-ppa or goose father; Kang, 2012). More problematically, the emotional stress that comes with the pressure to do well at school and in standardized examinations has led many scholars to question whether the exceptionally high suicide rates in Korea are a result of tests like the CSAT (Hu, 2015b). The intense desire to do well at school and in standardized tests partly explains the important role that English plays in Korea.

Evolving notions of educational and professional success, coupled with neoliberal policies introduced largely in the 1990s, were the catalyst for the ELT boom in Korea. Changing notions of the value of English are also occurring within families. Korean parents, for example, commonly view English as a neoliberal tool for their children to do well in life and to improve their family's standing in society (cf. M. Lee, 2016). Following Seth's (2002) observations of general education practices in Korea, language scholars apply terms like 'English frenzy' (J.S. Park, 2009) and 'English fever' (J.K. Park, 2009) to characterize the time and money spent learning and practicing English (for the amount of money spent on ELT instruction in Korea, see Chapter 6).

Frenzy and fever do not, however, capture the English language and learning in Korea over a century ago. Like many Asian countries, English existed initially as a way for outsiders, often White Westerners, to educate, proselytize and politicize (for a general discussion of Christian missionary work/linguistic imperialism, see Mühlhäusler, 1996: 139). A notable teacher at the time was Thomas Hallifax, an Englishman who taught at a school in 1883 dedicated to Western education, including ELT instruction. Hallifax, who had previously taught English in Japan, had a somewhat contentious career in education and was not highly regarded by his students. Henry Appenzeller was also a key figure in early ELT instruction. He founded one of the first academies dedicated to education based on Western beliefs and science, but the pedagogical efforts of the school were believed to be a cover for his missionary work (Davies, 1992). As with most early efforts to introduce Western approaches to teaching in Korea, enrollment at Appenzeller's school was very low. The school also experienced a high turnover of students because pupils had more pressing issues to deal with at the national level. In 1886, the Royal School of English was established as a new government institute of education (Lankov, 2007). Three instructors from the United States were hired – Homer Hulbert, Dalzell Bunker and George Gilmore – and were largely responsible for teaching privileged members of Korean society (for a more detailed account of Hulbert's missionary efforts in Korea, see Oak, 2010: 107–109). Years later, Annie Ellers, the partner of Bunker, provided English tutoring support for Syngman Rhee, who later became one of the most controversial presidents in Korea (Lankov, 2007).

The Christian missionary work that was associated with ELT instruction at the time stands in stark contrast to the current state of the profession. For example, numerous Korean media reports over the past decade or two have depicted ELT instructors from the United States and other English-speaking countries as social and sexual deviants (VanVolkenburg, 2010). The national imagination of language teachers getting into trouble and taking advantage of vulnerable Korean women provides some background to the current immigration law that requires ELT instructors to take HIV/AIDS tests before securing employment in Korea (Chapter 4 discusses immigration laws in more detail). Wagner and VanVolkenburg (2012), in their critical and landmark study of Korea's mandatory HIV/AIDS tests for ELT instructors, offers a concise overview of the situation:

> Increased social contact, especially between foreign English teachers and Korean women, has triggered traditional fears of cultural contamination and miscegenation. The resulting hostility and suspicion, in their most extreme forms, have been expressed through the metaphor of AIDS. An influential citizens' group has claimed that foreign teachers are infecting Koreans with HIV. Concomitantly, the South Korean government has instituted discriminatory HIV restrictions for foreign teachers that it claims are necessary to 'ease the anxiety of citizens' and 'assure the parents' of schoolchildren being taught by non-Koreans. (Wagner & VanVolkenburg, 2012: 179)

Mandatory HIV/AIDS testing for ELT instructors is not only a form of institutionalized discrimination, it is a projection of a larger, more complex relationship that Koreans have with foreigners and foreign languages (cf. J.S. Park, 2009). This relationship with 'outsiders' manifests in many domains of life. One such example is the preferential treatment given to Korean Americans seeking employment in Korea. Specifically, Korean Americans who are eligible for an F-4 visa need not undergo an HIV/AIDS test when seeking employment in Korea (they are, however, discriminated against in other ways; see the next chapter). Accordingly, although there is a deep-rooted preference for White teachers in the ELT profession in Korea (cf. Chapters 5–8), racial discrimination and privilege are not fixed phenomena nor do they function in the same way for different people and contexts. For example, many public schools have begun to cut the number of ELT instructors from places like the United States because of funding issues (cf. Chapter 5).

English in Korea

Koreans have a complex and complicated relationship with the English language. The need to learn English is made clear to Koreans at a very young age, and indeed the time and money spent on ELT instruction is a constant reminder of its importance. Yet, despite societal pressures to learn English, few spaces outside of institutional contexts actually require or compel Koreans to speak the language. This tension between learning and using can be partly explained by looking at Korea's political and economic relationship with the United States. Although Koreans understand that scoring well in the English portion of the national examination is obligatory for entry into a top university in Seoul, they also associate the language with 'Americans for whom they tend to harbor contradictory and unresolved feelings' (Min, 2013). Such feelings are an extension of the sociolinguistic landscape of Korea during Japanese colonial rule when assimilation policies forced Koreans to adopt over time the cultural and language practices of Japan (while at the same time decreasing the attention paid to ELT instruction and banning English-language signs; see Kim-Rivera, 2002). While the United States did not enforce the same type of top-down practices on language policy, the large US military presence is a constant reminder of Korea's colonized past. For many Koreans, this sociohistorical baggage creates the ideology that English is not the language of Korea, but rather the United States.

The discourse that speakers of English are from the United States (and other inner-circle countries, to a lesser degree) gets disseminated by the media and popular culture (e.g. Grant & Lee, 2009). Scholars have also examined ELT textbooks and demonstrated that racialized and hegemonic discourses are associated with Western images (e.g. H. Song, 2013). Furthermore, ELT textbooks may depict English as a language of wealth, power, globalization and capitalism (e.g. I. Lee, 2009). Koreans, in other words, are subjected to a number of discourses and ideologies from a range of sources that tell them that while English must be acquired in order to obtain cultural, social and economic capital (J. Lee *et al.*, 2010), it is also a language that is foreign, 'unspeakable' (cf. J.S. Park, 2009) and forever tied to the large US military presence in the country (N. Kim, 2008).

English Imperialism in Korea

It is commonly understood, and often discussed in sociolinguistic investigations, that Korea has never experienced colonialism by an English-speaking country (e.g. H. Shin, 2006). Despite extended periods of Japanese colonialism (J.W. Lee, 2014), this fact is sometimes used to characterize Korea as an ethnically homogenous and largely monolingual society. This characterization, however, belies a complex economic, political and military relationship with the United States. While it is true that Korea does not possess the same type of sociolinguistic history and relationship with English as places like Hong Kong and India, the United States has a significant presence in, and control over, the country (N. Kim, 2008). Korean–US relations, especially vis-à-vis military activities in the region, present a similar, if not more complex, sociolinguistic environment. The US military, the consumption of 'American culture' and economic policies between the two countries are salient points of consideration in a discussion of why English is viewed as an important language in Korea (H. Shin, 2007). Indeed, the historical relations between the two countries have shaped, in significant ways, the role English plays in Korean society.

For example, shortly after Korea's independence in 1945, the United States exerted its influence in the region through policy, foreign aid, military support and education (Seth, 2010). A post-colonial Korea, including the time during and after the Korean War, can be viewed as a turning point in the presence and perceived importance of English. Although English was introduced long before the 1950s, the Korean War brought with it a number of symbolic artifacts associated with the United States, including food, cultural practices and English signs. Figure 3.1, for example, was taken approximately one month before the Korean War ended and demonstrates how the linguistic landscape of a country can change as a result of war.

Figure 3.1 represents a radical symbolic change in the linguistic landscape of the country. Also noteworthy is the current linguistic landscape of urban areas like Seoul, where it is difficult to find a building or a block that is dominated by English signs such as the one in Figure 3.1. Closer examination reveals that although Chinese characters appear in several instances, which is not uncommon in contemporary Korea, and Korean signs are displayed less prominently in shop windows, with one exception at the bottom left-hand corner of Figure 3.1 that displays 'radio' in an outdated spelling convention (라듸오), English dominates this particular landscape. It is important to note that the presence of English signs in 1953 was not a random phenomenon (Shohamy & Gorter, 2009), but rather demonstrates a concerted effort to accommodate the thousands of English-speaking military personnel in the country at the time.

Figure 3.1

Figure 3.2

For instance, in Figure 3.2, taken in a different location nearly four months later (i.e. after the war ended), Korean shopkeepers and consumers are seen doing business with English signs conspicuously displayed in the background.

The linguistic accommodation that is represented in both images is driven by the need to sell goods and services to a large military community with greater buying power. Put differently, these English signs possess financial value (cf. Cenoz & Gorter, 2009). As noted in Chapter 1, Koreans experienced great financial despair in the time leading up to, during and after the Korean War. Aid from the United States provided much support to the economy, which was impoverished in the years leading up to the war (Seth, 2010), but economic hardship continued for many years afterward. Indeed, rapid economic development did not occur until the 1960s under the authoritarian rule of Park Chung-hee (Haggard *et al.*, 1991). Thus, for many Koreans, the understanding that English will lead to economic prosperity, or is necessary for financial survival, began with the US military shortly after Japanese colonialism ended. This discourse continues today, with the United States dictating international trade agreements and other global financial matters. Figures 3.1 and 3.2 are a reminder that the cultural symbols associated with the United States at the time were not limited to tanks and weapons, but were also symbolically tied to economic development and financial stability.

The US military operation around the time of the Korean War also resulted in a 'familiar' need to communicate between two linguistically diverse populations (for a discussion of the sociolinguistic effects of Japanese colonialism, see J.W. Lee, 2014). That is, the Korean War required Koreans not only to learn how to use weapons, but also to speak the language of its largest military 'ally'. The quotes surrounding ally signify the many Koreans who viewed US efforts before the Korean War as an extension of colonialism, which most notably came in the form of preselected government officials by the 'United States Army Military Government in Korea' (Robinson, 2007). During and after the Korean War, the United States played a significant role in training the rapidly growing Korean military, and the occupation of Korea by 'hundreds of thousands of GIs and civilian officials ... in this historically homogenous and sometimes xenophobic society insured that American culture would flow into the country. It also insured that South Korea would be linked with the Western world, economically as well as culturally' (Seth, 2010: 110).

The role of the US military around the time of the Korean War laid the political and economic foundations for English to prosper. M. Kim (1997: 360) makes a similar observation in her study of Korean nationalism: 'U.S. involvement in the Korean Peninsula largely coincides with the development of U.S. multinational capitalism, the economic internationalization promoted by American foreign policy in the mid-twentieth century, roughly between 1950 and 1970'. US military activities in the region during this time, and the role of the United States in influencing the use of English in Korea, are important empirical issues that deserve more attention in the literature. Neoliberal policies in Korea, a mere instrument, some would argue, of a larger American imperial agenda (cf. N. Kim, 2008), have been the most conspicuous in transforming the linguistic terrain of the country to accommodate the common-sense assumption that learning English will lead to academic and financial success. Recent attempts to reform the education system in Korea to closer reflect a free market ethos are observed in J.S. Park's (2013) investigation, where he considers how English is used to promote market liberalization and globalization. The observations made in subsequent chapters build on this work by examining how notions of who is an ideal ELT instructor become racialized as a result of a neoliberal mindset.

Conclusion

Korea is steeped in tradition, but it has experienced rapid development over the last six decades. These opposing forces limit what researchers can say about Korea. The country is, like most regions around the world, full of contradictions. Generalizations about Korea should be made with care, and situated in a wider understanding of the historical development of the country. To this end, it must be noted in closing this chapter that in discussing any aspect of Korea, including race, ethnicity, education and English, it is important, if not obligatory, to temper discussions, observations and findings with the understanding that while the country is, on the one hand, largely homogenous in ethnic make-up and language use, it is on the other hand rapidly changing and increasingly connected to the world – socially, politically and economically. Therefore, despite the desire to depict Koreanness as a fixed concept, bound to images of a racially and linguistically homogenous country dedicated to schooling and scared of 'foreign' languages, Korea is a transnational country with multiple ethnic identities and varying degrees of commitment to education and English (see Jenks & J.W. Lee, forthcoming).

4 White Normativity in ELT

Introduction

The English language in Korea has a history of being associated with military occupation, outsiders and cultural practices foreign to the lives of many Koreans, as discussed in the previous chapter. This historical fact is important for understanding how to view and discuss racism in the ELT profession in Korea, as discourses and ideologies regarding what a speaker of English looks and sounds like have been created through a history of encounters with, for example, British proselytizers and US military troops. As discussed throughout this book, racialized discourses and ideologies regarding the English language are further influenced by a range of modern political and cultural forces. Popular culture in the United States, for example, circulates notions of what prestigious varieties of English sound like, and indeed promotes the idea that speakers of such varieties possess certain ethnic and racial characteristics. These discourses are widely circulated in Korean society through movies, news broadcasts and television shows. Such racialized discourses and ideologies manifest in many domains of Korean life, including advertisements that promote the idea that Whiteness is a benchmark of beauty, intelligence and success. The symbolic power of Whiteness, and the importance and value associated with being White, also influence the ways in which the ELT profession in Korea is managed.

The aim of this chapter is to show how Whiteness operates as an organizing principle in the ELT profession. Specifically, the chapter reveals how White normativity discursively manifests in different spheres of the ELT profession, including most notably in immigration laws that rely not only on outdated notions of linguistic proficiency and language ownership, but also on racialized discourses and ideologies.

As noted at the beginning of this book, an examination of Whiteness is crucial to creating a better understanding of how the ELT profession is influenced by racialized discourses and power dynamics, as the bulk of critical race research in language teaching and learning is concerned with examining the cultural Other without adequate attention to White normativity (see, however, Liggett, 2009). Despite the growing body of work on critical White issues in several disciplines (e.g. Case, 2012; Guillem,

2014; Haney López, 2006; Hartigan, 1997; Keating, 1995), such scholarship has yet to make a significant impact on the ELT profession. ELT scholars, including applied linguists and sociolinguists, have by and large neglected the influential work being done in Whiteness studies. This empirical lacuna is curious given the ostensible desire within the ELT literature to promote multiculturalism and multilingualism. Barnett (2000) makes a similar observation regarding English Studies:

> One reason for this feeling of stagnation (despite intense theoretical interest in critical pedagogies) is that the discipline remains unable to question its own 'white ground' despite the very real gains scholars have made in coming to understand reading and writing in relation to human difference. That is, the discipline seems unable or unwilling to question 'whiteness' in all its complexity despite (because of?) the efforts of literary, creative writing, and composition teachers and scholars to bring to the foreground issues of race having to do with multiple 'Others'. (Barnett, 2000: 10)

In other words, English Studies scholars do not often question the inherent Whiteness of their discipline or the social and pedagogical implications of a disciplinary system that transmits racially homogenous discourses and images because the critical lens has historically been pointed away from the observer. Similar observations can be made of the ELT profession. Scholarship is, on the whole, aimed at helping the observed, often less linguistically proficient and darker-skinned, cultural Other. As a result of the critical lens being pointed *away* from the observer, empirical investigations concerned with Whiteness have historically been relegated to 'special issue' topics or taken up within the periphery by autoethnographers and critical race scholars (e.g. Guillem, 2014).

White normativity, which will be unpacked in the following section, adds to an already complex and complicated relationship that Koreans have with 'outsiders' (N. Kim, 2008), the English language (J.S. Park, 2009) and the cultural Other (Lo & Kim, 2011). The current discussion, as well as subsequent analytic chapters, applies critical theories of race and Whiteness, as explicated in Chapter 2, to identify and explore how the ELT profession is shaped by discourses and ideologies that privilege White instructors from so-called Western, English-speaking countries.

The following analysis draws from a number of different data sources, including Korean government documents, immigration policy statements, interviews with ELT instructors, news media reports and job-wanted postings. These data sources will be discussed in more detail as they are presented, though it should be said here that a considerable amount of time was spent analyzing a 342-page immigration publication by the Korean Ministry of Justice, as well as other government documents and statistics. In addition to applying critical race theories to the reading of these data sources, the discourse analysis conducted here and in subsequent chapters draws heavily from the idea that racism is the work of individuals, communities and organizations in positions of power (cf. van Dijk, 2008). That is to say, this book approaches the study of racism from the perspective that 'political, media, educational, academic, and corporate elites' reproduce inequalities and maintain power imbalances in and through racialized discourses (van Dijk, 2008: 8). For the ELT profession, White instructors with privileged varieties of English also produce elite discourses that may lead to racism, as demonstrated in subsequent sections and chapters. Although van Dijk (2008: 10) does not lay out a specific methodological framework or rubric, he nonetheless makes it clear in his writing that a study of racism must be based on the observation that because elites maintain the production and circulation of symbolic power, 'they also control the communicative conditions in the formation of the popular mind and hence, the ethnic consensus'. This book is thus an attempt to identify who is responsible for racialized discourses, the communicative conditions in which such language gets circulated and the social and pedagogical consequences of one of the most elite forms of discourse in the ELT profession: White normativity.

White Normativity in ELT

White normativity is a set of ideological commitments and social mechanisms that treat Whiteness as a barometer of all that is normal, authentic and exemplary. Whiteness is not necessarily about skin pigmentation or hair color, though physical appearance is important to how this institutionalized system of racism is determined and/or imagined; rather, Whiteness is 'a state of being' (Garner, 2007: vii) that exists only in relation to other racial and ethnic categories, such as Black and Blackness. Whiteness is a system of power and privilege that is rooted in a history of normalizing the cultural practices of White individuals while exoticizing, essentializing and subjugating other groups. White communities and institutions are able to maintain their positions of power because, in part, Whiteness presents itself 'as unraced individuality as opposed to a racialized subjectivity that is communally and politically interested' while 'reserving for itself the privilege of recognizing, defining, and denying difference on its own terms and to its own advantage' (Barnett, 2000: 10).

White normativity exists in many domains of life. In the United States (and beyond), for example, a primary perpetrator of White normativity is the Hollywood entertainment industry. By and large, the roles of heroes and protagonists are performed by White actors while peoples of color serve token roles, and films with a majority ethnic cast are placed on the periphery, often viewed as a 'genre' and/or produced so that stereotypical depictions are reinforced and therefore palatable to 'mainstream' consumers (Bernardi, 2008; see also Yang & Ryser, 2008). As a result of a racially homogenous entertainment industry, societal expectations of beauty, bravery and brawn are tied to notions of Whiteness (for specific movie examples, see Garner, 2007: 50). In the business profession, White privileging, and thus normativity, can also manifest in societal expectations of employability. In a highly influential paper, Bertrand and Mullainathan (2004) establish that when all employment credentials are otherwise equal, 'White-sounding' names (e.g. Emily and Greg) are 50% more likely to receive an interview request than 'Black-sounding' names (e.g. Lakisha and Jamal), which suggests that Whiteness is a preferential attribute in the labor market.

The preference for, and privileging of, Whiteness can extend to other regions and professions, including the teaching and learning of English around the world. For a number of reasons that will be discussed below and in subsequent chapters, many regions, including Korea, adopt White normativity discourses and ideologies when managing the ELT profession. Although the existence of White normativity in the global ELT profession is a multifaceted issue, it is largely rooted in, and shaped by, the social dynamics of so-called English-speaking countries like the United States, where the elite class that controls political power and possesses cultural capital is racially homogenous. In the United States, this elite class is both directly (e.g. English-only laws) and indirectly (e.g. popular culture) responsible for creating the fiction that the country is a monolingual society and that the English spoken by the White majority is the preferred and prestigious variety. Many people involved in the ELT profession in Korea, from school owners to parents, adopt this monolingual and monoracial fiction to formulate the belief that there is only one variety of English spoken in inner-circle countries that one must acquire, and that the best instructors and cultural ambassadors for the teaching of this variety are individuals with White qualities.

The privileging of such individuals in the ELT profession has long been associated with the understanding that native speakers are better equipped, linguistically and culturally, to provide 'authentic' and high-quality language teaching. Studies have only recently demonstrated that such associations are inherently racist because the image of an NES circulated around the world is usually of a White person (Holliday & Aboshiha, 2009). This image of a White speaker is rooted in a history of British colonialism and American imperialism, which gets circulated and taken up worldwide in different ideologies and discourses. For example, Golombek and Jordan (2005) establish how discourses of Whiteness are connected to the ways in which Taiwanese graduate students view the English language and their preference for White teachers when studying in the United States (for similar observations, see also Amin, 1997).

In the ELT profession in Korea, White normativity is based on a complex network of discourses and ideologies, such as the historical ties the country has with the United States, and modern political and cultural influences like American popular culture. However, White normativity in the ELT profession in Korea is actually put into practice through immigration laws that state that language instruction in English can only be performed by citizens from a small group of 'Western', stereotypically White nations (Mahboob, 2009). Specifically, the Korean Ministry of Justice states that the E-2 working visa, which permits legal employment at schools, institutions and corporations that deliver conversation courses, is only available to a 'national of a country' where English is used 'as a native language', which the government identifies as the United States, United Kingdom, Canada, South Africa, New Zealand, Australia and Ireland (Ministry of Justice, Korea Immigration Service, 2015a: 120). Interestingly, but perhaps not surprisingly, universities from these E-2 countries recognize each other as English speaking when admitting international students into various degree programs, but do not offer the same reciprocity to countries where English is also spoken from a very early age, such as Hong Kong, Singapore and India. In other words, this practice of reciprocity among universities in E-2 countries indirectly creates elite discourses by circulating the notion within higher education that students born and raised in places like Singapore or India are not legitimate speakers of English.

Although teachers of color from the United States are able to legally work in Korea, immigration officials do not dictate how employers must interpret the law when recruiting and hiring. For example, the Korean Ministry of Justice does not discuss anywhere in its 342-page document the need for instructors to submit photos when applying for job openings. Yet, nearly all employers require applicants to submit a recent passport-style photo, which then provides the space for racial discrimination. It must be noted that submitting photos for employment is commonly practiced in many professions in Korea. Nevertheless, requiring images of prospective employees allows employers and recruiters to easily and covertly dismiss instructors who do not fit a particular stereotypical image of an ELT instructor (see, for example, T. Lee, 2014a). Although the practice of requiring photos for recruitment purposes is not, in and of itself, discriminatory, this requirement has the potential to skew what is deemed valuable in the ELT profession (see Chapter 6).

In addition to immigration laws creating spaces for racism, elite racialized discourses come from teaching organizations. For example, the English Program in Korea (commonly known as EPIK), which works closely with the Korean Ministry of Education and places ELT instructors in public schools throughout the country (cf. JET Program in Japan), requires citizens from South Africa (i.e. an E-2 country) to demonstrate that they have received 10 years of English language instruction from seventh grade to university (EPIK, 2013). The Korean Ministry of Justice does not, however, state in its public documents that South Africans must demonstrate that they received their education in English; on the contrary, the Korean Ministry of Justice only states that South Africa is an English-speaking country (e.g. Ministry of Justice, Korea Immigration Service, 2015b: 132). This discrepancy points to a larger misconception within the ELT profession in Korea (and beyond) that multicultural and multilingual speakers within multiracial societies are inferior to monolingual NESs who belong to historically White nations because the English spoken by the former group may be influenced by other languages and cultures, such as Afrikaans. This view is criticized by an instructor discussing the new EPIK requirement for South Africans on a popular ELT website: Waygook.org. The data presented below is from the ELT website's public discussion forum that caters for instructors from E-2 nations. Anyone with a username and password can participate in these forums, though no discussion posts were made for the purpose of writing this book. The ELT website also allocates a considerable amount of space to job-opening posts written by both prospective employers and employees.

> So you want South Africans to prove they had education in English although the whole country speaks English. I understand the fact that a lot of people from South Africa had school in Afrikaans. But, have you ever heard of the term bilingual?

This observation is revelatory, despite its informality, in that it shows how White normativity is imagined and circulated within the

ELT profession. The discourse that South Africans must provide evidence of education in English while not requiring the same for speakers from the United States and the like is curious given that other E-2 countries are made up of large populations of immigrants and multilinguals. Viewing South Africa with skepticism when considering which countries can be considered English-speaking is problematic because the discourse suggests that bilingualism is an impediment to ELT instruction. Not asking prospective teachers from other E-2 countries that are viewed as stereotypically White the same question is also problematic because it creates the discourse that monolingualism is the best model for bilingual students. The underlying racism that exists in asking South Africans to submit proof that they have received their education in English, but ignoring the possibility that a citizen from the United States may have immigrated from a country that does not speak English to the same extent as South Africa, is evidence that racial, linguistic and national hierarchies are used in the ELT profession to shape expectations of who is an ideal speaker of English.

Although the evidence of systemic discrimination presented thus far suggests the possibility of widespread racism, it is important to note that the ELT profession in Korea is, like many aspects of life, made up of a complex set of social issues that require years of research, discussion and debate. That is to say, the point in identifying the problem with immigration laws is not to suggest that rampant discrimination occurs at different levels within the ELT profession; this is an empirical question that requires extensive, long-term research, including tracking the applications submitted for ELT positions and their country of origin; rather, the salient issue in pointing out current immigration laws and hiring practices is to argue that the legal and occupational systems that shape the ELT profession in Korea are inherently discriminatory and potentially racist. Moreover, these laws and practices demonstrate the need for government officials and ELT employers to adopt a more contemporary understanding of the English language that minimizes the possibility of racism.

Empirically demonstrating the existence of widespread discrimination against teachers of color from the seven E-2 eligible countries is a difficult task. Despite this, it is clear that work visa requirements shut out thousands of 'non-White' teachers from, for example, Asia and Africa. The privileging of teachers from countries that have been historically depicted as White is most evident in recent immigration law changes that allow nationals from India to teach English under the Comprehensive Economic Partnership Agreement (CEPA). While this is a positive step forward in the ELT profession in Korea, English instructors from India who obtain a work visa under CEPA are not categorized as an 'English native speaker assistant teacher' like their counterparts from the seven preferred countries, but rather an 'English assistant teacher' (Ministry of Justice, Korea Immigration Service, 2015a: 120). The omission of 'native speaker' is significant, as it demonstrates that the Korean Government does not consider ELT instructors from India to be the same as, or perhaps even thought inferior to, teachers from the original list of English-speaking countries. This is further evidenced in the need for instructors from India to have 'graduated from university and received a bachelor's degree (or higher) and teacher license' (Ministry of Justice, Korea Immigration Service, 2015b: 132). This insistence on a 'teacher license' is noteworthy, as citizens from the seven preferred countries are only required to possess an undergraduate degree (in any major), and need not demonstrate an ability to teach.

Recent changes to immigrations laws may allow instructors from Malaysia, the Philippines and Singapore to apply for ELT work in Korea, though the Korean Ministry of Justice has not updated its policy documents at the time of writing to reflect this; it is understood that ELT instructors from these South East Asian countries, like their Indian counterparts, will also be required to provide evidence that they have obtained a formal teaching license. In other words, the status of being an English speaker from an E-2 country carries with it a value that is greater than the ability to teach, while the status of being an English speaker from a Southeast Asian country does not possess a value larger than pedagogical acumen. This type of linguistic discrimination, or linguicism, is a common phenomenon, and has been reported on extensively in a number of different contexts (e.g. Mahboob & Szenes, 2010). Like the racial discrimination that is associated with, for example, the use of African American vernacular English in the United States, the E-2 visa requirement demonstrates that racism can be located within linguicism in ways that are not always visible.

Immigration laws help circulate the belief within Korea that English language instruction is best taught by White teachers, and this elite form of discourse is most evident when observing the racial landscape of the ELT profession. For example, North American instructors dominate the teaching landscape. Of the 16,560 E-2 visa holders in Korea as of September 2015 (Korea Immigration Service, 2015), 11,005 (or approximately 66%) are from the United States and Canada (8,455 and 2,550, respectively). Although the precise number of teachers of color from these countries is unknown, White normativity in the ELT profession in Korea exists irrespective of actual demographic totals because the pervasiveness of North American 'cultures' and dialects in classrooms helps circulate US racial hierarchies through pedagogical materials, instructor experiences and teaching philosophies (I. Lee, 2009; H. Song, 2013). I. Lee (2009), for example, shows that high school students in Korea are exposed to ELT textbooks that depict the 'West', and in particular the United States, as White, powerful, creative and entertaining. The mere presence of North American varieties of English in classrooms provokes images, discourses and ideologies of a 'White America' (cf. N. Kim, 2006; Yook & Lindemann, 2013) where Whiteness prevails as the baseline for all notions of what is socially and linguistically 'normal'.

The privileging of instructors from the seven E-2 countries, and the curricular decisions that are made as a result, lead to what Page and Thomas (1994: 111) refer to as a 'white public space', which comprises 'in its material and symbolic dimensions … all the places where racism is reproduced by the professional class. That space may entail particular or generalized locations, sites, patterns, configurations, tactics, or devices that routinely, discursively, and sometimes coercively privilege Euro-Americans over nonwhites'.

The privileging of NESs, as codified in immigration laws, creates a White public space in the ELT profession by making it possible for employers to interpret work visa requirements in a way that perpetuates societal expectations of what a speaker of English looks, and indeed sounds, like (for a discussion of White public spaces in the global ELT profession, including teacher training programs, see Chapter 7). For example, despite changes in immigration laws that allow citizens from India to teach English, employers have yet to actively recruit instructors from this region. A search conducted on 16 December 2015 found no employer or recruiter seeking instructors from India, as indicated by the type of work visa being advertised, among the 930 job postings on the popular recruitment website ESL Cafe (space does not permit an elaborate discussion of the significance of this website here, but it should be noted briefly that, over the last two decades, ESL Cafe has been one of a few premier sites for job searches and discussion). Further, employers can be seen interpreting immigration laws in such a circumscribed way that even some nationalities from the original list of E-2 nations are not given an opportunity to apply for employment. English Life, a pseudonym given to a private school on the same recruitment website, omits South Africa from its list of accepted nationalities: 'Nationality (USA, CA, UK, IR, AU, NZ)'. The omission of South Africa from job posts should not come as a surprise to many South Africans living in Korea given ongoing concerns regarding their ability to speak English (see above) and the recent Ebola virus outbreak that led some

Koreans to ban Africans from entering their places of business (C. Lee, 2014b).

The marginalization of teachers of color, or the fabrication of White normativity, is also visible in the language used by employers who accept job applications from overseas ethnic Koreans (e.g. Korean Americans). According to immigration laws, ethnic Koreans who live outside of Korea (commonly referred to as *gyopos*) can apply for an F-4 visa (for an interesting essay on transnational Korean adoptees working as English instructors in Korea as F-4 visa holders, see E. Kim, 2012: 310). Although overseas ethnic Koreans on F-4 visas are not tied to a specific place of employment like E-2 visa holders (i.e. immigration laws privilege *gyopos*), employers can be seen implicitly acknowledging the existence of White normativity in the ELT profession.

For example, searching the same 930 job postings listed on ESL Cafe, it is not difficult to find employers and recruiters using language such as 'F4 can apply also' or 'F4 visa Gyopos are Welcome' to note that in addition to the prototypical applicant, ethnic Koreans from E-2 countries are encouraged to apply. What is noteworthy about the language used in such job postings is the special or marked status given to overseas ethnic Korean instructors. For example, the use of 'also' in the first job posting demonstrates that overseas ethnic Korean instructors are on the periphery or are not considered in the prototypical pool of teachers. The use of 'also' and 'welcome' signals that there has either never been a tradition of accepting such instructors and/or that these teachers are sometimes excluded from consideration. Other job postings distinguish between 'normal' teachers and overseas ethnic Korean instructors in more explicit ways, as in the case of one employer searching for two positions: '(one F4 bilingual teacher and one native teacher)'. The juxtaposition between native and F-4 bilingual not only treats the two instructor types as different, but it also implies that the latter teacher is in some way not a 'native' of the English language.

It is encouraging to see employers considering overseas ethnic Korean instructors, yet only a small percentage of job advertisements state that F-4 visa holders may apply (7% or 65 out of 930 postings). Indeed, some employers state unequivocally in their job postings that F-4 visa holders are *not* wanted: 'Only American or Canadian - Native Speaker (Not Gyopo)'. Such comments are peculiar, as they treat overseas ethnic Koreans, despite growing up in North America, as people who are not the same as 'Americans' or 'Canadians'. According to this particular job post, overseas ethnic Koreans are neither North American nor native speakers. It is unclear whether this treatment and categorization of overseas ethnic Koreans applies to other racial groups.

While the descriptor *American* or *Canadian* can evoke a number of different racialized images apart from ethnic Korean, the notion that a *gyopo* cannot apply for teaching work suggests that there is a tacit racial hierarchy in the ELT profession. The outright dismissal of overseas ethnic Koreans in job postings demonstrates the extent to which racial discrimination exists in the ELT profession given that employers can simply reject applications from instructors of color after receiving their obligatory photo. That is, rather than veil their discrimination behind the practice of requesting photos with job applications, employers freely manufacture racism (and White normativity) in and through the language used to describe ideal candidates. Perhaps more importantly, such job postings circulate the perception that White normativity exists, which then gets taken up in various discursive spaces in the ELT profession. For example, it is not difficult to find instructors of color referencing their peripheral status or making relevant their ethnicity when seeking employment in Korea. The comments below are taken from job-wanted postings on the recruitment website Waygook.org.

> The elephant in the room? I'm Asian! While I've been told that blond haired, blue-eyed teachers are more easily marketable in Korea, American teachers of Asian ancestry are POWERFUL forces in the classroom who can offer your students a gift no others can.
> I can guarantee employers that if hired I will not disappoint them therefore please do not stray away because of my nationality, race, or gender.

Job-wanted posts like these are noteworthy because the common practice on this website, as well as others, is to exclude discussions of race and ethnicity. That is, instructors who seek employment by and large focus on work experience, teaching philosophies and employment preferences, to name a few. With the exception of one teacher who states 'I am a 25-year-old, white male from South Africa', when race is referenced it is often done so by teachers of color.

Asian American Native Speaker. Female Teacher w/ Experiences & TESOL Certified.

Korean American Female looking for post in Seoul.

Female Native-Speaker. Asian-American. English & Art teacher. Start: ASAP.

I am a British Chinese male with 1 year and 6 months of teaching experience at a elementary school.

With regard to the construction and circulation of White normativity, the language used to reference racial and ethnic information in these postings is significant, as it signals to other readers that being of color is a shortcoming or, at best, a marked characteristic. These five postings are also significant in that teachers can be seen, like recruiters and employers, to be contributing to the elite discourse that views race and ethnicity as professional 'qualifications'. While most job-wanted postings follow the same script of focusing on qualifications, the teachers quoted here use racial and ethnic categories to communicate their professional identities. While it is important for teachers of color to value and celebrate their diversity, especially when negotiating their professional identities, job-wanted posts like these unfortunately have the potential to place such instructors on the periphery. The discourse created as a result of marking or highlighting race and ethnicity manufactures White normativity by implicitly treating Whiteness as the 'unmarked norm'. That is to say, discourses that conflate teaching abilities with racial or ethnic features have the potential to simultaneously prop up White normativity and oppress teachers of color.

Associating race and ethnicity with desirable occupational characteristics in job-opening and job-wanted posts establishes, like immigration laws, 'a morally significant set of contexts that are the most important sites of the practices of a racializing hegemony, in which Whites are invisibly normal, and in which racialized populations are visibly marginal and the objects of monitoring' (Hill, 1998: 682). In other words, these posts function as White public spaces where descriptors, such as American, Canadian and native speaker, are understood to mean White instructor. The invisible, or unspoken, White-as-normal ideology is powerful, ubiquitous and hegemonic because it shapes what are understood to be valuable occupational characteristics. The mere reference to racial and ethnic categories in recruitment spaces, like Asian or Korean American, demonstrates this most vividly. White normativity is such an organizing principle in the ELT profession that instructors of color are compelled to engage in discursive practices that feed into, and prop up, the racial hierarchy within it (for a discussion of Whiteness as an organizing principle in race relations, see Lipsitz, 1995). While statements such as 'I am a British Chinese male' are ostensibly innocuous and/or are devoid of specific examples of institutionalized racism, the very disclosure of racial and ethnic information in job-wanted posts represents a more complex picture that is not immediately visible in the language used in immigration laws and recruitment spaces.

Immigration laws and recruitment websites are not the only spaces where White normativity gets manufactured and circulated. A number of media outlets report widespread racial discrimination in the ELT profession. Although caution must be taken when interpreting news reports (cf. van Dijk, 1988), the headlines presented below, irrespective of the extent to which they accurately reflect the realities of the profession, disseminate the view that there is a preference for White instructors:

Racial preference for white English teachers prevalent in Korea – Yonhap News Agency (Schroeder, 2011)

American rejected for job in Korea because of being black – *The Korea Observer* (T. Lee, 2014a)

Ethnic Bias Seen in South Korea Teacher Hiring – NPR (Strother, 2007)

Chungdahm April under fire for 'white only' recruitment ad – *The Korea Observer* (Hyams, 2015)

In addition to shaping societal expectations of the intersection of race and language, news media reports like the ones presented above explain in vivid detail how White normativity affects instructors of color. For example, as mentioned in Chapter 1, Sean Jones, an African American ELT instructor who no longer works in Korea, is said to have been rejected for two jobs in one week for possessing the wrong skin pigmentation (T. Lee, 2014a). In another example of racism, Chungdahm April, a private language institute, allegedly engages in frequent acts of discrimination, and in the last news report above, received criticism for including the expression 'Must be Caucasian' in a recent job posting (Hyams, 2015).

The discrimination against instructors of color is not only part of a larger system of White normativity, but it also fabricates a discourse that teachers belonging to the 'unmarked norm' are culturally and socially homogenous. Racial fabrication, in other words, is an ideological construct that states that a legitimate ELT instructor is White and all cultural Others are not. Haney López (1994: 55), in his discussion of the formation of a White–Black dichotomy in US history, states that 'Racial fabrication changes communities by emphasizing or even creating commonalities while eroding previously relevant differences'. Similar observations can be made of the ELT profession. Korean immigration laws, racialized recruitment spaces and discrimination against instructors of color, all help create an imagined, homogenous speaker of English by simultaneously ignoring the physical, social, linguistic and cultural differences that exist within and across so-called native-English-speaking countries and treating Whiteness as a referential baseline for all notions of what an ELT instructor should look like. That is to say, the ELT profession also creates false racial dichotomies by treating Whiteness and nativeness as fixed, stable and pure categories.

Racial fabrication is a process that is both shaped by society and shapes race-based belief systems. For example, societal expectations of what an ELT instructor should look like come from, and establish the conditions for, racial fabrication. This inherently ideological and socially derived manifestation of race is topicalized during the interviews of ELT instructors conducted for the present book, which took place online and over several months using semi-structured questions that were emailed to former colleagues, acquaintances and teachers with large social media followings. All four of the interviews with instructors of color revealed that their experiences led them to believe that White normativity organizes the ELT profession in Korea. All of the instructors of color also discussed the ways in which racial hierarchies and dichotomies carve out their lived experiences.

One interviewee, an African American with several years of teaching experience and knowledge of the Korean language, is cognizant of the ineluctable importance of race in her professional world. When asked whether she has experienced discrimination in Korea, Jennifer states the following:

Absolutely. Finding a job in Korea is super hard when you're not white. I found that Korean people tend to think that there are two types of English in America, white English and black English, the latter being less desirable. So even though I graduated from quite an elite university, many people just assumed that I wasn't as smart or educated as the white teachers applying for the same jobs. Even after having taught in Korea for 5 years, I got ignored by most recruiters, and a few times I was even directly told that they were only looking for white instructors. I won't lie, this really hurt. You have to attach a photo with all of your applications, and I found myself just dreading or even sometimes ignoring that part. After I changed my last name to a Korean one, I got a few more calls for interviews (if they hadn't seen my picture). But as soon I arrived, I could see the look of disappointment on their faces which always made me super uncomfortable.

Although Jennifer has been able to find employment in Korea, her professional experiences have not been without challenges. This is evidenced vividly in the beginning of her response, where she answers unequivocally in the affirmative to the question of experiencing discrimination. The initial one-word lexical element 'Absolutely' not only amplifies the answer (Tao, 2007), but it also frames (Goffman, 1984) the reality or experience that Jennifer constructs in her following response (cf. Tannen & Wallat, 1987). Jennifer continues by stating that it is 'super hard' to find a job 'when you're not white'. Her statement, by dichotomizing the experiences of instructors who are White and those who are not, casts her understanding of the ELT profession, and more specifically the process of finding employment, through a White normativity lens. Here, Jennifer can be seen actively engaging in the social construction of race, or racial fabrication, by defining her reality against, or in relation to, the experiences of White instructors. In other words, Jennifer racializes her professional life experiences by suggesting that instructors of color have a difficult time finding work because of White privilege.

Societal expectations of what an ELT instructor should look (and sound) like shape life experiences and ideological commitments in other ways. For example, Jennifer attributes her job-seeking experiences to the understanding that there are 'two types of English in America' according to Korean society: 'white English and black English'. Korean societal expectations of English varieties, as understood by Jennifer, point to a more complex interplay between language and race (cf. Crump, 2014). The ideology that 'black English' is 'less desirable' can be attributed most notably to the fact that the only exposure many Koreans have to African Americans comes from the US entertainment industry that culturally and linguistically essentializes Blackness in, for example, hip-hop music and Hollywood movies. This observation is supported by another interviewee who took part in the present study. Nathalie, an African American instructor, states the following in her description of being an object of scrutiny in Korea:

I do believe that the negative image of African Americans received by Koreans is a result of how the media decides to portray us. Ghetto, loud, hyper-sexualized criminals. At times I will see women move their purse and hold it tight when they realize I'm standing behind them in line waiting for the train ... Korean TV is no exception. There are regular depictions of Black people by Koreans in black face with afros, braids or dreads. It's supposed to be funny, but when they are 'pimp' walking, wearing a basketball jersey and talking 'black', it's really offensive. I honestly believe that it is just ignorance, but it's still widely done.

This perverse understanding of Black language and culture maintains White normativity by creating racial and linguistic dichotomies. African Americans are 'loud, hyper-sexualized criminals' while White Americans are positioned as ideal language instructors. For Jennifer, the existence of racial and linguistic dichotomies means that, despite being a highly educated individual with the ability to speak a 'standard' variety of English, ELT professionals assume that she is not 'as smart or educated as ... white teachers'. White normativity, therefore, has real-life consequences that extend beyond societal expectations of race and language: Jennifer was 'ignored by most recruiters' and even informed by them on some occasions 'that they were only looking for white instructors'.

The last section of Jennifer's answer provides important insights into how White normativity in the ELT profession is organized. Being on the job market with a Korean last name and refusing to submit photos with her applications allowed Jennifer to secure more job interviews, but this initial success led to disappointment when prospective employers discovered her racial background. In other words, her marriage to a Korean citizen and strategic omission of self-revealing information gave some employers the impression that she was a Korean American. The fact that employers were more willing to review her application because of her Korean last name, and their subsequent reluctance, demonstrates that White normativity is an organizing principle in the ELT profession; instructors of color experience discrimination as a result; and privilege and intolerance are part of, and based on, a racial hierarchy that affords Korean Americans more rights than African Americans.

While Korean Americans are situated above African Americans in the ELT racial hierarchy in Korea, White normativity dominates belief systems in the profession. For example, another interviewee, a Korean American named Lisa, reflects on her experience teaching at a school that offers lessons over the phone:

During my interview, the hiring manager made comments about how I had a 'great English native speaker voice' and I was hired on a trial basis a few days later. When I next met the hiring manager to review the job requirements and lesson plans, they instructed me to tell students that I was a White female from California and showed me (what looked to be a stock photo of) a picture of a blond female with blue eyes that they would be sending to all of my students. Their justification was that it fit with the company's mission statement of employing only 'English native speakers'.

The linguistic assessment given to Lisa is noteworthy, as it demonstrates that having 'great English' does not fulfill the requirements of being an ideal ELT instructor. For Lisa's employer, the ideal instructor must have linguistic proficiency, but this qualification is mutually dependent on being from California and having blue eyes. Although it is a difficult task to determine the extent to which this image represents the views of an entire ELT profession, Lisa's occupational constraints can be used to better understand why some instructors of color, such as Jennifer, experience discrimination. The belief that English is (best) spoken by White individuals with blue eyes, perhaps from California, does not materialize in a vacuum. Entertainment and media from the United States are major transmitters of English-language content in Korea (Shin & Stringer, 2005), and with an overall lack of ethnic diversity in American popular culture (e.g. Hunt & Ramón, 2015), Whiteness is transformed into a defining characteristic of English speakers. In addition, economic relations between the two countries, US military control in the region and a history of 'Western' Christian proselytizers have resulted in a belief system that assumes English is best taught by White 'Americans'. This limited view is exacerbated by the fact that Koreans have an uncomfortable relationship with the English language (J.S. Park, 2009); thus, ownership of English has not been taken up in any significant way in the country. English is still largely used only in educational and institutional settings where the presumed linguistic expert in the language is a 'non-Korean'.

Whatever the reason for asking Lisa to inform her students that she is a White instructor from the United States (for a neoliberal explanation, see Chapter 6), her employer in this particular request is actively engaging in the fabrication of White normativity. The company objective to employ not just 'native speakers' but blue-eyed instructors from California contributes to societal belief systems while concomitantly propping up the ELT racial hierarchy. This demonstrates that discrimination in the ELT profession extends beyond the linguistic level (cf. linguicism) to race, ethnicity and nationality. That is to say, discussions of linguicism, including critical evaluations of native and non-native categories (e.g. Rampton, 1990), should not be uncoupled from race, ethnicity and nationality (Amin, 1997; Leung et al., 1997).

While the interviews above establish how White normativity affects the professional lives of instructors of color as well as the ways in which they discursively construct their experiences, racial fabrication is not confined to discrimination. In understanding the architecture of

White normativity, it is important to examine not only the experiences of instructors of color and the ways in which employers propagate discrimination, but also how White instructors buy into, and circulate, the discourse in which they are the objects of privilege. This more inclusive approach to understanding racism is needed because discourses that are responsible for racial fabrication come from, and are transmitted to, all individuals of the ELT racial hierarchy. Understanding how White instructors participate in such fabrications is important because it demonstrate that responsibility for creating conditions for racialized privilege is not limited to individuals who practice discrimination. Those on the receiving end of privilege can also be seen actively engaging in racial fabrication in general, and in the creation of White normativity specifically (see, for example, Chapter 5).

Take, for instance, the following interview conducted for a public YouTube channel that provides general information for current and prospective ELT teachers in Korea. As a side note, the clip from which the following excerpt is taken has received over 130,000 views since 2013, and the over 700 comments posted on YouTube in response to this video include both positive appraisals and negative feedback.

The interviewee, a White instructor and one of three teachers participating in the YouTube video, responds to the question of experiencing racism in Korea by stating that she has not because she possesses the ideal physical characteristics for teaching English. Figure 4.1 captures the moment when the White instructor begins her response. Following Figure 4.1 is the response transcribed according to conversation analytic conventions (see Jenks, 2011).

This response raises several important issues regarding the organization of White normativity. The turn-initial construction 'for me' provides a window into the racial dynamics of ELT by suggesting that instructors in Korea have different experiences with racism. Her experience, as it turns out, reflects privilege and fortune. Although she does not explicitly promote discrimination in her response, statements such as 'I guess I'm lucky' and 'I have the look' perpetuate power imbalances and ethnic inequalities by reinforcing the idea that being White is nonpareil. Doane (2006: 256) talks about how such statements normalize racialized discourses within society by reinforcing existing belief systems. That is to say, simply stating that Koreans prefer White instructors, irrespective of whether this statement is true, may create the impression for some individuals, for example the two instructors of color sitting at the table, that White normativity exists in the profession. This does not mean

Figure 4.1 The look

1 **T3:**   uhm (1.2) I guess for me like I'm- I'm lucky because I- I have th:: I
2   have the. <u>look</u> that Koreans are looking for when they want like a
3   Western teacher so:: (.) I haven't I haven't had too much in the way
4   of racism.

that the interviewee, and other teachers who make similar statements, are consciously or strategically seeking to reinforce inequalities that promote White normativity. Such statements can, nonetheless, create the illusion – for both the speaker of this utterance and the thousands of viewers of this YouTube channel – that teachers of color must seek employment in the ELT profession in Korea with caution. For example, the use of 'lucky' implies that teachers located on the periphery because of their race or ethnicity are somehow unlucky for not being White, while the construction 'Koreans are looking for' suggests that employers and recruiters are not fortunate if they end up with, for example, an Asian American instructor. Although the construction 'Western teacher' opens up the possibility that this category can include more than one ethnic or racial group, the underlying message in her response is that Korean employers prefer White teachers and that such instructors are more fortunate than others because of this bias.

The admission that she is 'lucky' to possess 'the [right] look', and as a result has not experienced racism, may suggest at first reading that the interviewee is not involved in the reconstruction of racialized discourses, though these statements are inextricably connected to a larger system of racial hierarchies. That is say, although the interviewee has not experienced racism, her career has benefited from racial privilege and she is thus part of a larger system that discriminates against instructors of color. In this sense, White normativity is an issue that all instructors in the ELT profession must be aware of, especially teachers who reap the benefits of being located at the top of a racial hierarchy that discriminates on the basis of race and ethnicity. Further, the elite discourses that provide the means for the construction of White normativity come from, in addition to employers and recruiters who profit from stereotypical images of English speakers, instructors who are on the receiving end of privilege.

Conclusion

This chapter has demonstrated that White normativity is based on ideological constructs that treat Whiteness as an essential characteristic for good language teaching. Such belief systems come from, and are circulated by, different members of the ELT community. White normativity is circulated not only by professionals who are on the receiving end of privilege (e.g. employers and White instructors), but its elite discourses that lead to racism are also disseminated by instructors of color who exoticize race and ethnicity in and through job-wanted postings. This finding is significant, as critical race scholars have demonstrated that White normativity is typically reinforced by individuals who represent the 'unmarked norm' and/or benefit from such privilege. In the ELT profession in Korea, conversely, White normative discourses and ideologies are circulated and reinforced by employers and recruiters, White teachers *and* instructors of color. In other words, racism in the ELT profession in Korea is not only based on a White/non-White binary, but it also comes from hierarchies and a system of discourse that discriminate and privilege on the basis of race and ethnicity. Because immigration laws and recruitment practices create an institutional framework for racism to occur, White normativity transcends occupational spaces and thus represents the common-sense understanding of the profession.

White normativity is exceptionally problematic for the role of English in Korea. A system of White privilege hurts the relationship that Koreans have with English because it keeps the language 'foreign', attached to the cultural values of outside regions and forever unattainable given these reasons. The next chapter extends some of these observations by demonstrating that NES instructors and White teachers can reproduce elite discourses by transmitting colonial discourses that associate the English language with the cultural traditions and values of so-called inner-circle countries. These elite discourses provide a lens through which teachers can be seen working 'to legitimize and reproduce dominance by … marginalizing claims of subordinate groups, and moving to make dominant group understandings normative for the larger society' (Doane, 2006: 256).

5 White Saviorism in ELT

Introduction

The Spanish–American War of 1898, which was partly a result of US political efforts to end fighting in Cuba, led to the Treaty of Paris in December of the same year. Among a number of stipulations, the treaty required Spain to sell the Philippines to the United States. Rather than accept a change in colonial rule, Filipino nationalists decided to fight for independence. This three-year conflict (1899–1902), commonly referred to as the Philippine–American War, represents an important historical event in colonialism, imperialism and indeed White supremacy.

The discourses that were circulated at the time highlighted why, for some people, colonization was an important moral duty for Western countries. For example, during the time immediately leading up to the Philippine–American War, Rudyard Kipling, an English poet and writer, sent a poem 'to his friend Theodore Roosevelt, who had just been elected Governor of New York … to encourage the American government to take over the Philippines' (Brantlinger, 2007: 172). Kipling's (1899) poem, titled 'The White Man's Burden', speaks of racially bound moral principles and the need to help those who are culturally inferior to the White race. While the complete poem can be easily located and read online, it is worth quoting the first stanza here: 'Take up the White Man's burden – Send forth the best ye breed – Go bind your sons to exile/ To serve your captives' need;/ To wait in heavy harness/ On fluttered folk and wild–/ Your new-caught, sullen peoples/ Half devil and half child'.

Although the poem was published and widely circulated after the start of the Philippine–American War, it 'served [at the time and subsequently] as a lightning rod for both the supporters and the opponents of imperialism, as well as of racism and white supremacy' (Brantlinger, 2007: 172). Indeed, with characterizations like 'Your new-caught, sullen peoples, Half devil and half child' and 'Go mark them with your living, And mark them with your dead,' it is clear that justifications for imperial rule at the time, but more specifically for Kipling, were rooted in both moral elitism and racism. That is to say, colonialism and racism are inextricably connected.

The historical significance of Kipling's poem lies not in its influence on the US military – such a connection is tenuous at best – but rather in how it represents some of the ideological commitments that were circulated at the time. For example, media coverage of the ongoing war in the Philippines, both in the United States and the United Kingdom, created 'an Anglo-Saxon brotherhood that prized blood over politics and that imagined itself as the epitome of modern order and benevolence' (S. Harris, 2007: 261). The notion that the 'White man' is morally responsible for bringing about civilization to countries deemed *by him* to be uncivil, unruly and the like, is in fact an ideology that the United States learned from the British Empire (S. Harris, 2007). This belief system shaped colonial and imperial efforts in the many decades leading up to the Philippine–American War, both in the United States and beyond, including, notably, atrocities committed against Native Americans (cf. 'manifest destiny'). Thus, Kipling's poem is not the first to popularize or disseminate racially informed paternalism; the exceptionally contentious though highly popular nature of Kipling's stanzas can be partly attributed to the fact that the belief systems underpinning 'The White Man's Burden' were, have been and continue to be a central organizing principle for 'Western' colonialism and exceptionalism. Indeed, 'terms such as "noble savage", "manifest destiny", "white man's burden", and "great white hope" refer to previous iterations of the complex relationship between the tropes of the white savior and the dysfunctional and dark "other" in need of saving' (Hughey, 2014: 8).

Closer examination of social processes and cultural phenomena, both historical and contemporary, reveal that the ideologies underpinning 'The White Man's Burden' are in fact present in many domains of life. For example, the idea that White individuals are morally responsible for saving or rescuing the cultural Other is a common trope still present in, and disseminated by, the Hollywood film industry (e.g. *The Help* with Emma Stone or *The Blind Side* with Sandra Bullock). Such narratives, which 'construct whites as heroic and virtuous and nonwhites as dysfunctional and dangerous' (Hughey, 2010: 481), help circulate the belief that peoples of color are unable to save or rescue themselves. This White saviorism, or what T. Cole (2012) refers to as the White Savior Industrial Complex, is bound to a national imaginary that sees its own cultural practices and ways of life as nonpareil. Put differently, White saviorism is intricately connected to national identities and, as such, represents a cogent reason for individuals to justify their paternalism. White saviorism in Hollywood films is particularly powerful and influential, as the trope is so widely circulated (and done so unproblematically) that it becomes the common-sense understanding of the nation (for a detailed look at White saviorism in film, see Hughey, 2014).

White saviorism stems from a number of psychologies, chiefly sentimentality, self-righteousness and chauvinism. These saviorist discourses are rooted in an epistemology that situates ethnocentric and egocentric ambitions within larger narratives of kindness, generosity and the like (e.g. victimization); such narratives will be unpacked with empirical examples in the next section. White saviorism may manifest in the desire of a country or individual to cultivate democracy, spread Christianity, introduce modern technology or teach English, to name a few examples. A saviorist agenda is underpinned by larger issues of race, ethnicity and nationality, but has serious political, religious, cultural, technological, educational and linguistic consequences for those who are 'saved' or 'rescued'.

White saviorism manifests in, or is used in response to, social events, problems and issues. For example, Kipling's poem responded to the issue of whether the United States should colonize the Philippines and was located in a broader discussion of Western imperialism. Thus, social events, problems and issues provide a window into the 'racial ontologies' of a nation or individual. A racial ontology is a belief system predicated on race. In this sense, White saviorism is a racial epistemology. That is to say, White saviorism is used by people to make sense of *how* their participation in, and contribution to, a social event or issue justifies their existence. In the next section, the analysis will explore how White saviorism is used as a discursive resource to argue that recent budget cuts in education are a mistake, given NES teachers' participation in, and contribution to, the ELT profession.

White Saviorism in ELT

At the end of 2014, media outlets reported a significant drop in NES teachers in Korean public schools (e.g. H. Kim & Han, 2014). Between 2011 and 2013, the number decreased from 9320 to 6785 (T. Lee, 2014b). This decrease, as revealed by several government branches, including the Seoul Metropolitan Office of Education, was a result of nationwide budget cuts and changes to spending priorities, including additional monies spent on offering free daycare services in some districts. The loss of over 2500 instructors follows many years of growth in the ELT profession, starting from 2002 when there were only 131 NES instructors in public schools (H. Hong, 2010). While this most recent drop is significant, fluctuations in the size of the ELT market are not new, and budgetary constraints can indeed affect hiring practices on a yearly basis.

In the years since 2010, ELT instructors have expressed their frustration at the possibility of further budget cuts and at how these would affect hiring practices in subsequent years. These budget cuts, as well as the responses from instructors to such changes, are well documented in the media and online ELT forums. As demonstrated below, social events, problems and issues that have far-reaching and significant implications, such as budget cuts, force individuals to evaluate how they contribute to their profession. Put differently, such events, problems and issues provide discursive spaces for individuals to construct, and make sense of, their understanding of the world. The data examined in this section addresses how White saviorism is used as an epistemological tool by instructors to simultaneously qualify their value in the profession and critique the decision to cut spending on ELT instruction. Thus, the responses given by ELT instructors to recent budget cuts provide a better understanding of how White saviorism is discursively constructed.

The first example is a response to a report on the recent budget cuts published by an English-language newspaper read by many ELT instructors. The response, provided in the comments section of the article, provides a reason why the Korean government has decided to scale back on the number of ELT instructors from 'English-speaking' countries:

This all comes down to [sic] 12 year-old Korean male mentality angry at taller, more socially suave, economically developed Westerners.

The argument that government officials are spending less on NES instructors because Koreans are envious of, and/or feel threatened by, Westerners reveals how Orientalism can be used to make sense of the cultural Other (Said, 1985). The saviorism here is based on chauvinism and, more specifically, the notion that Koreans are, in relation to their Western peers, immature, emotional, short, socially inept and economically feeble. Although the author does not use any race-based categories, such as White, the juxtaposition of 'Westerners' and 'Korean male' is a form of racialized discourse. That is, the notion that Westerners are taller than Koreans is based on the assumption that individuals with Asian ancestry from so-called Western countries do not belong to places like the United States. The comment, accordingly, circulates the common assumption that Western equals White (as well the more profession-specific ideology that NES instructors are Westerners, and therefore White).

The data example above demonstrates that White saviorism, here based on the view that funding cuts undermine the important work provided by NES instructors, can be used as an analytic lens through which to identify how the savior condemns or problematizes the actions or characteristics of the cultural Other. Specifically, the author of the saviorist comment views the funding cuts as a decision based on the insecurities of Korean men. In this instance, White saviorism is based on a racial hierarchy that places the savior above the cultural Other in relation to desirable human characteristics (e.g. the physical, social, economic and emotional advantages and privileges Westerners have over Koreans). The common-sense understanding that Westerners possess more desirable human characteristics than Asians is woven into the very fabric of society, as argued in Chapter 4 (cf. Haney López, 1994). While it is beyond the scope of this book to examine how such belief systems are created and circulated within English-speaking countries, it can be said that the more specific ideology that Koreans are insecure about their social and physical standing in relation to Westerners is *learned* in and through the discursive formations of White-dominant nations.

The next data example comes from a discussion created on a popular ELT website in response to one of the many media reports on the budget cuts. The comment thread, which received over 6000 views, dealt with the merits of reducing the number of NES instructors in Korea. Although several remarks in the comment thread made use of some form of saviorist discourse, the following observation provides one of the most powerful examples of saviorism:

> Great maybe these fluent Korean English teachers can teach the students great phrases like this one found in my school above the English room … Besides the spelling and grammar, confusing feet with feel, that's a far cry from fluent.

This characterization of Korean ELT teachers refers to a picture of the contributor's place of employment that is uploaded with the discussion. The photo, which is not included for copyright reasons, is of a sign with an inspirational statement about learning English:

> To learn English fast and effectively [sic] you have to see it, hear it and to feet it.

The comments pertaining to this inspirational statement (which is accompanied by a Korean translation in the photo), like the previous example of White saviorism, reveal how racial hierarchies are maintained through various discursive means (cf. Nakayama & Krizek, 1995). Here, the contributor can be seen making visible the racial hierarchy used to make sense of the cultural Other. This is noteworthy from a theoretical point of view, as CRT scholarship is preoccupied with how racial hierarchies are made *invisible* (cf. colorblindness) in and through racialized actions and practices. In the comment above, by contrast, the contributor ridicules the competence of Korean ELT instructors and thus reinforces and makes *visible* the ubiquitous assumption that NES teachers are linguistic experts who can, as a result of their superior knowledge, evaluate other educators in the profession.

The saviorism in this example is based on the suggestion that the budget cuts will hurt the profession because Korean ELT instructors are not as 'fluent' as NES teachers; this observation is underpinned by chauvinism, which the contributor uses to indirectly promote the idea that NES instructors should be valued more in the profession. The use of humor to disparage Korean ELT instructors allows the contributor to maintain existing power structures (i.e. the notion that NESs are fluent), establish discursive control over the debate (i.e. Korean ELT instructors are not fluent) and mobilize support from other readers of this comment thread (cf. Hay, 2000). An intriguing interplay between White saviorism and linguicism also exists within this comment, which demonstrates that White saviorism can be driven by linguistic hierarchies and discrimination. Specifically, the notion that Korean ELT instructors are 'a far cry from fluent' because of a few 'errors' is based on the assumption that such mistakes were not intentional and/or were not simply typos (J.W. Lee, 2016). That is, the assumption here is that when Korean ELT instructors engage in spelling mistakes, they do so because of some linguistic deficiency. In revealing this ideological commitment, the contributor racializes the budget debate by collectively describing Korean ELT instructors as disfluent speakers of English responsible for making humorous spelling mistakes.

The next set of saviorist observations come from a different comment thread posted on the same popular ELT website. The comment thread deals with the same budget cuts, but received less attention (approximately 2300 views) because the discussion centers on a specific region in Seoul. The first comment deviates from the two previous examples of saviorism in that the observation below is situated in a larger victim narrative:

> Most of my students can't afford to go to a private school. My co-teachers have been okay to pretty good, but without me, the students would never have progressed as far as they have.

While access to, and the affordability of, ELT instruction in Korea is an important point of consideration when discussing the consequences of budget cuts in public schools, the writer of this post uses his self-proclaimed ability to teach more effectively than Korean ELT instructors to suggest that students will suffer linguistically from the budget cuts. In so doing, the author positions himself as a saviorist or, in other words, a teacher who takes students to levels of linguistic proficiency unattainable through the teaching conducted by Korean instructors. The way the teacher constructs this discourse is noteworthy, as he relies on sentimentality to justify his position. That is, he expresses sympathy for the linguistic welfare of his students, but the larger discursive action being accomplished functions to validate the widespread belief (as demonstrated by the overwhelming majority of NES teachers expressing their dissatisfaction in different online forums) that the budget cuts are wrong.

This sentimentality is also expressed in the next saviorist example taken from the same comment thread as above:

> These kids are fortunate to have the opportunity to learn English with us. I never had that foreign language opportunity in my elementary school.

In this example, the contributor does not rely on chauvinism in criticizing the budget cuts, or specifically on the argument that NES teachers are better than Korean EFL instructors; the teacher does, however, suggest that students are 'fortunate to have the opportunity to learn English' with NES instructors. Underpinning this suggestion is an attempt to demonstrate a degree of sentimentality, which is accomplished by implying that language learners in Korea are in a unique situation where they can learn English from NES teachers and will therefore be less fortunate after the budget cuts. The author of the comment exhibits a concern for the well-being of 'these kids', and indeed this worry may be genuine, but like many instances of saviorism, the underlying belief is that the savior is in the best (or privileged) position to help the cultural Other. By and large, such belief systems unproblematically assume that the cultural Other, in this case the students, are better off with the saviorist in their lives.

In addition to expressions of chauvinism and sentimentality, saviorism may possess self-righteous discourses. Self-righteousness in the context of the ELT profession is the belief that one's viewpoint regarding language teaching and learning is unequivocally and irrefutably correct. This belief is often connected to the notion that nativeness in a language results in superior teaching.

In a different, but much longer, comment thread viewed by over 66,000 readers, many instructors can be seen using self-righteous discourses to criticize the budget cuts. Three instructors provide their observations below:

> ... by not hiring foreign teachers the school systems will saving [sic] a lot of money and you know where most of the MOE's [Ministry of Education] heart [sic] are. Certainly not with the quality of language acquisition.
>
> I think in the long run it will be to the detriment of Korean English Education...
>
> ... there will always be a place for us in the hagwon [private institute], where mothers will still pay a premium to have their child taught by a real, live Native Speaker.

Each contributor provides a different observation regarding the budget cuts, though all of the examples rely on the belief that nativeness in a language leads to superior learning outcomes. The first example of self-righteous saviorism, for example, argues that by cutting the budget for NES instructors, the government demonstrates a lack of concern for 'the quality of language acquisition'. Here the assumption is that alternative approaches, such as using more Korean ELT instructors, are inferior. The self-righteousness is the conviction that NES instructors are the only group of teachers who can provide 'quality' language education. This belief system is also visible in the second example: the teacher argues that spending less money hiring NES instructors 'will be to the detriment of Korean English Education'. Superiority in teaching, or the perception of superior teaching, can also be expressed in relation to value. Specifically, the ideology that nativeness in a language results in superior teaching is confirmed when parents 'pay a premium' for NES instruction, as evidenced in the third example (for a discussion of how value is determined in the ELT market, see Chapter 6). In other words, the amount of money spent on NES instruction demonstrates, for some instructors, that they are making a significant contribution to the ELT profession.

Indeed, closer examination of the examples above reveals that self-righteous saviorism is underpinned by the ideology that NES instructors are vital for the betterment of society. Collectively, the comments argue that spending money on NES instructors elevates the standard of ELT instruction in Korea, and this belief is substantiated by the amount of money spent on said teachers by some parents. In addition to these discourses, self-righteous saviorism intersects with chauvinism. Implicit in the three comments above, for example, is the belief that instructors who do not belong to the NES category provide inferior language instruction. The following comment provides a vivid example of how self-righteousness and chauvinism intersect in saviorist discourses. This example is from the same comment thread viewed by over 66,000 readers:

> ... guess Korea wants to keep sucking at English ... Let's increase English classes and decrease teachers that actually know how to speak it. Brilliant.

The author of this comment first characterizes the language proficiency of an entire nation as substandard (i.e. chauvinism), and then suggests that NES instructors are the only professionals who 'actually know how to' use English correctly (i.e. self-righteousness). In so doing, the teacher intimates that in order for Koreans to improve their English, they must continue to use NES instructors. This betterment of society argument is a discursive tool commonly used in imperial efforts (cf. Chapter 6); accordingly, many of the comments made in response to the budget cuts can be characterized as promoting linguistic discrimination in, and through, the ideology that NES instructors are superior ELT professionals. That is to say, White saviorism in the context of the ELT profession is a discursive tool for linguistic imperialism.

Although many of the comments examined in this section do not explicitly reference White racial categories, a significant number of the criticisms provided in response to the budget cuts are based on a false NES–non-native English speaking (NNES) dichotomy founded on racialized images and discourses (e.g. Amin, 1997). More importantly, the denunciations expressed in the saviorist discourses in this section shape, and are shaped by, a larger professional context that promotes White normativity (cf. Chapter 4). The racialized discourses that influence the hiring of, and preference for, White instructors are the same as those that provide a lens through which ELT professionals conceptualize the teaching and learning of English in Korea. Saviorist discourses in the ELT profession, in other words, are inherently racialized because they are based on a racial hierarchy that privileges White instructors.

Many reasons exist as to why individuals adopt White saviorist discourses, including the widespread belief within the United States that 'Americans' are exceptional, morally superior and must therefore help the world become a better place. In the ELT profession, the existence of

White saviorism can be partly attributed to the ubiquitous assumption that English must be taught alongside 'culture'. The coupling of language and culture, while ostensibly innocuous and widely promoted in teacher training programs around the world (Kumaravadivelu, 2006), can be used to promote the idea that English is bound to the cultural practices of a few countries. Specifically, the language–culture link encourages the belief that learning English requires adopting the cultural practices of, for example, the United States (cf. Gray, 2010). Such belief systems may lead to White saviorism, or specifically the idea that instructors from, say the United States, are in the best position to teach English because they own both the language and the culture that will be used to 'liberate' students. Take, for instance, the following observation provided in the same comment thread on the budget cuts discussed above:

> Native teachers provide invaluable English experience that Korean teachers (unless they have spent a significant time living abroad) simply cannot offer. For example, native teachers are able to fully teach about culture, pronunciation, and expressions/idioms that Korean teachers may not know much about.

Like all of the examples presented thus far, the saviorism here is the belief that NES teachers are capable of providing exceptional learning experiences for students. This example is different, however, in that it makes use of the language–culture argument. Specifically, the contributor assumes that NES teachers, unlike Korean English as a foreign language (EFL) instructors, 'are able to fully teach about culture'. This small variation in how saviorism is expressed is significant, as it promotes the misconception that English can only be used correctly when produced according to the cultural and communicative norms and practices of inner-circle countries. More problematically, the comment ignores the possibility that Korean ELT instructors can incorporate local cultural and communicative norms and practices in the teaching of English. Put differently, the comment establishes that Korean ELT instructors are not, 'unless they have spent a significant time living abroad', 'able to fully teach about culture' because they do not belong to or are not familiar with the 'culture of English'. By conceptualizing the teaching of English according to the cultural and communicative norms and practices of a few Western countries, NES instructors can position themselves as teachers who offer unique and superior learning experiences.

The ideology that English belongs to, or is owned by, a small group of Western countries is part of the common-sense understanding of many ELT professionals. This should come as no surprise, as the belief that culture should be taught alongside language is a pedagogical concept that is widely disseminated and promoted in teacher training programs across the United States and other 'English-speaking' countries (see Chapter 8). Modiano (2001b), for example, warns the ELT profession against promoting the idea that language teachers are so-called 'cultural ambassadors' (cf. course book as ambassador; see Gray, 2000). The danger in promoting the concept of cultural ambassadors is that ELT instruction can consequently become an exercise in imperial conditioning, where students are instructed to acquire culture-specific forms and varieties of English. As Modiano (2001b) reminds the profession:

> One does not learn a language solely as a system of lexical usage, grammar, and pronunciation utilized to express meaning, but also as a vehicle for the conveying of ideologies which seek to define the individual, the world, and the social realities which frame human experience. In the process of learning a language, one is ontologically colonized by the ideologies which flourish in the acquired tongue. (Modiano, 2001b: 162)

Thus, saviorist discourses represent much more than the belief that merely being a citizen from a particular country results in better teaching. Teaching guided by saviorism has the potential to shape how students come to an understanding of who they are in relation to English, and what this may mean for their future interactions. Put differently, saviorist discourses reveal a great deal about how teachers position themselves within the ELT profession and in relation to their peers and students. The issue of how instructors discursively position themselves is crucial to the advancement of critical ELT scholarship, but the possibility that White saviorism has a profound impact on what and how students learn is perhaps a more significant area of study that must be addressed in future research.

From the perspective of the student, White saviorism, especially the type that relies on chauvinism and self-righteousness, can reinforce linguistic and racial hierarchies, or what Endres and Gould (2009: 429) refer to as the 'cultural deficit model' that denigrates language learners for sounding 'foreign' or different from the 'target' speaker. That is, White saviorism creates conditions for failure because it is built on linguistic and racial hierarchies that do not allow students to ever achieve the 'gold standard', which is based on, and policed by, the so-called 'native' teacher.

Power imbalances are created by concomitantly assuming that nativeness in English leads to superior teaching and requiring students to achieve native-like standards. That is to say, nativeness as a social construct is a form of oppression because it creates a standard for Korean teachers and students that can never be achieved. These power imbalances are exacerbated by the fact that White normativity is a central organizing principle in the ELT profession in Korea. The privilege that is afforded to NES instructors, the prestige associated with sounding like a native speaker and the preference for a particular skin color manufacture 'elite' members of society (cf. van Dijk, 1993). In other words, NES instructors are elite members of the ELT profession because of, in part, White normativity (cf. Chapter 4). The discourses of elite members of society are germane to a discussion of White saviorism, as such individuals often do not see themselves as active participants of racism despite manufacturing and maintaining hierarchies that disadvantage others (van Dijk, 1993). By constructing saviorist discourses, NES instructors not only feed into existing White normative ideologies, but such actions also help them control the dominant narrative that they are superior teachers because of their nativeness in English. That is, White saviorism is both a discursive tool that produces racism and a social action that regulates dominant ways of thinking about race, ethnicity and linguistic proficiency. As noted by van Dijk (1993: 10), 'elites have a leading role in shaping the production [of] and interpretation framework' for racism. Saviorist discourses, such as the notion that NES instructors are superior teachers because they can teach American cultural practices alongside the 'correct' way of communicating, create an analytic lens through which other members of the ELT profession see themselves and their colleagues. With very few counter-narratives and opposing ideologies in the ELT profession, NES instructors can maintain their positions of power by circulating saviorist discourses.

In this sense, White saviorism is a discursive formation (Foucault, 1972: 31) or an institutionalized way of thinking and knowing about how race intersects with language teaching. Assumptions about how nativeness in English leads to superior teaching, for example, which are inherent in all saviorist discourses, create what Foucault (1972: 38) refers to as 'rules of formation' or, in other words, the ways in which ELT professionals identify and understand characteristics and attributes that are valuable in language teaching and learning. Put differently, by promoting the value of nativeness in ELT instruction, White saviorists create and reinforce the logic that second language development is best achieved through the instruction of NESs. White saviorism is predicated on a number of institutional discourses that position NES instructors as elite members of the profession (cf. Chapter 4), and such teachers, by engaging in saviorist discourses, help circulate the idea that White speakers of English are not only the ideal model for second language development, but that their contribution to the ELT profession in Korea also plays an important role in the economic, social and educational advancement of Korean society.

Conclusion

This chapter has demonstrated that 2010 education cuts provide a window into the ideologies and discourses of the ELT profession. Although the government's decision to decrease the number of NES instructors working in public schools over recent years may suggest that Korea is placing more value on the local pool of Korean ELT teachers, this budgetary move does not mean that the profession is moving away from the native speaker model. For example, immigration laws and recruiting practices have not changed significantly since these cuts were first reported in 2010. Despite this, the budget cuts represent a counter-narrative to the White normative discourses that are widely circulated in the profession. That is, the budget cuts are partly based on the assumption that Korean ELT teachers can conduct the same job assigned to NES instructors. This counter-narrative questions the superiority of NES instructors, provides an alternative model and discursively undermines the White normative discourses and practices that shape the profession. The budget cuts also provide a space for NES instructors, and namely those who are White, to maintain the dominant discourse that nativeness in English results in superior language teaching and learning. White saviorism represents one of possibly many discursive tools that maintain dominant narratives and forms of oppression.

Like all of the observations made in this book regarding racism in the ELT profession, the objective of this chapter was not to argue that White saviorism is a widespread problem in Korea. Many ELT instructors do not promote saviorist discourses; more importantly, White saviorism is not necessarily a deliberate act of linguicism and racism. However, the different belief systems – such as sentimentality, chauvinism and self-righteousness – that make up White saviorism are rooted in a profession that institutionalizes racism and privilege, as demonstrated in Chapter 4. That is to say, White saviorism is simply a projection of a larger occupational system that privileges instructors who possess a certain skin color and facial morphology. White normativity, which again is disseminated and promoted by recruiters, school owners, immigration policy makers, teachers and students, provides the space for White saviorism to occur. Put differently, the saviorist discourses reported here feed into and represent the common-sense understanding of the profession. The following chapter builds on this observation by examining how White normativity and neoliberalism operate within the ELT profession.

6 White Neoliberalism in ELT

Introduction

The English language has helped create an economy in Korea in which the racial and ethnic backgrounds of foreign teachers are essentialized, objectified, commodified and, as a result, used as a resource to exploit instructors who fit an 'ideal' image, while excluding from the ELT market entire nations of qualified teachers. As established in Chapter 4, the privileging of certain teachers in hiring practices is possible because Korean immigration law states that the only foreign nationals legally permitted to teach English in Korea are citizens from Kachru's (1985) inner-circle countries, as well as South Africa and Ireland. The law is not only based on the misconception that so-called NESs are the most suitable language instructors, or indeed the erroneous belief that a passport from an inner-circle country implies a certain linguistic superiority, it also excludes thousands of linguistically proficient and highly experienced teachers from South East Asia and beyond (Mahboob, 2009).

This skewed understanding of who is an 'authentic' ELT instructor is partly a result of, and feeds into, the discourse that English belongs to peoples with certain facial morphological features and skin pigmentation (for a discussion of how the NES category is associated with Whiteness, see Holliday, 2008). The view that English is spoken by White speakers is rooted and shaped by Korea's brief but complex history with 'ethnic outsiders'. Studies of race and ELT that have been conducted in different countries have attempted to explain the preference for White teachers by arguing that the motivation is pedagogically driven. That is, the assumption in the literature is that White instructors are preferred around the world because they are NESs and therefore more 'qualified' to teach the language (Amin, 1997; Holliday & Aboshiha, 2009; Mahboob, 2004; Sung, 2011). Holliday and Aboshiha (2009: 670) note, for example, 'that "nonnative speakers" have been discriminated against in employment because of a historical widespread belief in the dominance of presumed "native speaker" standards in language and language teaching methodology'.

Although in Korea there exists the flawed pedagogical belief that NESs are better teachers, an ideology that is often used to privilege White instructors, this chapter argues that such understandings are also driven by racial capitalism and the commodification of ELT. That is to say, this chapter aims to show that preferential treatment given to White teachers is largely a business decision. This argument is established by exploring how neoliberalism, often presented under the guise of competition and educational reform, has fueled the perceived importance of English in Korea, and examines how the sense of urgency to speak English well and become global participants has created a preference for White teachers in the ELT profession.

Capitalism Backdrop

Financial times were ostensibly good in 2007. The Dow Jones Industrial Average opened the year above 12,000 and ended over 13,000. In the decades before, deregulation and financial risk-taking, two hallmarks of free-market dogma, had created images of financial success and growing wealth. It seemed that the dominant economic ideology – less state more private – would yield continued financial success for many years to come.

By the end of 2008, however, the economy had taken a significant hit. Thousands of jobs were lost and the Dow fell, and continued to do so, for most of the year. Contributing factors included, but of course were not limited to, the subprime mortgage crisis and the declared bankruptcy of Lehman Brothers. The free-market party was over, or at least temporarily. Paradoxically, proponents of the free-market enterprise supported state involvement in bailing out financial giants, including AIG and Bear Stearns, in what represented a great socialist redistribution of resources, only this time in the wrong direction. The bailout demonstrated, more so than ever, the extent to which the state was willing to place the needs of corporations ahead of ordinary people (Chomsky, 1999). Backlash against corporate greed and ineptitude started in Europe more than a year later, which eventually led to the Occupy Wall Street 'moment' (Calhoun, 2013). Not much was done to remedy the failures of the past, and protests around the world did little to create change. Despite this, the US$700 billion given mostly to banks brought to the fore once again the dominant economic ideology: that is, the prosperity of corporations will lead to individual prosperity, even at the expense of social welfare programs.

The years leading up to and contributing to the 2008 financial crisis were characterized by lax, or even negligent regulations, unfounded economic optimism, large returns on unsubstantiated speculation, and callous loans in the form of predatory lending (Demyanyk & Van Hemert, 2011; Spiegel, 2011). The mantra, deregulation for the prosperity of all, turned out to require financial casualties on a large scale. The economic policies that led to what can be safely characterized as a tyrannical and fanatical quest for wealth can be traced back to the 1970s recession, which affected a number of different countries (Harvey, 2005). Putting aside the very complex financial environment of the 1970s, the policies and practices that led to the 2008 financial crisis started with an overall disappointment with the ability of Keynesian economics to remedy, among other things, high inflation and stagnant growth. Using stagflation and government inefficiency as a springboard for ideological dissemination, economists in the 1970s, including Milton Friedman, and politicians in the 1980s, including Ronald Reagan and Margaret Thatcher, argued for more deregulation and privatization, or what would later be characterized as neoliberalism (Harvey, 2005).

Commodification of Race and Ethnicity

An intense desire to learn the language of neoliberalism exists in Korea, a collective psychology commonly referred to as 'English fever' (J.K. Park, 2009) or 'English frenzy' (J.S. Park, 2009). This fever or frenzy to learn English has created a commercially rewarding ELT market. In a country where examinations for entry into universities nearly shut down the country each year (Seth, 2002) and private education occupies a large part of students' time outside of 'normal' school hours (S. Kim & Lee, 2010), large sums of money can be made by promising to offer concerned parents an effective way for their children to learn English, and indeed great financial resources are used to market and otherwise manage the ELT profession. The ELT market in Korea, which consists largely of for-profit after-school language academies (*hagwon*), has grown sharply since Keynesian economics fell out of favor several decades ago. From 1970 to 2008, the number of after-school language academies increased from approximately 1,400 to just over 70,000 (Moon, 2009). This growth is remarkable given that private education was prohibited by Chun Doo-hwan in the 1980s, a ban that was only lifted in the 1990s under the International Monetary Fund (IMF) banner of market liberalization (J. Song, 2009). Figure 6.1 provides an illustration of this growth in private English education and the immensity of the ELT market.

The sheer concentration of education signs in Figure 6.1 symbolizes the money spent on ELT in particular and on learning in general. It is estimated that Koreans spend US$15 billion each year on English language instruction,

Figure 6.1 *Hagwon* signs

or 1.9% of the country's 'nominal' gross domestic product (GDP) (Jeon, 2006). For comparison purposes, Japan, a country with nearly three times the population of Korea, spends approximately US\$5 billion annually on English education (Jeon, 2006). China, a country with 27 times Korea's population, outlays half of Korea's annual expenditure (Education First, 2013). While it is unclear whether the market has grown in the last decade, the billions of dollars spent on education not only demonstrate the extent to which Koreans invest their time, money and energy in English language instruction, but also point to larger sociolinguistic forces that have come to shape the ELT profession in Korea.

As the financial calculations above demonstrate, English is a commodity and, as such, operates within a market (Cameron, 2012). The ability of English to function as a commodity stems, in part, from aspects of new capitalism, as discussed in Chapter 2 (also referred to as 'late capitalism' or 'high modernity'; see Heller, 2010). New capitalism includes, but of course is not limited to, the movement and mobility of labor, the blurring of national boundaries and a shift in economic production from products to services.

In Korea, new capitalism shapes economic and educational policies in and through the discourse of globalization. J.S. Park (2013) argues, for example, that Lee Myung-bak's presidency from 2008 to 2012 led to less state involvement in education; universities could more freely select applicants based on factors that had been shaped heavily by socioeconomic variables (e.g. regional schools in affluent areas of Seoul), and competition was encouraged between educational institutions. Education driven by a free-market ethos also helped create private schools that privileged the wealthy and ruling classes. The ideology underpinning these attempts to engage in free-market education, as observed in J.S. Park (2013: 291), is the notion that promoting fairness through government intervention hinders learning potential by 'blocking students' proper development as individuals with skills and competence appropriate for the global age'.

Educational policies that reflect neoliberalism existed in Korea before Lee Myung-bak, including, notably, in the form of concerted globalization (세계화/se-gye-hwa) efforts following Kim Young-sam and the 1997 Asian financial crisis (D. Seo, 2011). During this period, competition and globalization were just beginning to enter into public discourse, and much political work was needed to move away from an educational system in which the Korean government, for example, 'not only maintained strict guidelines regarding how to establish and operate a higher education institution, it also controlled the number of students in each department for each school, as well as student selection methods' (S. Kim & Lee, 2006: 559). Although heavy regulation was the norm prior to 1997, the Asian financial crisis (with the help of IMF measures) made it possible for policy makers to argue for more competition in education. Education in a post-1997 Korea shifted from a somewhat horizontal market to a system that is exceptionally hierarchical (S. Kim & Lee, 2006).

The 1997 Asian financial crisis is an important turning point in the liberalization of education in Korea. Competition, individualism and nationalism – though important issues for Koreans prior to the 1990s (cf. the Seoul Olympics in 1988) – symbolized future prosperity and growth, both individually and collectively, and English was a way to achieve this success. Families, taking note of the neoliberal discourse that learning English will lead to financial success and career advancement, have made, and continue to make, enormous sacrifices to acquire the language of the global economy. In addition to the money spent on English language instruction in the country, approximately 500,000 families have a *'gireogi appa'* or 'goose father' (Kang, 2012; J.Y. Song, 2011; Onishi, 2008). This situation involves one parent, typically the father, earning a wage in one country, generally in Korea, while the other family members, including the children, live abroad for educational purposes.

While it is clear that English is a highly valued commodity in Korea, and Koreans make exceptional sacrifices to acquire this linguistic capital, the present discussion has yet to identify the exchange mechanisms that create value, support profit-making and commodify race in the ELT profession. The value associated with race is created in and through several occupational practices. That is to say, the commodification of race occurs in different spheres of the ELT profession, is accomplished in many ways and is reflected in specific business values and policies. For example, most, if not all, employers require instructors to submit at least one photograph when applying for a job. In a recent job advertisement on a popular ELT website, a recruiter asks for the following:

> I would like to have couple clear color face and full length pictures, if you don't mind. A director will get a first impression by picture. so if you can offer several pictures to decide. Then It will make director job easy.

The photograph requirement represents a crucial aspect of the commodification process. In asking candidates to submit a photograph, recruiters and employers attribute value to physical characteristics and, in doing so, reconfigure what is traditionally understood as the marketable characteristics of an ideal language instructor. That is, by placing value on facial features and the like (e.g. age and beauty), recruiters and employers alter the market's perception of what is valuable in language instruction; the value of a language instructor in the ELT market thus shifts from professional qualifications and experience to physical characteristics. Hiring practices that are based on physical characteristics represent a form of linguistic imperialism because they allow recruiters and employers to shape the ELT market according to outdated, 'occidental' images of an English speaker. That is to say, this pre-employment screening process allows recruiters and employers to, if they wish to do so, hire language instructors based on race and ethnicity. This form of racial preference is important for some employers because it allows them to use White teachers to sell linguistic 'authenticity' and a 'Western' experience (for similar observations in a Japanese context, see Appleby, 2013: 136–138). It is important to note, however, that the observation here is not that rampant discrimination occurs (this is an empirical question that would be extremely difficult to quantify because school owners are unlikely to disclose how many applications they receive from instructors of color), but rather the photograph requirement allows employers to create market value based on skin color, facial morphology and other physical characteristics deemed desirable.

When recruiters and employers hire language instructors according to physical features, their actions feed into, and represent, a larger discourse in Korea that not only sells English as a form of new capitalism and a means of upward mobility, an ideal that is perpetuated by many factors but most prominently by language academy names like 'Wall Street English', but also racially and ethnically exoticizes and valorizes the people who speak the language of neoliberalism. Numerous advertisements for language academies can be found both in Korea and online that depict speakers of English as White, successful, well-dressed, attractive and/or competitive (for similar observations of the Japanese ELT profession, see Piller & Takahashi, 2006; Takahashi, 2013), as shown in the advertisement for a private academy in Figure 6.2.

In the advertisement, like many others, English is associated with ostensibly intelligent, well-informed and industrious individuals, as suggested by the newspapers, business suits and MacBook computer. While these attributes and characteristics are enough to sell the idea that learning English will lead to financial success, the advertisement uses White actors to convey the neoliberal image. In so doing, it promotes the idea that English is a means of achieving upward mobility, and that the people who are visually experiencing and thus representing this economic

Figure 6.2 English is life

success are White, young, attractive and cheerful. Similarly, online reports exist of school owners engaging in hiring practices that explicitly seek out beautiful Korean female teachers, with some academies asking their instructors to wear provocative outfits while teaching (Y. Hong, 2015). Hiring practices that are based on physical characteristics and features are thus neither new nor a mystery.

The commodification of ELT creates a sense of allure and prestige around the English language that is not too dissimilar to the way some people ascribe fascination with products that have traditionally been seen as utilitarian but now have a very high markup and are thus valorized beyond their functional value (e.g. iPhones and Louis Vuitton bags). That is, the exchange of money for language instruction, including the financial cost of promoting the ELT market, perverts the 'use-value' associated with English. Through market forces, the value associated with the English language is no longer limited to the ability to communicate (i.e. the use-value of any language); the commodification of the English language creates a new value system based on what the ELT market determines should be valorized (i.e. exchange-value). The shift from use- to exchange-value has several pedagogical consequences (see below), including notably the misconception that the challenges of learning a language can somehow be overcome with money (or worse, that an attractive and/or white face can provide the best opportunities to learn English).

Unlike excessively overpriced phones and bags, where consumers have little or no access to the proletariat class of workers producing such fetishized commodities, the exchange of money for English language instruction positions the consumer (i.e. the student) in the same room as the 'worker' in the ELT profession (i.e. the language instructor). It can be said, accordingly, that the allure and prestige associated with the English language does not simply and solely come from the exchange of money for instruction, as some Marxists would argue (cf. commodity fetishism; Marx, 1976: 163), nor from the social disconnect that exists between the proletariat class and the consumer, but rather from a larger neoliberal discourse that sells the idea that being successful in life means accumulating wealth, enrolling in an elite school and securing a job with international relevance.

Within this neoliberal structure, English has become, and is, the commodity exchanged for material wealth and upward mobility. English is alluring and prestigious because it is associated with the ability to live a comfortable life and purchase commodities that are valued by society, an ideology that is transformed into various discursive practices in ELT hiring and advertising. That is to say, hiring and advertising practices create discourses in the ELT profession that exoticize or fetishize the English language. These discourses tell Koreans that English does not belong to them (cf. ELT advertisements with an ethnically Other teacher and a Korean student), an idea that is exacerbated by an expat teaching community that is disproportionately White (and from North America), but that proficiency in the language can be purchased for what amounts to a small fortune over a lifetime of learning (J.K. Park, 2009). Thus, hiring and advertising practices alienate Koreans from English by creating stereotypical, ethnically homogenous images of an ELT teacher.

The commodification of English and the privileging of White teachers in the ELT market are a result of a free-market approach to education: employers are effectively able to manage their schools (i.e. businesses) with little government intervention. Indeed, the only legal requirement that shapes hiring practices in the ELT market is a proxy for racial and ethnic discrimination (for an investigation of how immigration laws discriminate against E-2 language instructors, see Wagner & VanVolkenburg, 2012). Specifically, the Ministry of Justice requires that all English language instructors seeking work in private academies apply for an E-2 working visa; the sociolinguistic issues and problems associated with limiting the teaching pool to a small group of E-2 nations that are stereotypically 'White' and/or 'non-Asian' is a topic of discussion in Chapter 4. What is germane to the present discussion is how the owners of, and recruiters for, private language academies interpret the law for hiring practices.

The privileging of speakers from E-2 nations creates a space for school owners and recruiters to exploit the neoliberal mindset. While a number of different ethnic groups come from E-2 nations, school owners and recruiters are able to use immigration laws to privilege language instructors who 'look the part'. With its close military and political relations with the United States and consumption of American popular culture, 'looking the part' of an English teacher in Korea often means having white skin, blue eyes and light-colored hair (for reasons why this stereotype may exist in Korea, see Chapter 3). The stereotypical image of an English speaker is used as a resource to both exploit White instructors (see below) and disadvantage teachers who do not possess the ideal skin pigmentation and facial morphology.

Racial discrimination in hiring practices is tied to various images created in different domains of life (e.g. Hollywood, ELT advertisements, US military presence in Korea), but manifests primarily in the discourse that an instructor should be an NES. Numerous studies and reports have explored how the term NES, again a legal requirement for employment in Korea, has become racialized in the ELT profession. For example, rather than explicitly asking for White teachers, school owners and recruiters use the term NES to seek out instructors of a particular ethnic background (Holliday, 2008). As a result, school owners and recruiters can engage in discrimination while hiding behind immigration laws.

The TESOL and applied linguistics literature often characterizes the preference for NES teachers as flawed pedagogical decision-making (Amin, 1997; Holliday & Aboshiha, 2009; Mahboob, 2004; Sung, 2011). That is, racial discrimination that arises out of the need to hire an NES stems from the misconception, often perpetuated by people with little or no knowledge of good ELT research and practice, that White teachers have the best spoken English and instruct the most effectively. In Korea, this discourse is partly shaped by the lack of representation of peoples of color speaking 'good' English (J.S. Park, 2009), but must be understood within a larger historical context in which the United States continues to shape political and economic policies in the region (N. Kim, 2008).

While the pedagogical explanation for racial discrimination in hiring practices may apply to some school owners and recruiters who have a fallacious understanding of what an NES instructor can offer professionally, linguistically and communicatively, it is argued here that a more contextually appropriate explanation includes the understanding that financial growth in the ELT profession, which has been driven largely by a neoliberal agenda, has created a privileging of White instructors. Put differently, can the boom in private language instruction be explained by a genuine pedagogical concern to equip students with the necessary linguistic skills to become 'global competitors' or has the growth been driven by opportunistic school owners who understand how to capitalize on the largely unregulated ELT market? Both explanations are valid, though the pedagogical explanation for racial discrimination must still account for the forces of neoliberalism. That is to say, all capital in Korea, including the English language, operates within a larger neoliberal framework. This capital has been used by employers and consumers to create a market where aptitude in English and teaching experience are valued less than skin pigmentation and facial morphology. One report, for example, notes that the preference for blond hair and blue eyes comes from parents' flawed understanding that English belongs to the White community, as revealed in the following quote by an ELT recruiter (Strother, 2007):

> The mothers are the ones who kind of dictate what they want, because it's them who are making the decision as to what school they're going

into a top university and be seen as cosmopolitan has elevated the status of English in Korea. English, in other words, represents the language of neoliberalism. It is not merely a tool for communication; English is a means to achieve, and allows individuals to engage in practices related to, neoliberal citizenship. The free-market ethos adopted in the ELT profession, and concurrent efforts to globalize the Korean economy, has led to the commodification of race and ethnicity. For example, the market forces (e.g. hiring practices and immigration laws) that shape the selling and buying of language instruction have led to a preference for White teachers. The common-sense understanding behind this preference is that White teachers provide the most pedagogically sound and authentic learning experience for students. The chapter maintained that while White normativity can be, and has been, interpreted as a flawed pedagogy that favors NES instructors, the larger and more salient issue in understanding Whiteness in ELT is how race and ethnicity are bound to the business decisions made when recruiting and hiring ELT teachers, as well as to the ways in which school owners market and advertise their instructional services.

The preference for White teachers should not, however, be generalized beyond the ELT profession. In Korea, the racial climate is indeed complex, dynamic and context specific (N. Kim, 2008). Koreans at best have a complicated relation with White foreign nationals and they do not have a particular reverence for Western individuals with fair skin, both historically and in contemporary times (N. Kim, 2006). It is not difficult to find, for example, anti-American discourse (G. Shin & Izatt, 2011), discrimination against White teachers (L.G. v. Republic of Korea, 2015), including stereotypes of White women as Russian prostitutes, and a general disdain for and/or fear of non-Koreans (M. Kim, 1997; J. Lee, 2015). Nor is it prevalent in Korean society to characterize White teachers as upstanding visitors, and indeed the opposite, where such instructors are portrayed as social deviants, can be found in the media (McCauley, 2014; Rauhala, 2010).

Despite this complex and complicated relationship, White preference exists in the ELT profession because school owners and recruiters operate within a largely unlegislated market that exploits the ubiquitous ideology that the English language is best taught by a particular racial group (for how Whiteness is objectified and commodified in a Japanese context, see, for example, Appleby, 2013; Kubota, 2011). The commodification of race and ethnicity has created a market where physical characteristics are valued more than teaching credentials. The free-market ethos adopted in the ELT profession creates an environment in which all teachers, especially White instructors, are used as marketing tools to increase recruitment, retain students and sell language education. Employment exists for some of these teachers because an unknown number of parents (and students) associate a blond, blue-eyed teacher with not only speaking English, but doing it well. This association is partly a result of ethnic inequalities, racial stereotypes and a lack of representation of peoples of color in American popular culture and media (Marchetti, 1993), which get disseminated back to Korea and represent the only exposure many Koreans have to the English-speaking world (N. Kim, 2008). Consequently, White instructors are privileged for possessing the 'right' skin pigmentation and facial morphology. With that said, however, instructors from all racial and ethnic groups are bound to the neoliberal logic in that it is ultimately the free market that determines who possesses wealth, power and privilege in the ELT profession. For example, recent government cuts in public education (including English instruction) are a reminder that the ELT profession is dictated by global economic forces (see M. Jung, 2014). Although all instructors are to some extent exploited, oppressed or alienated, it must not be forgotten that students are affected by neoliberalism in that the market also ultimately dictates the extent to which the English language is taught as a reflection of multiple voices and cultures.

7 Beyond Korea: Racial Capitalism and White Public Spaces

Introduction

The analysis has thus far drawn from critical race and discourse scholarship to examine how White normativity, a central organizing principle in the ELT profession in Korea, contributes to the formation of racism and linguicism. The analysis conducted in Chapter 4 revealed that a number of different ideologies and discourses imagine and enforce White normativity. Race-based discrimination and privilege in the ELT profession, and more specifically White normativity, come from immigration laws that narrowly define who can be considered an NES, are put into practice by Korean recruiters and school owners who are responsible for hiring teaching staff, and represent the ideologies of many teachers, including instructors of color. Because racism and race-based privilege occur in many domains of the profession and are promoted by a range of ELT professionals, it can be said that White normativity is a discursive formation (Foucault, 1972). That is, the notion that English monolingualism and White teachers are ideal models of ELT instruction represents the common-sense understanding of the profession.

Chapter 5 argued that White saviorism is a projection of White normativity. Specifically, the analysis showed that White saviorism, which is often based on sentimentality, chauvinism or self-righteousness, provides a window into how instructors make sense of their position in, and contribution to, the ELT profession. It was demonstrated that White saviorism is connected to racial and linguistic hierarchies that privilege NES instructors. Specifically, saviorist discourses stem from the ideology that nativeness in English is synonymous with superior teaching. The chapter argued that White saviorism creates power imbalances in the profession between NES and NNES instructors; maintains dominant narratives that assume English is a language of the 'West'; compresses race, language proficiency and nationality into a single way of thinking about teaching; denies students the possibility that their cultural norms and practices are relevant to the learning process; and thus produces racism.

Chapter 6 revealed how White neoliberalism both stems from, and contributes to, White normativity. The chapter showed that White normativity comes from a number of different ideologies and discourses that construct and present the English language as symbol of power, wealth, success and upward mobility. The discussion provided a historical account of how free-market principles evolved over time in Korea and developed alongside US economic and military interest in the region. The status of English has evolved over time because of ongoing societal pressures on individuals to accumulate material wealth, become competitive international professionals, gain entry into a top university and be seen as worldly.

In other words, English functions as a cultural toolkit for individuals to engage in practices related to neoliberal citizenship. While embracing free-market principles in Korea has allowed some individuals to become 'successful', this orientation to neoliberalism not only props up White normativity in the ELT profession, but it also commodifies race and ethnicity in all domains of society. Hiring practices and immigration laws, for example, provide the space for the ELT market to circulate the belief that English speakers are White and from a 'Western' country. Market forces that dictate the selling and buying of language instruction are partly responsible for White normativity. Put differently, White normativity is based on business decisions and value-based exchange mechanisms.

These observations will be further explored in the present chapter by applying an understanding of racial capitalism to the ELT profession. It is important to examine racial capitalism in the global ELT context as the profession has a long history of benefiting from White normativity and linguicism.

Racial Capitalism

Leong (2013: 2153) defines racial capitalism as 'the process of deriving social or economic value from the racial identity of another person'. Racial capitalism occurs in many parts of the ELT profession, including teacher training programs. In Korea, for example, owners of language schools who are of ethnic Korean heritage may create value and thus benefit financially from White ELT instructors. Although White ELT professionals may benefit financially from their privileged status as well, as revealed in the previous analytic chapters, for some scholars this is not a form of racial capitalism. That is to say, some critical race scholars argue that racial capitalism is limited to creating value or accumulating capital from the cultural Other. As Leong (2013: 2153) notes, for instance, 'individuals may also derive value from their own racial identities, [but] this practice is not racial capitalism'.

Although this chapter is concerned primarily with how the ELT profession benefits economically and institutionally from the cultural Other, it is difficult to detach the racialized discourses and hierarchies that allow an individual to benefit from one's own race from the social structures that allow 'the racial identity of another person' to be exploited for financial gain. It will be established, in other words, that racial capitalism is a process that generates value and capital from a system of racialized discourses and racial hierarchies: while some racial groups may be privileged more than others, racial capitalism can only operate within a hierarchy of exploitation. For instance, while some segments of the ELT profession may benefit financially from the cultural Other (e.g. Western universities that are predominantly White receiving income by recruiting international students from Asia), this benefit arises because of the existence of White normativity, cultural and linguistic imperialism and a history of colonialism. Put differently, individuals and institutions cannot benefit from the cultural Other without racialized discourses and racial hierarchies, such as White normativity.

In most ELT contexts, language learners represent the cultural Other. The economic and institutional value that is generated from language learners comes from, somewhat predictably but paradoxically, the objective to help students learn English. By and large, these students are less proficient in English than their instructors, come from regions and countries outside of the 'inner circle' and do not share the same cultural and linguistic norms and practices of teachers who manage learning activities in the classroom. Value is thus created when students are not only conditioned to believe that English is necessary for their future academic and professional success, but that they must also learn the language in a way that conforms to the cultural and linguistic norms of a few select countries. That is to say, ELT institutions profit when students believe that they possess deficiencies in the target language, the profession circulates the discourse that competence in exogenous or non-local linguistic norms is necessary for living a meaningful life, and teachers promote the view that 'foreignness' in English, such as accents, is undesirable. In the ELT profession in Korea, for example, the widespread belief that English is simultaneously a neoliberal tool and a language spoken by outsiders allows ELT institutions to profit from racial hierarches. ELT institutions generate profit, create value and produce capital when linguistic, communicative and cultural deviations occur from the standards that they establish for language learners. In other words, linguistic and racial hierarchies create a demand for language instruction.

The global spread of English, fueled by neoliberal economic policies, has created an ELT profession that is influenced by, and takes advantage of, market forces. For example, the ELT profession uses market forces to transform 'soft skills', such as linguistic proficiency, communicative competence and cultural awareness, into commodities (cf. Education Testing Service). Racism facilitates the business of language teaching and learning, as the ELT profession is built on White normativity and linguicism, as will be discussed in more detail below. Leong (2013: 2154) makes similar observations regarding racial capitalism in the United States: 'In a society preoccupied with diversity, nonwhiteness is a valued commodity. And where that society is founded on capitalism, it is unsurprising that the commodity of nonwhiteness is exploited for its market value'.

In relation to the ELT profession, the commodity of the English language is undoubtedly exploited for its market value, and the exchange values of this commodity are based on the valorization of Whiteness. This ideological commitment to Whiteness within the ELT profession is situated within a larger narrative that promotes the idea (or myth) that English is the language of the world and that speakers of other languages must acquire the global tool of communication for survival. This narrative has created a market in which English, and the pedagogical tools that are used to disseminate and promote the language, are transformed into commodities. In discussing the historical developments of language commodification, Watts (2011: 263) observes how discourses pertaining to the perceived need to become multilingual speakers create language markets:

> Languages had become abstract commodities, which could be put on sale in the sociocultural and symbolic sectors of the marketplace, and the means through which those commodities could be sold to others (e.g. teaching materials, teaching methods, teacher training courses) become part of what we might call the 'language industry'. Languages as commodities began to develop different social, cultural, and instrumental values with respect to one another.

The possibility that languages possess different values according to global factors is important to an understanding of racial capitalism in the ELT profession. Proficiency in English is a highly valued commodity, a phenomenon from which the ELT profession benefits because it represents an investment that is believed to be easily converted into social, cultural and economic capital (Tan & Rubdy, 2008). For example, a high score on a standardized test not only suggests an ability to communicate well in English, but it also allows Koreans to more competitively vie for a place at a top university and better market themselves as intelligent and worldly. English maintains a value that is greater than other 'abstract commodities' because it is commonly accepted in many regions of the world that proficiency in the language is necessary for modernity (i.e. participation in a global economy; cf. Cameron, 2012). The status of English as the pre-eminent world language creates the conditions necessary for racial capitalism to occur in the ELT profession. That is, historical, colonial and imperial processes (Pennycook, 1998) and current global forces (Block & Cameron, 2002) have created discourses and images that associate English with White speakers from inner-circle countries (see, for example, Chapter 2). These discourses and images condition speakers of other languages into believing that not only are their varieties of English inferior (Amin, 1997), but that ELT instruction is also the business of White teachers instructing the cultural Other (Kubota, 2002).

Although the belief that English is best taught by a small group of racially homogenous teachers is the source of value in Whiteness (e.g. Ruecker & Ives, 2015), linguistically 'inferior' and often 'darker' students, say from Africa or Asia, also contribute to the commodification process because they benefit from participating in a market that privileges individuals who are 'fluent' in the global language. Tupas (2008: 98), for example, examines how the value associated with English in the Philippines has led to educational and economic reforms that privilege individuals with 'good American English'. In the same edited volume, Tan (2008) explores how the value of English in Malaysia has increased in recent years, together with societal ambitions to become more competitive in the global market. In both situations, speakers of English are ideologically committed to, and thus participate in, the ELT market. Racial capitalism in the ELT profession, accordingly, is a process in which language learners commit to the belief that learning English from, say, a North American teacher, will result in economic, educational, social and/or cultural benefits (cf. White neoliberalism in Korea).

In this sense, the ELT profession benefits from circulating discourses and images of language learners buying into, and reaping the benefits of, White normativity. Universities in inner-circle countries, for example, will use discourses and images of international students, often from Asia, to promote diversity. On the web pages of most universities, it is not difficult to find biographies and photos of Asian students espousing the benefits of learning English in, and pursuing a degree at, a particular academic institution. Further, the International English Language Testing System (IELTS) website and promotional materials are adorned with images of Asian students appearing happy, sociable and studious. Similar images can be found on the website and promotional materials of the test of English as a foreign language (TOEFL). The 'Learn English' section of the British Council website, though not as Asian-centric, uses racially diverse images to promote the idea that learning English will lead to success and happiness. While the cultural Other in such marketing endeavors represents the efforts of institutions to attract the 'consumer', language learners become a part of the commodification process when images of racial diversity are used to sell teaching and learning services. While racial diversity is not inherently problematic, it can lead to structural inequalities when used for marketing purposes.

In discussing the promotion of diversity in US universities, Leong (2013: 2155) notes the problems associated with racial capitalism. Her observations of US universities are particularly relevant to ELT institutions:

> The efforts of colleges and universities ... to promote racial diversity should be celebrated, not disparaged. But problems with racial capitalism arise when white individuals and predominantly white institutions seek and achieve racial diversity without examining their motives and practices ... This superficial view of diversity consequently leads white individuals and predominantly white institutions to treat nonwhiteness as a prized commodity rather than as a cherished and personal manifestation of identity ... This instrumental view is antithetical to a view of nonwhiteness – and race more generally – as a personal characteristic intrinsically deserving of respect. Worse still, the instrumental view of nonwhiteness inhibits efforts at genuine racial inclusiveness and cross-racial understanding.

ELT institutions use the instrumental view of the cultural Other to promote the belief that English must be acquired in a particular way (the next section explores how the instrumental view can be addressed). That is, ELT institutions benefit economically when it is commonly accepted around the world that English is the 'global language'.

Marxist notions of exploitation and oppression are particularly germane to the present discussion. For Marx, race and racism are based on the division (and exploitation) of labor. That is to say, 'Capitalism is an inherently racist system because of its structural tendency to historically expand in search of profitability and the dependence of this profitability on finding exploitable labor' (Paolucci, 2006: 643). The selling and buying of human beings as slaves, for example, provided the impetus, or moral justification, to see the cultural Other through a race-based prism. Although language teaching does not have a history of labor exploitation to the extent experienced in and through slavery, the market-driven nature of the ELT profession has facilitated asymmetrical divisions of power in relation to English (cf. Chapter 4). In its efforts to expand institutionally and grow economically, the ELT profession has relied on, or at least benefited from, White normativity. In other words, White normativity exists because survival, and indeed success, in capitalism requires expanding the global demand for ELT instruction. For many ELT institutions, this means promoting the myth that English is best spoken and taught by speakers from inner-circle countries. The ELT profession is thus inherently oppressive in that teachers of color and speakers of less-valued varieties of the language are denied teaching opportunities, and even privileged instructors with the 'right' skin color are commodified, objectified and thus dehumanized (for a Marxist discussion of alienation and oppression, see Bakan & Dua, 2014).

The preceding discussion confirms that the ideological foundation of racial capitalism in the ELT profession transcends race-based belief systems. In language teaching and learning, benefiting from the racial identity of the cultural Other also relies on linguicism or, more specifically, linguistic hierarchies. Such hierarchies, and their underlying belief systems (e.g. native speakerism), explain how language ideologies shape exchange mechanisms in the ELT market. Value is derived from the social and cultural capital that English provides. The social and cultural capital that is attached to a particular variety of English varies according to communicative context, but value is always based on an exchange mechanism, such as the decision to enroll in an ELT course with a teacher from the United States. It can be said, therefore, that language teaching and learning are bound to economic factors, such as the occupational benefits that come from achieving a high score on a standardized language test; yet these ostensible gains are based on a set of racialized ideologies and discourses. For example, in deciding to learn English in the United States, rather than say Hong Kong, a student makes an ideological statement about his/her preference for inner-circle varieties. Here, the value of a North American variety of English is created by transferring economic resources into a language ideology. This exchange mechanism is a form of racialized discourse, as perceptions regarding the value of studying in inner-circle countries are bound to the racially homogenous discourses and images created by the predominantly White institutions, including the ELT profession, that control the social and cultural capital associated with the English language. Simply put, racial capitalism in the ELT profession is based on White normativity. The economic benefits derived from buying and selling ELT instruction come from hierarchies that privilege White individuals proficient in inner-circle varieties of English. Eradicating White normativity in the ELT profession is thus one way of addressing racial capitalism.

Decolonizing White Public Spaces

Racial capitalism cannot be fully eradicated because of the extent to which neoliberalism controls different segments of the ELT profession. Put differently, eradicating racial capitalism in the ELT profession requires replacing globalism and neoliberalism with an economic model that ensures equity and equality for all. Although it may be difficult to move the profession away from an economic model that treats English as a commodity (i.e. taking the commodification out of racial capitalism), there are ways of handicapping the market forces that capitalize on racial and linguistic hierarchies. The profession can, for example, increase racial diversity in teacher training programs, promote bilingualism in language pedagogy and decolonize the images and discourses used to circulate the importance of ELT instruction, which may include promoting varieties of English located on the periphery. These suggestions are part of a larger project that is referred to as 'decolonizing White public spaces', which is the focus of discussion in this section.

As noted briefly in Chapter 4, a White public space 'may entail particular or generalized locations, sites, patterns, configurations, tactics, or devices that routinely, discursively, and sometimes coercively privilege Euro-Americans over nonwhites' (Page & Thomas, 1994: 111). The plural form of space in this section, as in White public spaces, is used to denote the many and varied ways in which Whiteness operates within the ELT profession. That is, Whiteness is not a monolithic social construct that has the same meaning in different ELT contexts. White public spaces in the ELT profession may entail anything from ideological commitments that privilege White speakers from inner-circle countries to textbooks and other teaching materials that depict speakers of English as a racially homogenous group. It will be argued below that White public spaces restrict instructors of color from seeking employment and advancing within their respective fields of work. In other words, White public spaces marginalize outsiders while privileging the elite class. Page and Thomas (1994: 112) frame this discrimination as a form of racial self-entitlement: 'White privilege is institutionally and interpersonally constructed in white public space when social closure takes place in the interest of the dominant group'. The authors' use of (Max Weber's) 'social closure' is particularly germane to an understanding of how White public spaces lead to racial discrimination (and capitalism). For Weber (1968: 342), social closure entails an individual, group, organization or profession taking 'some externally identifiable characteristic of another group of (actual or potential) competitors – race, language, religion, local or social origin, descent, residence, etc. – as a pretext for attempting their exclusion ... its purpose is always the closure of social and economic opportunities to outsiders'.

Decolonizing, or de-monopolizing (to use Weber's nomenclature) White public spaces involves resisting and extinguishing dominant ideologies, oppressive discourses and discriminatory practices in the ELT profession. For Kubota (2015b: 3), this may involve 'moving beyond [the] white vs. non-white dichotomy' that is omnipresent in the profession. For the present discussion, the term *decolonizing* is not used in the traditional sense of the word. To decolonize a White public space does not entail removing a settler group from an indigenous setting or context, for example; rather, it involves unsubscribing from discourses that privilege (or disadvantage) cultural groups on the basis of race and language. Decolonizing the mind is an ideological struggle that requires individuals, and indeed the ELT profession, to reconceptualize what it means to be a speaker of English.

Creating new discourses and ideologies that resist and challenge dominant racial and language hierarchies, or decolonize White public spaces, provides a way for ethnically diverse individuals to position themselves in society as legitimate speakers of English and meaningful members of the ELT profession (for similar observations regarding the linguistic struggles of African peoples, see wa Thiong'o, 1981). A decolonizing methodology also challenges discourses and ideologies that view knowledge production in the ELT profession as a 'Western' right and responsibility. Knowledge production in this sense refers to creating teaching materials, dictating curricular goals, training teachers, conducting research and delivering workshops, among other activities. The work of Smith (2012: 2) on indigenous peoples of Africa, which provides a lens through which the observations below are viewed, speaks of the inherent social tensions that exist 'between the interests and ways of knowing of the West and the interests and ways of resisting of the Other'. A Western European anthropologist, for example, may set out to examine an African region using analytic tools that make sense in the researcher's country of origin, but such ways of knowing and understanding may ultimately dehumanize and oppress the cultural Other, especially in colonial situations (Smith, 2012). In many ways, the colonial nature of research conducted in Africa by countries in positions of political and economic power is similar to the tensions that exist in knowledge production in the ELT profession. Edge (2006: xiii), in his thought-provoking book on ELT in an age of empire, frames the discussion around US imperialism when he argues that

> it is impossible to be engaged in the teaching of English to speakers of other languages at the beginning of the twenty-first century without at one and the same time being engaged in helping one's students achieve their aspirations *and* in supporting the linguistic, cultural, commercial and increasingly military dominance of the USA and its allies.

Like European settlers conducting research in Africa (cf. Rothermund, 2006), the colonial and imperial discourses and ideologies that are circulated in the ELT profession deny the cultural Other the same privileges and rights that are given to the dominant group (Pennycook, 1998; Phillipson, 2009). While dominant groups in the ELT profession should not be discussed as a fixed category, such people are, by and large, in positions of power and privilege because of some benefit derived from exploiting the belief that English is owned by a small group of inner-circle, often historically White, countries (for a study that examines how the United States is constructed as racially homogenous country that is 'owned' by White males in privileged positions, see Kennedy, 1996). In other words, dominant groups in the ELT profession are not White individuals (Kubota, 2015b) as such, but organizations directly or indirectly promote the discourse that English is a White language. Power and privilege are further accumulated by dominant groups because they can capitalize on the common-sense view that English is the global language one needs to learn.

One of the most immediate actions that can be taken in attempting to decolonize the ELT profession is to address the inherent racism that exists in the many regions of the world that require students to learn English. This book is one such attempt at understanding how race and racism operate within a particular region. Scholarship must continue to examine the ELT profession in different regions, provide comparative analyses of countries and use such observations to make connections with wider global language teaching and learning issues. The underlying argument here is that while uncovering race and racism within a particular region is important to advancing critical race scholarship in language teaching and learning, further research must establish how discriminatory practices within regions are connected to the ELT profession as a whole.

Zooming out from an analysis of a region to the global ELT profession helps uncover the many discourses and ideologies that contribute to the production of White public spaces.

The first step in a decolonization project is to address the issue of whether scholars view race and racism as important empirical issues in ELT research. Specifically, language scholars and practitioners must not hide from race and racism or treat such issues as taboo topics if they wish to begin decolonizing the White public spaces of the ELT profession. For example, if the bulk of the knowledge production in the ELT profession is coming from, or feeding into, Western cultural imperialism (Edge, 2006), then language scholars and practitioners from such regions have a responsibility to give priority to issues of race and racism in their scholarship and pedagogical materials. Put differently, if much of the world is looking, for better or worse, to these so-called inner-circle countries for knowledge production, and very little is being discussed about race and racism within this body of work, then it should come as no surprise that regions like Korea import racial and linguistic hierarchies when dealing with ELT issues. It is, of course, not the sole responsibility of scholars from the United States and the like to engage in critical race scholarship. Researchers based in Korea and beyond must also devote more attention to how race, racism, Whiteness and racialized discourses operate within the ELT profession. This requires, in part, individuals who are gatekeepers of knowledge production (e.g. journal editors) to not only make issues of race and racism a priority in their writing, but also create easier paths for language scholars and practitioners working at the periphery (i.e. outside the inner circle) to contribute to the profession. In the same vein, the innovative work of Zhang et al. (2015) reminds scholars that knowledge production in Asia must be reimagined as a legitimate form of scholarship and placed outside of Western cultural imperialism (for similar observations of African scholars, see Smith, 2012).

To this end, H. Shin (2006: 162) speaks of decolonizing the ELT profession by creating 'counter-hegemonic' discourses 'through the legitimation of SOL's [speakers of other languages] indigenous knowledges'. The indigenous epistemology that she speaks of involves resisting the colonial temptation to see the ELT profession through the eyes of Western scholarship. While H. Shin (2006) does not directly address race in her discussion of an indigenous epistemology, the colonial history of English and ELT cannot be separated from the racialized discourses that existed during the expansion of the language and profession. Said's (1979) work is a reminder that colonial histories are not only inextricably connected to racialized discourses, but they form an epistemological foundation on which many people see the world today. To resist the colonial discourses that operate within the profession – for example, the notion that communicative language teaching is a superior form of instruction or the belief that learners should mimic NESs – is to oppose the racial and linguistic hierarchies that allow such hegemony to operate.

Decolonizing White public spaces also entails critically examining the value associated with, and the meaning of, Whiteness. Motha's (2014) body of work provides an exemplary approach to understanding how racial and linguistic hierarchies operate within the profession and the ways in which such power imbalances can be addressed. Her work follows several teachers as they attempt to understand how their racial identities are situated in an inherently racist profession (see also Motha, 2006). Her findings, like other similar observations made in the critical race literature (see Chapter 2), demonstrate that nativeness in English and Whiteness are interconnected social constructs that endow certain teachers with privilege and power. The notion that language and race are inseparable social constructs is important to a decolonizing effort, as the ELT profession is in the business of delivering instruction in a way that privileges certain varieties of English over others (Holliday, 2008; Rampton, 1990). If this observation can be accepted, or if, in other words, it is true that the ELT profession is predisposed to linguistic hierarchies, then it must also be concluded that the business of language teaching is in some way racially biased (cf. Holliday & Aboshiha, 2009). Thus, decolonizing White public spaces involves promoting discourses that depict the ELT profession as racially diverse and open to varieties of English located on the periphery. As Motha (2006: 514) argues, 'Portraying the TESOL profession as racially neutral is part of a larger social movement toward a liberal multiculturalist ideology that professes to be antiracist but actually serves to sustain racism'. Liberal multiculturalism champions diversity by claiming that individuals are all equal regardless of race and ethnicity, but this view, as discussed in Chapter 2, is a form of colorblindness because it erases the privilege afforded to White members of society while ignoring the discrimination experienced by peoples of color (for an insightful study that indirectly addresses colorblindness in the ELT profession by asking White student teachers to live and study in Mexico, see Marx & Pray, 2011).

Before language scholars and practitioners can begin to produce counter-narratives, they must acknowledge that the ELT profession is bound to a colonial history as well as racialized discourses (cf. Liggett, 2009). But simply professing that all teachers are equal regardless of race and ethnicity, as just mentioned, does little, if anything at all, to create a more horizontal structure that does not privilege one race or language variety over another. Cochran-Smith (1995), for example, argues that teacher education must require student teachers to be more cognizant of the values and practices of the cultural Other; and while this endeavor is inherently good, it does nothing to change the racial and linguistic hierarchies that shape teacher education. One way of acknowledging and moving beyond these racial and linguistic hierarchies is to promote diversity within those segments of the profession that dictate knowledge production. Teacher training programs in countries that are in positions of political, economic and cultural power can, for instance, increase the racial diversity of their teaching staff. Increasing the racial diversity in higher education institutions would help instill confidence in younger generations of language scholars and practitioners that the business of knowledge production is not the exclusive responsibility of predominantly White institutions. In the United States, for example, a recent demographic study showed that out of over 400,000 professors in 1500 higher education institutions, 75% are White, and the lack of diversity is worse at private colleges and for higher professorial ranks (Myers, 2016).

Further, experts who speak English as an additional language can be hired in teacher training programs that recruit 'international students' to demonstrate that linguistic proficiency, pedagogical expertise and knowledge production in the ELT profession are not limited to a particular race and language background. Informing a new generation of language scholars and practitioners of the inherently colonial epistemologies of the profession is a form of decolonization, but a deeper more impactful approach would additionally entail exposing students to a range of voices and experiences from a diverse group of teachers, including White instructors. Put differently, although predominantly White institutions can successfully engage in decolonization efforts, students and future language professionals ought to be exposed to different life experiences.

To this end, Kubota (2015b) shows that decolonizing racial and linguistic hierarchies, or what she calls 'critical antiracism', can be carried out by engaging in self-reflection. In reflecting on her own privileged status as a settler of color in Canada in response to being on the receiving end of racism, Kubota (2015b: 6) shares the following observation regarding decolonization: 'When we view ourselves as the victim, we tend to overlook the possibility that we might be the victimiser in hierarchical relations of power ... Critical self-reflection helps us become aware that we exist at a certain space and time in a colonial power hierarchy'. This observation brings to mind the interconnectedness of the ELT profession. Individuals and individual actions are all part of a larger system of discourses and ideologies. Self-reflective practice creates the space for language scholars and professionals to explore how their participation in the profession is connected to a range of critical issues. Asking students to critically reflect on their language identities in relation to English and experiences with race, racism and linguicism can also be used to decolonize White public spaces in ELT (cf. Pennycook, 1998: 207). For Kubota (2015b: 7), this interconnectedness is uncovered for her by reflecting on how living and working in an indigenous region involves some economic exploitation – even if there exists an effort to help address racial and linguistic discrimination – of 'aboriginal people's lives, land, culture and rights'.

The upshot is that decolonization requires of language scholars and practitioners an awareness of their own participation in, and production of, colonial narratives (e.g. critical self-narratives like the one in Chapter 1). This can be implemented by promoting critical self-reflections in teacher training programs as part of professional development efforts, and through journals and other publications as special topics and issues. Although critical self-reflections are inherently personal and reflect unique encounters (Liggett, 2009), the individualized experiences of language scholars and practitioners are often connected to societal, professional and/or institutional structures, such as racial and linguistic hierarchies, colonial discourses, cultural imperialism and global capitalism (cf. Kubota & Lin, 2009a).

A central effort in decolonizing White public spaces also entails rejecting a liberal approach to bilingualism. Such an approach promotes the view that learning English as an additional language is beneficial for students, but paradoxically does not value the linguistic and communicative deviations that may occur during the process. A more radical approach to bilingualism moves linguistic standards and curricular goals away from a monolingual model that views English as an autonomous linguistic system that does not interface with other languages and cultural identities. This may entail reconceptualizing standardized tests that ignore the unique, yet relevant, ways in which Englishes are used in local contexts (Shohamy, 2013); it may also involve an approach to the development of language teaching materials that does not incorporate outdated notions of what it means to be a speaker of English in a globalized world (Gray, 2010). Decolonizing bilingualism, as it is currently imagined in the ELT profession, requires scholars and practitioners to reject the view that nativeness in English is necessary for successful language learning. Bilingual ELT instructors closely reflect the experiences of language learners and should thus be championed more in the profession. Finally, and perhaps more importantly, rejecting a liberal approach to bilingualism involves eradicating the myth that inner-circle countries, such as the United States, are monolingual English-speaking nations. This objective is particularly important for decolonizing White public spaces in the ELT profession, as it directly addresses the widespread misconception that peoples of color and speakers of additional languages in countries like the United States are non-natives and/or foreigners (Reyes & Lo, 2009).

Conclusion

The preceding discussion has not identified all of the possible ways to decolonize White public spaces in the ELT profession. Other decolonizing efforts may include, for example, applying critical race theory to immigration laws (e.g. Chapter 4) and critically examining how institutions promote the notion that English is a 'brand' (Holliday, 2008). Despite these acknowledged shortcomings, the primary objective of the previous section was to explore how racial capitalism can be compromised by uncovering the discourses and ideologies that control the social and cultural capital associated with the English language.

It was argued that racial capitalism entails creating economic wealth not from a particular race or ethnic community, but rather from racialized discourses. In other words, racial capitalism involves the financial exploitation of at least one racial or ethnic group, but this type of oppression is connected to discourses that afford rights and privileges to some communities while denying them to others. Race exists because of the subjective realities generated through encounters with other cultural groups and the primordial need to use such interactions to create power imbalances. That is to say, racial capitalism only exists because of race-based hierarchies. For instance, the discussion above provided several examples of how the ELT profession benefits from racial capitalism because of White privilege (or normativity) in language teaching and learning. Racial capitalism must be addressed in future research, as it keeps dominant groups in power by maintaining racial and linguistic hierarchies. The chapter suggested that while English will be treated as a commodity in the foreseeable future, there are actions that individuals (and the profession) can carry out to improve this situation.

One way of addressing the financial exploitation of teachers and students is to be cognizant of how racial and language ideologies are tied to market forces in the ELT profession. As discussed extensively in relation to Korea in previous chapters, the business of language teaching and learning benefits financially from a small set of racial and language ideologies.

For example, as a predominantly White cohort, the ELT profession benefits financially when the common-sense assumption around the world is that English must be taught by speakers from inner-circle countries. In this respect, value in the ELT market is created when discourses and ideologies promote the view that English leads to social, economic and cultural capital. This value is bound to exchange mechanisms, such as the buying and selling of language instruction (and teacher training programs). This business transaction, as just noted, is not simply about the exchange of money for an ELT service; such transactions are centrally about the exchange of racialized discourses and language ideologies (e.g. the notion that a White instructor from the United States is better equipped to teach English). Thus, exchange mechanisms in the ELT profession are inherently discriminatory, both racially and linguistically speaking. Because ELT institutions control, to a large extent, the discourses and ideologies that are circulated to promote the value of English, it is necessary to critically examine what these belief systems may look like when addressing racial capitalism. To this end, the chapter proposed a decolonization of White public spaces in the ELT profession (for a similar proposal in anthropology, see Brodkin *et al.*, 2011; for English studies, see Barnett, 2000).

Finally, the discussion of the interconnectedness of race and language in this and previous chapters, and the proposal that racial capitalism is not about the exploitation of a cultural group, but rather racialized discourses, demonstrate that notions of Whiteness in the ELT profession must move beyond race-based social constructs, such as White (for a similar proposal that discusses Whiteness in relation to class, see Arat-Koç, 2014). For example, predominantly White institutions are not the only participants in the ELT market that are reaping the benefits of racial and linguistic hierarchies. Whiteness in the ELT profession is imagined and reinforced by any participant of the ELT market who engages in the buying and selling of language teaching and learning, including teachers and students of color. Therefore, Whiteness is not only a social construct that is owned, managed and used for the benefit of White individuals, groups and institutions. It is a social construct that is used as a discursive resource to exploit labor, race and language for economic advantage. Therefore, Whiteness is as much a marketing tool as it is a marker of identification.

8 Conclusion and Future Directions

Concluding Remarks

This book has argued that White normativity is an ideological commitment and a form of racialized discourse that comes from the social actions of those involved in the ELT profession; this normative model or ideal standard constructs a system of racial discrimination that is founded on White privilege, saviorism and neoliberalism. Using Korea as a case study, and relying principally on critical race and discourse scholarship to examine racism, the findings established that race, ethnicity and citizenship are central aspects of how immigration laws are discursively constructed, employers manage hiring practices and teachers imagine their contribution and value to the profession. Although Korea was the starting point and main analytic focus of several chapters, the discussion throughout the book has attempted to make connections to the entire ELT profession. The previous chapter, for example, applied an understanding of White normativity and neoliberalism in Korea to a discussion of how the ELT profession as a whole engages in racial capitalism.

The observations made throughout this book contribute to the ELT literature by showing how critical race and discourse scholarship can be used to uncover the ways in which White privilege shapes common-sense understandings of language teaching and learning. ELT research must continue to be more self-reflective and explore issues, such as White normativity, as widespread discrimination exists in many segments of the profession beyond Korea (Kubota & Lin, 2009a; Motha, 2014). Furthermore, racial capitalism and White normativity continue to oppress under-represented professionals, including instructors of color. Critical race scholarship is especially needed, as racial capitalism and White normativity in the ELT profession close off employment opportunities to highly competent teachers because of linguistic hierarchies that are based on, as well as perpetuate, colonial and racialized discourses, such as outdated notions of what a speaker of English looks and sounds like.

The dearth of critical race scholarship in the ELT literature, and the apparent low priority it receives in the profession, is unfortunate given the real-life consequences that racial discrimination has for researchers, language practitioners and students. For decades, ELT scholars have favored methodological approaches that point the analytic lens outward, away from the Self and onto the cultural Other. While the propensity to observe, rather than to be observed, partly explains the comparatively small number of studies examining racism, this tendency has not stopped scholars in other disciplines from investigating race and racialized discourses. Indeed, many disciplines, from education to anthropology, possess a long history of examining structural and institutional racism (e.g. Appiah, 1985; Barnett, 2000; Bonilla-Silva, 2006; Crenshaw, 1991; Delgado & Stefancic, 2012), and scholars working within and across these disciplinary boundaries have indeed led the way in investigating racial discrimination and privilege (e.g. Bakan & Dua, 2014; DiAngelo, 2011). It is time for ELT scholars to contribute more to this body of work. Language scholars and practitioners possess expertise in language that can be used to advance an understanding of race and racialized discourses (e.g. Appleby, 2013; Chun, 2016; Fleming, 2015; Ruecker & Ives, 2015). Given the opportunities that exist to contribute to the rich body of critical race scholarship (Crump, 2014; Liggett, 2014), coupled with the ostensible lack of urgency in addressing racial discrimination in language teaching and learning, it can be said that the ELT profession is complicit in maintaining racial and linguistic hierarchies (cf. Mahboob, 2009).

An ELT profession that is more cognizant of racialized discourses, racism and race will involve decolonizing White public spaces, as outlined in the previous chapter. This may entail, among other things, journals, publishers and professional organizations actively seeking out work done on racial discrimination and privilege (cf. Kubota & Lin, 2009a). Teacher training programs, especially in the United States and other inner-circle countries, can also incorporate mandatory coursework on racism, seek ways to promote a more racially diverse teaching staff and reject liberal bilingualism and multiculturalism (e.g. Motha, 2006). These suggestions, as explicated in previous chapters, all feed into a larger, and perhaps more important, disciplinary task of engaging in critical applied linguistic work.

That is, an examination of White normative discourses and racial capitalism in the ELT profession is helpful in uncovering the political, social and cultural issues and conditions that shape, and sometimes hinder, access to teaching opportunities and students' ability to learn. The latter issue is particularly relevant to critical applied linguistic work. Although this book has not devoted much attention to student perspectives, the developmental consequences of White normativity in language teaching and learning are clear. An ELT profession that lacks racial and linguistic diversity hurts students by exposing them to language and cultural input that may not reflect their immediate communicative and social needs. In this sense, an ELT profession that is shaped by White normative discourses is inherently oppressive in that it does not provide students with the knowledge and tools to become legitimate participants in their local communities. More problematically, White normativity creates unrealistic linguistic standards and cultural expectations that set students up for failure (e.g. Phan, 2008). One way of addressing unrealistic linguistic standards is to adopt a critical pedagogy that is aimed at eradicating the social inequalities, power imbalances and hegemonic and neoliberal forces in education (cf. Freire, 2000).

Critical pedagogy, as conceptualized in the present book, is not concerned with replacing one subjective reality with another. That is to say, this book does not treat critical pedagogy as a tool to convince language scholars and practitioners that their way of thinking is incorrect. Critical pedagogy is fundamentally about better understanding the ways in which social structures and mechanisms, such as the racial and linguistic hierarchies that shape the ELT profession, provide or restrict opportunities to learn, be successful and participate in society in meaningful ways. The contents of this book, therefore, should not be interpreted as an accusation of wrongdoing, but rather as a critical reflection on how language scholars and practitioners can create a more humane profession (cf. J.Y. Song, 2016). As highlighted in Chapter 1, a critical pedagogy is about the struggle to achieve humanization: 'emancipation of labor', 'overcoming of alienation' and 'affirmation of men and women as persons' (Freire, 2000: 44).

The critical pedagogical elements of this book can be found in the analysis that demonstrated how neoliberalism and racial capitalism in language teaching and learning rely on the exploitation, oppression and exclusion of ELT instructors. The dehumanizing elements of the ELT profession are based on racial and linguistic hierarchies and come from the ideology that nativeness in English is synonymous with good, and indeed superior, teaching (cf. Aneja, 2016). These hierarchies explain how racial and language ideologies shape exchange mechanisms in the ELT market. The exploitation and oppression of language instructors occurs when free-market (or neoliberal) forces allow the social, cultural and economic values associated with English to be aligned with individuals, groups and organizations in positions of power, such as the predominantly White institutions in the profession that dictate linguistic standards. In this racialized context, critical race and discourse approaches provide tools to reconfigure the White normative discourses that circulate within and beyond the profession.

Moving beyond a system of exploitation, oppression and exclusion requires language scholars and practitioners to be not only aware of how racialized ideologies are tied to market forces, but also cognizant of the pedagogical implications of an ELT market that benefits from racial discrimination and linguicism. This may entail, for example, understanding that predominantly White institutions in the ELT profession benefit financially when the common-sense assumption around the world is that English must be taught by speakers from inner-circle countries. Transformative practices that address the pedagogical consequences of such racial discrimination and linguicism involve reconfiguring how the ELT profession circulates discourses and ideologies of what it means to be a speaker of English. This is the chief objective of a decolonizing effort in the ELT profession, which includes, but is not limited to: informing a new generation of teacher trainees of the inherently colonial and imperial epistemologies of language teaching and learning; exposing learners to a range of voices and experiences from a diverse group of teachers, including White instructors (see, for example, a recent 2016 special issue on teacher identity in *TESOL Quarterly*); and asking language scholars and practitioners to critically reflect on their own participation in, and production of, hegemonic discourses.

While White normativity is a central theme of this book, the preceding chapters contribute to several areas of ELT scholarship, including linguistic imperialism, colonialism, neoliberalism and critical applied linguistics. The contribution made in this book to these areas of ELT scholarship is discussed below as ten different, but overlapping, empirical issues.

(1) The global spread of English has done little to compromise the ubiquitous belief that English is the language of, and owned by, a small group of Western countries. The United States in particular plays a significant role in circulating the belief that English is a symbol of power that is controlled by predominantly White institutions. For example, the production of popular culture and management of international affairs, two global phenomena that are by and large mediated in English, are controlled by US institutions that are racially homogenous. These predominantly White institutions (e.g. the Hollywood industry) create images and discourses of the ideal speaker of English (i.e. what a speaker of English should look and sound like). In Korea, these images and discourses can be located in immigration laws that oppress speakers of

English from outer-circle and expanding-circle countries, recruiting and hiring practices that privilege White teachers, and the language ideologies constructed by ELT instructors. An examination of White saviorism in Chapter 5, for instance, demonstrated that instructors from inner-circle countries see themselves as superior teachers because their Korean colleagues did not grow up using English. Saviorist discourses rely on the same ideologies used by predominantly White institutions in the United States to promote the ethnocentric view that the cultural Other is inferior. When race and ethnicity are used to construct discourses and images of an ideal speaker of English, it is often done because dominant groups wish to maintain their positions of power, and/or individuals, groups or organizations seek to capitalize economically on these racial and linguistic hierarchies.

(2) The rapid expansion of the Korean economy over the past six decades, the country's increasing role in global politics and US military and political interest in the region have shaped in significant ways how English is imagined and used in Korea. Chapter 6 established that neoliberalism represents an idea from which Koreans make important life and education decisions, a language used to achieve success, and material wealth and cultural capital. This chapter demonstrated that the adoption of neoliberal policies in Korea coincided with a sharp increase in for-profit after-school language academies. In three decades, the number of such academies increased from approximately 1,400 to just over 70,000 (G. Moon, 2009). This growth helps explain the vast amounts of money spent on ELT instruction in Korea each year, which equals to approximately US$15 billion (H. Jeon, 2006). The desire to become a neoliberal citizen has created a profitable ELT market in which race, ethnicity and the English language are commodified. The commodification of English proficiency and the privileging of White teachers in the ELT market are tied to immigration laws that act as a proxy for racial and ethnic discrimination. School recruiters and owners exploit immigration laws that privilege speakers from inner-circle countries to create and circulate racialized discourses, such as the belief that ELT instructors are White and from Western countries. These discourses exist because of White racial hegemony.

(3) Kubota (2015b: 3) reminds the profession that race and racism are topics that lead to 'discomfort and a sense of threat in both everyday and academic discourses'. This partly explains why ELT scholars and practitioners spend comparatively little time investigating critical race issues. Researchers run the risk of being accused of 'race baiting' and their professional integrity can be called into question as a result. This lack of

serious uptake has created a profession that is illiterate in critical race theories. The critical race scholarship reviewed in Chapter 2 is an attempt to provide some knowledge of the topic to the ELT profession. In a field that prides itself on being interdisciplinary, ELT scholars and practitioners are encouraged to consider how CRT scholarship can be used to advance language teaching and learning. The central objectives of CRT scholarship are indeed aligned with much of what language scholars and practitioners value in the ELT profession. Critical race scholars are, for example, devoted to addressing the oppression of disadvantaged communities and analyzing how individual acts of discrimination and privilege are situated in a broader social context. The discussion in Chapter 2 explored how these critical race objectives, as well as the 10 CRT empirical themes, provide a theoretical template for an examination of racialized discourses, colonialism and imperialism in the ELT profession.

(4) A central analytic focus of this book has been on the exchange mechanisms in the ELT market that shape discourses and ideologies pertaining to the English language. The discussion in Chapter 6 in particular established that the value associated with race is created in and through several exchange mechanisms (or occupational practices). Exchange mechanisms, for example the requirement that applicants submit at least one photograph of themselves when applying for a teaching position, reconfigure what is traditionally understood to be valuable qualities and characteristics of an ideal language instructor. By placing value on physical features (e.g. skin color) rather than teaching experience and educational qualifications, ELT professionals alter the market's perception of what a speaker of English looks and sounds like. Exchange mechanisms, in other words, provide the space to hire language instructors based on race, ethnicity and language variety. When recruiters and employers hire ELT instructors according to physical features, and base their choice on a preference for a particular variety of English, they are not only treating individuals as a commodity (Holborow, 2012), but their actions also feed into a wider narrative that promotes the view that English is the language of inner-circle countries and should, accordingly, be taught by teachers from places like the United States. Such exchange mechanisms are also part of a larger discourse circulated in Korea that sells English as a form of new capitalism, a means of upward mobility and an integral aspect of being a neoliberal citizen.

(5) The notion that expertise in a language is tied to a nationality has been criticized over several decades of ELT scholarship. In particular, researchers have argued and demonstrated that the unfortunate dichotomy of native/non-native speaker perpetuates the belief that speakers from

outer-circle and expanding-circle countries are unable to speak English well and therefore cannot teach the language as competently as their inner-circle counterparts (e.g. Holliday, 2006; Llurda, 2006). However, the same researchers have established that speakers from outer-circle and expanding-circle countries are indeed competent in English and possess learning experiences that better equip them to engage in ELT instruction. This book has taken this discussion a step further by demonstrating that race and ethnicity are factors in how competence in English is imaged and used as a marketing tool. The analysis of immigration laws, for example, established that while policies that privilege speakers from inner-circle countries represent a form of linguicism, school owners and recruiters use such legal spaces to hire ELT instructors based on physical features. While immigration laws are based on outdated ideologies that associate linguistic competence with citizenship, hiring practices are carried out with the underlying belief that the ability to speak (and teach) is tied to race and ethnicity. Thus, the interface between linguistic competence, race, ethnicity and citizenship is highly context dependent and negotiable; yet, it is hoped that the analysis conducted in this book will encourage researchers interested in issues of nativeness to explore the possibility that race is an underlying issue in their studies.

(6) Race has no genetic validity. For example, it has been observed that there is more genetic variation within a race than there are differences between racial groups. Despite this, however, race is a social construct that many individuals use to understand and explain similarities and differences within and across cultural groups. The practice of evaluating the cultural Other through an ethnocentric lens is not new, and has in fact been occurring for millennia. Although the historical significance of ethnocentrism does not make racism acceptable, it does explain the existence of racial hierarchies. Western European colonizers, for example, used their cultural norms and practices to determine where indigenous people should be located in a number of different hierarchies, including intelligence, creativity and morality (Said, 1979). Such hierarchies also apply to languages. English was introduced in many regions of the world through colonization, but the language has since extended to other nations because of US imperialism, as well as its association with globalism, neoliberalism and social progression. For many people, the English language conjures up images of US power and culture. Accordingly, notions of what are acceptable forms of communication are tied to countries in positions of power. A Korean, for example, may view his/her competence in English in relation to the norms and conventions of North American English.

She/he may also construct her/his English language identity according to the discourses and images of people who either speak North American English or are from countries in positions of power. The racial and linguistic hierarchies that exist in relation to English stem from such ideological commitments and provide the foundation for the economic exploitation of race and ethnicity in the ELT market.

(7) Racial capitalism is the underpinning market-driven system that controls how race and ethnicity are commodified. It is a system that is used for the exploitation and oppression of ELT instructors and English language learners. Deriving economic value from racial and ethnic identities is a widespread phenomenon in the ELT profession, but the consequences of racial capitalism extend beyond the economic exploitation of a particular cultural group. Although it is important to address the unique issues that stem from the economic exploitation of specific communities within society, it was argued in this book that the more pressing concern is understanding how racial capitalism exploits the discourse that language instruction and teacher training must be carried out by a particular individual, group or institution. This discourse is partly responsible for White normativity in the ELT profession. Therefore, confronting racial capitalism requires decolonizing White public spaces, which are largely propped up by the belief that speakers from inner-circle countries are superior teachers. A decolonization effort entails eradicating discrimination and moving away from a linguistic hierarchy that does not value bilingual speakers of English and other varieties of the language that do not conform to inner-circle standards. Decolonizing White public spaces will not end racial capitalism, but promoting linguistic and racial diversity within the profession will make it more difficult to exploit and oppress language instructors.

(8) Critical discussions of race and ethnicity often benefit from the author or researcher providing a reflexive account of how personal life experiences, professional encounters and subjective realities have shaped the research process. Such accounts help establish the inherently political nature of conducting research and provide, both aesthetically and stylistically, an important literary element. Methodologically, such reflections have a long history in how CRT scholarship is disseminated. Accordingly, critical applied linguists can strengthen their research by engaging in a discussion of how their positions of power and privilege not only influenced their research, but also help address issues pertaining to discriminatory practices in the profession. Chapter 1 provided such an account by identifying how personal life experiences, professional encounters and subjective realities influenced the decisions made while conducting the present

study. It was demonstrated, for example, that personal and professional experiences with racism shaped the choice of analytic topics investigated and how the research was conducted. Furthermore, the decision to place the issue of Whiteness at the center of this book was influenced by both the dearth of research in this area and personal experiences dealing with White normativity in the ELT profession. As argued in Chapter 1, this self-reflexive component of doing research is a key feature of critical applied linguistics.

(9) Whiteness as a unit of analysis receives little attention in the ELT literature. This is a curious situation, as predominantly White institutions, such as teaching training programs in Western countries and organizations that administer standardized language tests, ostensibly control the flow of knowledge production in ELT scholarship and create discourses of what an expert (and person of power) in the profession looks and sounds like. While some attention has been given to the colonial history of the ELT profession (e.g. Pennycook, 1998), which represents a time when racialized discourses were central to how the British Empire understood the cultural Other (Said, 1985), little research has been, or is being, conducted on how Whiteness operates within language teaching and learning as a privileged status. This book has addressed the issue of Whiteness by describing what White normativity is, who benefits from it, how it operates within a market-driven profession and why it exists in language teaching and learning. For example, Chapter 4 traced White normativity in the ELT profession to, among other social events and organizations (e.g. the US military presence in Korea after the Korean War), a racially homogenous Hollywood entertainment industry that is responsible for attributing Whiteness to notions of beauty, bravery and brawn (cf. White saviorism; see Chapter 5).

(10) Finally, eradicating discrimination requires language scholars and practitioners to first acknowledge that oppression and exploitation of racial, ethnic and linguistic groups exists in the ELT profession. The next step involves understanding what racial, ethnic and linguistic discrimination looks like, who is responsible for carrying it out and how it is used to oppress and exploit language teachers. Although it is difficult to imagine many scholars and practitioners rejecting the need to investigate discriminatory practices in the profession, ELT scholarship has not moved far beyond the first step in eradicating racial, ethnic and linguistic discrimination. That is to say, while most language scholars and practitioners support a more racially inclusive profession, the ELT literature is still in the very beginning stages of understanding how race-based discrimination and privilege operate within the business of

language teaching and learning. ELT scholarship must continue to seek out ways to uncover, address and eradicate discriminatory practices in all segments of the profession. The investigation of race and ethnicity in the ELT profession in Korea represents one of many examples of how an understanding of the racial climate of one region can provide the empirical foundation to make sense of discriminatory practices in general. More analytic exercises like the one conducted in this book are needed, as the profession cannot stop discrimination and privilege without knowing what forms of racialized discourses feed into such discriminatory practices.

Future Directions

The objectives addressed in this book move the discussion of race in the ELT profession beyond the uncritical acknowledgement that racism is simply bad to an understanding of how racialized discourses interface with language teaching and learning. A number of empirical issues that are critical to an understanding of race and racialized discourses have not, however, been addressed while conducting the present study. Furthermore, several empirical issues, theoretical constructs and investigatory themes have been discussed superficially or tangentially, but deserve some concluding remarks because other disciplines have found them useful in advancing understandings of race and racism. This section concludes the book by identifying, in no particular order, empirical issues, theoretical constructs and investigatory themes that build on the findings established in this book and collectively represent growth areas in critical ELT scholarship. It will be argued that such empirical issues, theoretical constructs and investigatory themes have the potential to reconfigure how race and racism are approached and understood in ELT scholarship. In other words, the following discussion represents a collection of 'preferred futures' (Pennycook, 2001), or specifically what language scholars and practitioners can do to help address and eradicate racial discrimination in the ELT profession.

First, as alluded to in the discussion of White public spaces above and in the previous chapter, teacher training programs, and particularly those in the United States and other inner-circle countries that are viewed by the ELT industry as the source of expert knowledge in the profession, have the power to transform the oppressive hierarchies that exist in language teaching and learning. What teacher training programs do for and with critical issues in language teaching and learning represents a growth area in ELT scholarship. Researchers can examine, and reflect on, how curricular materials encourage teachers to be more conscious of race and racism, for example. Understanding the process that underpins the design, implementation and evaluation of such materials will also be helpful in eradicating racial discrimination in the ELT profession. Language scholars and practitioners should be able to discuss which critical issues and themes work best for promoting race-conscious teachers (future research must also examine how student learning is affected by racialized discourses, such as White normativity and saviorism). At the time of writing, very little work has been done in these areas. In other words, language scholars and practitioners are collectively not in a position at present to state which teacher training (and learning) materials are the most productive in creating a racially harmonious profession.

ELT scholarship is also in the early stages of understanding how the racial and linguistic ideologies of student teachers from outer-circle and expanding-circle countries evolve as they complete their graduate degrees in places like the United States. This type of research is needed because, while teacher training programs ostensibly have good intentions in delivering course materials that are based on 'Western scientific knowledge', such information has the potential to reinforce dominant and oppressive narratives (Mignolo, 2009; Said, 1979). Are teacher training programs responsible for identifying, addressing and sometimes altering the racial and linguistic ideologies that student teachers possess prior to beginning their education? If so, how can this be accomplished? Future research must explore the extent to which teacher training programs promote or resist oppressive narratives. Equally important is understanding how students respond to, and transform as professionals as a result of, training materials that question the very theories and concepts that define the profession (cf. Motha, 2006).

To this end, language scholars and practitioners can advance the discipline by providing more critical perspectives on the often problematic connection that is made throughout the profession between language and culture. Kumaravadivelu (2006: 19) offers an appropriate starting point to this discussion in the following excerpt:

> While the world at large seems to be treating English as a vehicle for global communication, a sizable segment of the TESOL profession continues to be informed by an anachronistic anthropological belief in the inextricability of the language–culture connection. TESOL textbooks continue to use the English language as a cultural carrier. There are instances where academic papers presented at professional

conferences propagate an ethnocentric view of culture learning and culture teaching.

With regard to race, racism and racialized discourses, the assumption that English must be taught alongside, say, 'American culture' can lead to a number of problematic outcomes. An uncritical discussion of the language–culture connection in ELT and teacher training courses encourages language students and student teachers to view their instructors or themselves as cultural ambassadors. An approach to ELT that is based on the cultural ambassador model promotes (White) saviorism among ELT professionals and creates a permanent deficit in how language students view their English. Accordingly, scholarship must continue to critically examine the racialized discourses and ideologies that are disseminated in the profession. For example, how can teachers identify such discourses and ideologies, and what can they do to resist them (cf. Gray, 2010)? How do language students and student teachers discursively construct their linguistic identities when given opportunities to confront racialized discourses and ideologies? Future research that follows this line of investigation must be careful not to assume that simply giving students opportunities to engage with, and make use of, race issues will promote critical multiculturalism. For instance, in their investigation of Whiteness as charity, Endres and Gould (2009) demonstrate that students do not necessarily adopt critical stances after being exposed to scholarship that is meant to provide a more nuanced understanding of different cultural experiences.

While it is not clear what the best approaches are to using critical race scholarship as a pedagogical tool, theorists working in disciplines outside of ELT have established that much can be gained from CRT. A critical race concept not utilized in this book, but worth exploring in future research, is W.E.B. Du Bois' (2007) notion of *double consciousness*. This term was originally used to understand how the multiple identities that an individual possesses operate within his/her everyday sense-making practices, and the psychological consequences of dealing with different, socially relevant categories, such as nationality (American) and ethnicity (African American). The idea that we all possess multiple identities is not new, but the term is helpful in remembering that experiences vary according to the relevance of a particular social category for a specific context. Double consciousness may assist researchers in understanding how, for example, linguistic imperialism and colonialism present different psychological and social challenges within marginalized groups in the ELT profession. Advancing ELT scholarship along this line of investigation requires using double consciousness as a theoretical lens for the examination of how teachers and students possess and manage their multiple, and sometimes conflicting, social categories. How does, for example, a Korean American ELT instructor in Korea manage his/her ethnic identities when notions of English and Americanness are tied to racially homogenous discourses and ideologies? What pedagogical tensions exist, if any, when a White instructor confronts racialized discourses and ideologies, such as saviorism and linguistic imperialism? Relevant to this discussion is Mazrui's (2006) sociolinguistic investigation of double consciousness and Fanon's (1986) two-part Black persona. Both scholars consider, albeit in different ways, how racialized discourses colonize the individual consciousness. Given the great and abundant literary and scholarly work conducted prior to, and immediately after, the 1960s civil rights movement, researchers may wish to consider how the struggles experienced by Africans and African Americans can be used as analytic tools to engage in critical race scholarship, including reflexive practices.

Homi Bhabha's (1994) understanding of *hybridity* and *hybridization* – terms used to capture the fluid and liminal nature of cultural identities – is needed to advance the ELT profession. Both terms offer insights into how the discourses and ideologies of colonialism and imperialism are inherently contradictory and forever changing. Bhabha's (1994) work assists in understanding the historical developments of colonial discourses and what this may say about racism and linguicism in today's society. Despite the contributions made by scholars working on similar issues (e.g. Pennycook, 1998), further research is needed to understand how phenomena associated with modernity, like globalization, neoliberalization and English as an international language, to name a few, conceal oppressive discourses and narratives. Specifically, within this area of investigation, research must continue investigating how globalization, neoliberalization and English as an international language propagate racism and linguicism.

In the spirit of postcolonialism, language teaching and learning scholarship must look beyond Western knowledge when attempting to understand how racialized discourses marginalize and oppress individuals, groups and communities within the ELT profession. Scholarship must draw from a range of perspectives from minority groups (e.g. Fujikane & Okamura, 2008), not least because the ELT profession is centrally about promoting cultural diversity. Indeed, this observation that more cultural diversity is needed can be applied to this book: postcolonial theorists, for example, may find the discussions in previous chapters somewhat problematic because more could have been done to include the perspectives of underrepresented communities, including indigenous scholars. Although the theoretical boundary between critical race scholarship and postcolonialism is blurred, if not nonexistent, this book has favored scholarship from the former body of work. Moving forward, scholarship may benefit from examining how spaces and bodies are reconfigured according to 'the asymmetrical and frequently violent processes of settler colonialism' (Mar & Edmonds, 2010: 3). The importance of building on this body of work lies in the unfortunate consequences of an expanding neoliberal agenda that consumes all that is in the way of its trajectory (Veracini, 2010). That is to say, racial discrimination is a product of neocolonialism. The ELT profession is an associate of this economic system, and thus language scholars and practitioners must do more to confront its inherently oppressive business model.

The connection between Marxism and critical race scholarship, while discussed to some extent in Chapter 2, is a largely underdeveloped empirical issue in language teaching and learning research in general, and in this book in particular. This connection has not been fully explored in the literature not only because of the common view that Marxism has little to offer critical race studies (Bakan & Dua, 2014), but also because of the more specific failure of scholars to adequately account for the importance of social class in language teaching and learning (Block, 2013). However, as this book has demonstrated, a Marxist understanding of value can be used to uncover the commodification of race in a market-driven ELT system. Paolucci (2006: 618) also demonstrates that Marx's understanding of an 'inverted' capitalist society, flawed scientific reasoning and 'the historico-structural dynamics of capitalism' are helpful in examining racialized discourses. Labor exploitation and oppression, two central features of Marx's understanding of capitalism, will serve as important areas of investigation as the world becomes more globalized and the ELT profession continues to be enmeshed in an economic network that is inherently discriminatory.

Also of potential benefit to an understanding of race and racism in the ELT profession is *identity salience*. This theoretical concept pays special attention to the liminal nature of identities. According to Turner (2012: 333), 'identities are designations that people make about themselves in relation to their location in social structures and the roles that they play by virtue of this location'. This notion of identity was originally developed by Stryker (1968), who argued that self-identification is a process organized within a hierarchy of saliency. Individuals possess a number of different identities, but the relevance of any given social category changes from one context to another. In other words, identities lie dormant until a contextual issue triggers their relevance. Identity salience can be used to explore how the identities of ELT instructors evolve as their professional and personal circumstances change. For example, the saliency of gender may become more apparent when an instructor moves to a teaching context where there is a preference for women professionals. Although this book does not examine gender, this limitation should not discourage other researchers from exploring how White women instructors from inner-circle countries experience great pleasure (or frustration) in places like Korea as a result of their identities becoming immediately relevant in their personal and professional lives. In the same vein, it is also worth exploring how the professional experiences of women and men differ in the ELT profession, and how gender roles in places like Korea intersect with a number of issues, including social class, education, religious affiliation and sexual orientation. This line of research would help uncover how ELT instructors reflect on, and deal with, racism, White privilege, linguicism, linguistic imperialism, colonialism and sexism. ELT scholarship can add to, or build on, the work done in identity salience by using the notion of sociolinguistic scales to investigate how social identities and interactional resources shape, and are shaped by, personal and professional conditions (cf. Blommaert, 2007).

Finally, a key growth area in ELT scholarship is the issue of how racialized discourses make racial and linguistic hierarchies visible (or invisible). In this book, for example, the study of how ELT teachers responded to budget cuts demonstrated that White saviorism makes Whiteness and linguicism visible objects. This line of research, which uncovers the social processes that make racism visible, deviates from much of the work done in critical race scholarship. That is, much critical race work examines how colorblind ideologies make race, racism and racial hierarchies *invisible* (e.g. Haney López, 2006). The impact of racialized discourses in societies, within professions and on the lives of real people is an empirical topic that can be examined by looking at the extent to which dominant groups downplay the importance of race. Denying the importance of race in society – whether by ignoring racial discrimination or denying its existence – is a form of oppression. Although some work has looked at how the NNES category is a form of racialized discourse and at the ways in which this construct oppresses many highly capable teachers, ELT scholarship has made a comparatively small contribution to the larger discussion of how race and racism are part of a profession (or system) that is inherently discriminatory. If the ELT profession is founded on the idea of providing equitable learning opportunities, then it would behoove scholars to pay closer attention to race and racism, as discriminatory practices and racialized ideologies not only hurt teachers, but also students.

References

Aghion, P. and Bolton, P. (1997) A theory of trickle-down growth and development. *The Review of Economic Studies* 64 (2), 151–172.

Ajayi, L. (2011) Exploring how ESL teachers relate their ethnic and social backgrounds to practice. *Race Ethnicity and Education* 14 (2), 253–275.

Amin, N. (1997) Race and the identity of the nonnative ESL teacher. *TESOL Quarterly* 31 (3), 580–583.

Aneja, G. (2014) Disinventing and reconstituting native speaker ideologies through the classroom experiences of international TESOL students. *Working Papers in Educational Linguistics* 29 (1), 23–39.

Aneja, G. (2016) (Non)native speakered: Rethinking (non)nativeness and teacher identity in TESOL teacher education. *TESOL Quarterly* 50 (3), 572–596.

Appiah, A. (1985) The uncompleted argument: Du Bois and the illusion of race. *Critical Inquiry* 12 (1), 21–37.

Appleby, R. (2013) Desire in translation: White masculinity and TESOL. *TESOL Quarterly* 47 (1), 122–147.

Arat-Koç, S. (2014) Rethinking Whiteness, 'culturalism,' and the bourgeoisie in the age of neoliberalism. In A.B. Bakan and E. Dua (eds) *Theorizing Anti-Racism: Linkages in Marxism and Critical Race Theory* (pp. 311–339). Toronto: University of Toronto Press.

Atkinson, D. (2002) Comments on Ryuko Kubota's 'Discursive construction of the images of U.S. classrooms'. A reader reacts. *TESOL Quarterly* 36 (1), 79–84.

Austin, T. (2009) Linguicism and race in the United States. In R. Kubota and A. Lin (eds) *Race, Culture, and Identities in Second Language Education: Exploring Critically Engaged Practice* (pp. 252–270). New York: Routledge.

Bakan, A.B. and Dua, E. (eds) (2014) *Theorizing Anti-Racism: Linkages in Marxism and Critical Race Theories*. Toronto: University of Toronto Press.

Bangou, F. and Wong, S. (2009) Race and technology in teacher education. In R. Kubota and A. Lin (eds) *Race, Culture, and Identities in Second Language Education: Exploring Critically Engaged Practice* (pp. 158–175). New York: Routledge.

Barker, V. and Giles, H. (2004) English-only policies: Perceived support and social limitation. *Language & Communication* 24 (1), 77–95.

Barnett, T. (2000) Reading 'Whiteness' in English Studies. *College English* 63 (1), 9–37.

Barton, D. and Tusting, K. (2005) *Beyond Communities of Practice: Language, Power, and Social Context*. Cambridge: Cambridge University Press.

Bashir-Ali, K. (2006) Language learning and the definition of one's social, cultural, and racial identity. *TESOL Quarterly* 40 (3), 628–639.

Behar, R. (1996) *The Vulnerable Observer: Anthropology That Breaks Your Heart*. Boston, MA: Beacon Press.

Bell, D. (1992) Reconstruction's racial realities. *Rutgers Law Journal* 23, 261–270.

Bernardi, D. (2008) *The Persistence of Whiteness: Race and Contemporary Hollywood Cinema*. London: Routledge.

Bertrand, M. and Mullainathan, S. (2004) Are Emily and Greg more employable than Lakisha and Jamal? A field experiment on labor market discrimination. *American Economic Review* 94 (4), 991–1013.

Bhabha, H.K. (1994) *The Location of Culture*. London: Routledge.

Block, D. (2013) *Social Class in Applied Linguistics*. London: Routledge.

Block, D. and Cameron, D. (eds) (2002) *Globalization and Language Teaching*. London: Routledge.

Block, D., Gray, J. and Holborow, M. (2012) *Neoliberalism and Applied Linguistics*. London: Routledge.

Blommaert, J. (2007) Sociolinguistic scales. *Intercultural Pragmatics* 4 (1), 1–19.

Bonilla-Silva, E. (2006) *Racism without Racists: Color-Blind Racism and the Persistence of Racial Inequality in the United States*. Lanham, MD: Rowman & Littlefield.

Bonilla-Silva, E., Goar, C. and Embrick, D.G. (2006) When Whites flock together: The social psychology of White habitus. *Critical Sociology* 32 (2–3), 229–253.

Bourdieu, P. (1977) *Outline of a Theory of Practice*. Cambridge: Cambridge University Press.

Bourdieu, P. (1984) *Distinction: A Social Critique of the Judgement of Taste*. Cambridge, MA: Harvard University Press.

Brantlinger, P. (2007) Kipling's 'The White Man's Burden' and its afterlives. *English Literature in Transition, 1880–1920* 50 (2), 172–191.

Brodkin, K., Morgen, S. and Hutchinson, J. (2011) Anthropology as White public space? *American Anthropologist* 113 (4), 545–556.

Burke, D. (2007) An autoethnography of Whiteness. Unpublished doctoral dissertation, Oregon State University.

Butler, Y.G. (2007) How are nonnative-English-speaking teachers perceived by young learners? *TESOL Quarterly* 41 (4), 731–755.

Calhoun, C. (2013) Occupy Wall Street in perspective. *The British Journal of Sociology* 64 (1), 26–38.

Cameron, D. (2012) The commodification of language: English as a global commodity. In T. Nevalainen and E.C. Traugott (eds) *The Oxford Handbook of the History of English* (pp. 352–361). Oxford: Oxford University Press.

Capaccio, A. and Gaouette, N. (2014) U.S. adding 800 troops for South Korea citing rebalance. *Bloomberg*, 7 January. See www.bloomberg.com/news/2014-01-07/u-s-adding-800-troops-for-south-korea-citing-rebalance.html (accessed 16 November 2014).

Case, K.A. (2012) Discovering the privilege of Whiteness: White women's reflections on anti-racist identity and ally behavior. *Journal of Social Issues* 68 (1), 78–96.

Cenoz, J. and Gorter, D. (2009) Language economy and linguistic landscape. In D. Gorter and E. Shohamy (eds) *Linguistic Landscape: Expanding the Scenery* (pp. 55–69). New York: Routledge.

Central Intelligence Agency (2016) *The World Factbook: South Korea*. See https://www.cia.gov/library/publications/resources/the-world-factbook/ (accessed 28 March 2017).

Chacón, C.T. (2009) Transforming the curriculum of NNESTs. In R. Kubota and A. Lin (eds) *Race, Culture, and Identities in Second Language Education: Exploring Critically Engaged Practice* (pp. 215–233). New York: Routledge.

Charlebois, J. (2008) Developing critical consciousness through film. *TESOL Canada Journal* 25 (2), 124–132.

Chomsky, N. (1999) *Profit over People: Neoliberalism and Global Order*. New York: Seven Stories Press.

Choo, H. (2016) *Decentering Citizenship: Gender, Labor, and Migrant Rights in South Korea.* Stanford, CA: Stanford University Press.

Chun, C.W. (2016) Addressing racialized multicultural discourses in an EAP textbook: Working toward a critical pedagogies approach. *TESOL Quarterly* 50 (1), 109–131.

Clark, D.N. (2003) *Living Dangerously in Korea: The Western Experience, 1900–1950.* Norwalk, CT: EastBridge.

Cochran-Smith, M. (1995) Color blindness and basket making are not the answers: Confronting the dilemmas of race, culture, and language diversity in teacher education. *American Educational Research Journal* 32 (3), 493–522.

Cole, M. (2009) *Critical Race Theory and Education: A Marxist Response.* Basingstoke: Palgrave.

Cole, M. (2012) Critical race theory in education, Marxism and abstract racial domination. *British Journal of Sociology of Education* 33 (2), 167–183.

Cole, T. (2012) The White-savior industrial complex. *The Atlantic*, 21 March. See www.theatlantic.com/international/archive/2012/03/the-white-savior-industrial-complex/254843/ (accessed 16 January 2016).

Connolly, E. (2014) An ethnicity conversation your adoptive child wants you to have. *Huffington Post*, 12 September. See www.huffingtonpost.com/elizabeth-connolly/an-ethnicity-conversation-your-adoptive-child-wants-to-have_b_5768150.html (accessed 16 November 2014).

Crenshaw, K.W. (1988) Race, reform, and retrenchment: Transformation and legitimation in antidiscrimination law. *Harvard Law Review* 101 (7), 1331–1387.

Crenshaw, K. (1991) Mapping the margins: Intersectionality, identity politics, and violence against women of color. *Stanford Law Review* 43 (6), 1241–1299.

Crookes, G. and Lehner, A. (1998) Aspects of process in an ESL critical pedagogy teacher education course. *TESOL Quarterly* 32 (2), 319–328.

Crump, A. (2014) Introducing LangCrit: Critical language and race theory. *Critical Inquiry in Language Studies* 11 (3), 207–224.

Crumpler, T.P., Handsfield, L.J. and Dean, T.R. (2011) Constructing difference differently in language and literacy professional development. *Research in the Teaching of English* 46 (1), 55–91.

Crystal, D. (2012) *English as a Global Language.* Cambridge: Cambridge University Press.

Cummins, J. (2000) *Language, Power, and Pedagogy: Bilingual Children in the Crossfire.* Clevedon: Multilingual Matters.

Curtis, A. and Romney, M. (2006) *Color, Race, and English Language Teaching: Shades of Meaning.* Mahwah, NJ: Lawrence Erlbaum Associates.

Davies, C.A. (1999) *Reflexive Ethnography: A Guide to Researching Selves and Others.* London: Routledge.

Davies, D.M. (1992) Henry G. Appenzeller: Pioneer missionary and reformer in Korea. *Methodist History* 30 (4), 195–205.

Day, D. (1998) Being ascribed, and resisting, membership in an ethnic group. In C. Antaki and S. Widdicombe (eds) *Identities in Talk* (pp. 151–170). London: Sage.

Delgado, R. and Stefancic, J. (1989) Why do we tell the same stories? Law reform, critical librarianship, and the triple helix dilemma. *Stanford Law Review* 42 (1), 207–225.

Delgado, R. and Stefancic, J. (1993) Critical race theory: An annotated bibliography. *Virginia Law Review* 79 (2), 461–516.

Delgado, R. and Stefancic, J. (2012) *Critical Race Theory: An Introduction.* New York: New York University Press.

Demyanyk, Y. and Van Hemert, O. (2011) Understanding the subprime mortgage crisis. *Review of Financial Studies* 24 (6), 1848–1880.

Denney, S. (2015) South Korea's migrant workers in the public eye. *The Diplomat*, 10 September. See http://thediplomat.com/2015/09/south-koreas-migrant-workers-in-the-public-eye/ (accessed 10 March 2016).

DiAngelo, R. (2011) White fragility. *International Journal of Critical Pedagogy* 3 (3), 54–70.

Doane, A. (2006) What is racism? Racial discourse and racial politics. *Critical Sociology* 32 (2), 255–274.

Doogan, K. (2009) *New Capitalism? The Transformation of Work*. Cambridge: Polity.

Du Bois, W. (2007) *The Souls of Black Folk* (edited by B.H. Edwards). Oxford: Oxford University Press.

Edge, J. (2006) *(Re-)locating TESOL in an Age of Empire*. Basingstoke: Palgrave.

Education First (2013) *South Korea: Massive Investment with Limited Return*. Cambridge, MA: EF Education First.

Ellwood, C. (2009) Uninhabitable identifications: Unpacking the production of racial difference in a TESOL classroom. In R. Kubota and A. Lin (eds) *Race, Culture, and Identities in Second Language Education: Exploring Critically Engaged Practice* (pp. 101–117). New York: Routledge.

Endres, D. and Gould, M. (2009) 'I am also in the position to use my Whiteness to help them out': The communication of Whiteness in service learning. *Western Journal of Communication* 73 (4), 418–436.

EPIK (2013) Required documents. See www.epik.go.kr/contents.do?contentsNo=60&menuNo=293#optional_sub9 (accessed 28 November 2015).

Fanon, F. (1986) *Black Skin, White Masks*. London: Pluto.

Ferguson, G. (2006) *Language Planning and Education*. Edinburgh: Edinburgh University Press.

Fernández, P.G. (2004) Linguistic imperialism in the ELT profession? *Vigo International Journal of Applied Linguistics* 1, 113–150.

Ferreira, A.J. (2007) What has race/ethnicity got to do with EFL teaching? *Linguagem & Ensino* 10 (1), 211–233.

Fleming, D. (2015) Citizenship and race in second-language education. *Journal of Multilingual and Multicultural Development* 36 (1), 42–52.

Foucault, M. (1972) *The Archaeology of Knowledge*. New York: Pantheon Books.

Fought, C. (2006) *Language and Ethnicity*. Cambridge: Cambridge University Press.

Frank, C.R., Kim, K-S. and Westphal, L.E. (1975) Economic growth in South Korea since World War II. In K. Kim (ed.) *Foreign Trade Regimes and Economic Development: South Korea* (pp. 6–24). Cambridge, MA: National Bureau of Economic Research.

Freire, P. (2000) *Pedagogy of the Oppressed*. London: Continuum.

Fujikane, C. and Okamura, J.Y. (eds) (2008) *Asian Settler Colonialism: From Local Governance to the Habits of Everyday Life in Hawai'i*. Honolulu, HI: University of Hawai'i Press.

Garner, S. (2007) *Whiteness: An Introduction*. London: Routledge.

Gebhard, M. (2004) Fast capitalism, school reform, and second language literacy practice. *The Modern Language Journal* 88 (2), 245–265.

Goffman, E. (1984) *Frame Analysis: An Essay on the Organization of Experience*. Boston, MA: Northeastern University Press.

Goldberg, D.T. and Solomos, J. (2002) General introduction. In D.T. Goldberg and J. Solomos (eds) *A Companion to Racial and Ethnic Studies* (pp. 1–12). Oxford: Wiley-Blackwell.

Golombek, P. and Jordan, S.R. (2005) Becoming 'black lambs' not 'parrots': A poststructuralist orientation to intelligibility and identity. *TESOL Quarterly* 39 (3), 513–533.

Grant, R.A. and Lee, I. (2009) The ideal English speaker: A juxtaposition of globalization and language policy in South Korea and racialized language attitudes in the United States. In R. Kubota and A. Lin (eds) *Race, Culture, and Identities in Second Language Education: Exploring Critically Engaged Practice* (pp. 44–63). New York: Routledge.

Gray, J. (2000) The ELT coursebook as cultural artefact: How teachers censor and adapt. *ELT Journal* 54 (3), 274–283.

Gray, J. (2010) *The Construction of English: Culture, Consumerism and Promotion in the ELT Global Coursebook.* Basingstoke: Palgrave.

Guillem, S.M. (2014) Going 'global', (re)locating privilege: A journey into the borders of Whiteness, foreignness, and performativity. *Journal of Multicultural Discourses* 9 (3), 212–226.

Haggard, S., Kim, B. and Moon, C. (1991) The transition to export-led growth in South Korea: 1954–1966. *The Journal of Asian Studies* 50 (4), 850–873.

Hall, R.E. (2008) *Racism in the 21st Century: An Empirical Analysis of Skin Color.* New York: Springer.

Hammond, K. (2006) More than a game: A critical discourse analysis of a racial inequality exercise in Japan. *TESOL Quarterly* 40 (3), 545–571.

Haney López, I.F. (1994) The social construction of race: Some observations on illusion, fabrication, and choice. *Harvard Civil Rights–Civil Liberties Law Review* 29, 1–62.

Haney López, I.F. (2006) *White by Law: The Legal Construction of Race.* New York: New York University Press.

Hansen, A.D. (2005) A practical task: Ethnicity as a resource in social interaction. *Research on Language & Social Interaction* 38 (1), 63–104.

Haque, E. and Morgan, B. (2009) Un/marked pedagogies. In R. Kubota and A. Lin (eds) *Race, Culture, and Identities in Second Language Education: Exploring Critically Engaged Practice* (pp. 271–285). New York: Routledge.

Haque, E. and Patrick, D. (2015) Indigenous languages and the racial hierarchisation of language policy in Canada. *Journal of Multilingual and Multicultural Development* 36 (1), 27–41.

Harris, C.I. (1993) Whiteness as property. *Harvard Law Review* 106 (8), 1707–1791.

Harris, S.K. (2007) Kipling's 'The White Man's Burden' and the British newspaper context, 1898–1899. *Comparative American Studies* 5 (3), 243–263.

Hartigan, J., Jr (1997) Establishing the fact of Whiteness. *American Anthropologist* 99 (3), 495–505.

Harvey, D. (2005) *A Brief History of Neoliberalism.* Oxford: Oxford University Press.

Hay, J. (2000) Functions of humor in the conversations of men and women. *Journal of Pragmatics* 32 (6), 709–742.

Heller, M. (2010) The commodification of language. *Annual Review of Anthropology* 39, 101–114.

Herrera, S. and Morales, A.R. (2009) Colorblind nonaccommodative denial. In R. Kubota and A. Lin (eds) *Race, Culture, and Identities in Second Language Education: Exploring Critically Engaged Practice* (pp. 197–214). New York: Routledge.

Hill, J.H. (1998) Language, race, and white public space. *American Anthropologist* 100 (3), 680–689.

Hobbs, A. (2014) *A Chosen Exile: A History of Racial Passing in American Life.* Cambridge, MA: Harvard University Press.

Holborow, M. (2006) Ideology and language: Interconnections between neo-liberalism and English. In J. Edge (ed.) *(Re)locating TESOL in an Age of Empire* (pp. 84–103). Basingstoke: Palgrave.

Holborow, M. (2007) Language, ideology and neoliberalism. *Journal of Language and Politics* 6 (1), 51–73.

Holborow, M. (2012) Neoliberalism, human capital and the skills agenda in higher education: The Irish case. *Journal for Critical Education Policy Studies* 10 (1), 93–111.

Holliday, A. (2006) Native-speakerism. *ELT Journal* 60 (4), 385–387.

Holliday, A. (2008) Standards of English and politics of inclusion. *Language Teaching* 41 (1), 119–130.

Holliday, A. and Aboshiha, P. (2009) The denial of ideology in perceptions of 'nonnative speaker' teachers. *TESOL Quarterly* 43 (4), 669–689.

Hong, H. (2010) 원어민 보조교사 배치 현황. *서울신문*, 8 November. See www.seoul.co.kr/news/newsView.php?id=20101109023001 (accessed 23 January 2016).

Hong, Y. (2015) Academies with 'pretty female teachers' begin a controversial trend. *Nate: No Cut News*, 2 February. See http://netizenbuzz.blogspot.com/2015/02/academies-with-pretty-female-teachers.html (accessed 11 April 2015).

Howatt, A.P. and Widdowson, H.G. (2004) *A History of English Language Teaching*. Oxford: Oxford University Press.

Hu, E. (2015a) Even the planes stop flying for South Korea's national exam day. *NPR*, 12 November. See www.npr.org/sections/parallels/2015/11/12/455708201/even-the-planes-stop-flying-for-south-koreas-national-exam-day (accessed 10 March 2016).

Hu, E. (2015b) The all-work, no-play culture of South Korean education. *NPR*, 15 April. See www.npr.org/sections/parallels/2015/04/15/393939759/the-all-work-no-play-culture-of-south-korean-education (accessed 10 March 2016).

Hughey, M.W. (2010) The White savior film and reviewers' reception. *Symbolic Interaction* 33 (3), 475–496.

Hughey, M.W. (2014) *The White Savior Film: Content, Critics, and Consumption*. Philadelphia, PA: Temple University Press.

Hunt, D. and Ramón, A.-C. (2015) *2015 Hollywood Diversity Report: Flipping the Script*. Los Angeles, CA: Ralph J. Bunche Center for African American Studies.

Hyams, J. (2015) Chungdahm April under fire for 'white only' recruitment ad. *The Korea Observer*, 30 March. See www.koreaobserver.com/chung-dahm-under-fire-for-employing-whites-only-27547/ (accessed 23 December 2015).

Ibrahim, A. (2009) Operating under erasure: Race/language/identity. In R. Kubota and A. Lin (eds) *Race, Culture, and Identities in Second Language Education: Exploring Critically Engaged Practice* (pp. 176–194). New York: Routledge.

Ibrahim, A. (2015) Body without organs: Notes on Deleuze & Guattari, critical race theory and the socius of anti-racism. *Journal of Multilingual and Multicultural Development* 36 (1), 13–26.

Jenks, C.J. (2011) *Transcribing Talk and Interaction: Issues in the Representation of Communication Data*. Amsterdam: John Benjamins.

Jenks, C.J. (in press) The semiotics of learning Korean at home: An ecological autoethnographic perspective. *International Journal of Bilingual Education and Bilingualism*, doi:10.1080/13670050.2015.1070788.

Jenks, C.J., Bhatia, A. and Lou, J.J. (2013) The discourse of culture and identity in national and transnational contexts. *Language and Intercultural Communication* 13 (2), 121–125.

Jenks, C.J. and Lee, J.W. (eds) (forthcoming) *Korean Englishes in Transnational Contexts*. Basingstoke: Palgrave.

Jeon, H. (2006) *The Economics of English*. Seoul: Samsung Economic Research Institute.

Jung, M. (2014) More native teachers to lose jobs. *The Korea Times*, 13 November. See www.koreatimes.co.kr/www/news/nation/2014/11/116_168089.html (accessed 27 May 2015).

Kachru, B.B. (1985) Standards, codification, and sociolinguistic realism: The English language in the outer circle. In R. Quirk and H. G. Widdowson (eds) *English in the World: Teaching and Learning the Language and Literatures* (pp. 11–30). Cambridge: Cambridge University Press.

Kang, Y. (2012) Any one parent will do: Negotiations of fatherhood among South Korean 'wild geese' fathers in Singapore. *Journal of Korean Studies* 17 (2), 269–297.

Katz, L. and DaSilva Iddings, A. (2009) Classroom positionings and children's construction of linguistic and racial identities in English-dominant classrooms. In R. Kubota and A. Lin (eds) *Race, Culture, and Identities in Second Language Education: Exploring Critically Engaged Practice* (pp. 139–157). New York: Routledge.

Keating, A. (1995) Interrogating 'Whiteness', (de)constructing 'race'. *College English* 57 (8), 901–918.

Kennedy, L. (1996) Alien nation: White male paranoia and imperial culture in the United States. *Journal of American Studies* 30 (01), 87–100.

Kim, E. (2012) Human capital: Transnational Korean adoptees and the neoliberal logic of return. *Journal of Korean Studies* 17 (2), 299–327.

Kim, H. and Han, C. (2014) [무상복지 논란] 보육 예산 때문에… 원어민 교사들 "오 마이 갓". *서울신문*, 13 November. See www.seoul.co.kr/news/newsView.php?id=20141113003005 (accessed 23 January 2016).

Kim, J. (2014) National identity under transformation: New challenges to South Korea. *The ASAN Forum* 2 (5).

Kim, M. (1997) Moments of danger in the (dis)continuous relation of Korean nationalism and Korean American nationalism. *Positions: East Asia Cultures Critique* 5 (2), 357–389.

Kim, N.Y. (2006) 'Seoul–America' on America's 'soul': South Koreans and Korean immigrants navigate global white racial ideology. *Critical Sociology* 32 (2), 381–402.

Kim, N.Y. (2008) *Imperial Citizens: Koreans and Race from Seoul to LA*. Stanford, CA: Stanford University Press.

Kim, P. and Vogel, E.F. (2011) *The Park Chung Hee Era: The Transformation of South Korea*. Cambridge, MA: Harvard University Press.

Kim, S. (2014) Number of multiracial students on rapid rise. *The Korea Times*, 21 September. See www.koreatimes.co.kr/www/news/nation/2014/09/116_164971.html (accessed 16 November 2014).

Kim, S. and Lee, J. (2006) Changing facets of Korean higher education: Market competition and the role of the state. *Higher Education* 52 (3), 557–587.

Kim, S. and Lee, J. (2010) Private tutoring and demand for education in South Korea. *Economic Development and Cultural Change* 58 (2), 259–296.

Kim-Rivera, E.G. (2002) English language education in Korea under Japanese colonial rule. *Language Policy* 1 (3), 261–281.

King, R. (2007) North and South Korea. In A. Simpson (ed.) *Language and National Identity in Asia* (pp. 200–234). Oxford: Oxford University Press.

Kipling, R. (1899) The white man's burden. *McClure's Magazine* XII (4), 290–291.

Kobayashi, Y. (2006) Interethnic relations between ESL students. *Journal of Multilingual and Multicultural Development* 27 (3), 181–195.

Korea Immigration Service (2015) 국적 및 신체류자격별 장단기체류외국인. See http://
immigration.go.kr/doc_html/attach/imm/f2015//20151022239138_3_03.xls.files/
WorkBook.html (accessed 3 December 2015).

Krinsky, J. (2007) *Free Labor: Workfare and the Contested Language of Neoliberalism.* Chicago,
IL: University of Chicago Press.

Kubota, R. (2001) Discursive construction of the images of U.S. classrooms. *TESOL
Quarterly* 35 (1), 9–38.

Kubota, R. (2002) The author responds: (Un)raveling racism in a nice field like TESOL.
TESOL Quarterly 36 (1), 84–92.

Kubota, R. (2003a) New approaches to gender, class, and race in second language writing.
Journal of Second Language Writing 12 (1), 31–47.

Kubota, R. (2003b) Critical multiculturalism and second language education.
In B. Norton and K. Toohey (eds) *Critical Pedagogies and Language Learning* (pp. 30–52).
Cambridge: Cambridge University Press.

Kubota, R. (2004) Critical multiculturalism and second language education. In B. Norton
and K. Toohey (eds) *Critical Pedagogies and Language Learning* (pp. 30–52). Cambridge:
Cambridge University Press.

Kubota, R. (2011) Learning a foreign language as leisure and consumption: Enjoyment,
desire, and the business of eikaiwa. *International Journal of Bilingual Education and
Bilingualism* 14 (4), 473–488.

Kubota, R. (2013) Critical race theory and qualitative research. In C. Chapelle (ed.)
The Encyclopedia of Applied Linguistics (pp. 1520–1525). Oxford: Wiley.

Kubota, R. (2015a) Introduction: Race and language learning in multicultural Canada.
Journal of Multilingual and Multicultural Development 36 (1), 1–2.

Kubota, R. (2015b) Race and language learning in multicultural Canada: Towards critical
antiracism. *Journal of Multilingual and Multicultural Development* 36 (1), 3–12.

Kubota, R. and Chiang, L.T. (2012) Gender and race in ESP research. In B. Paltridge and
S. Starfield (eds) *The Handbook of English for Specific Purposes* (pp. 481–499). Oxford:
Wiley-Blackwell.

Kubota, R. and Lin, A. (2006) Race and TESOL: Introduction to concepts and theories.
TESOL Quarterly 40 (3), 471–493.

Kubota, R. and Lin, A. (2009a) *Race, Culture, and Identities in Second Language Education:
Exploring Critically Engaged Practice.* New York: Routledge.

Kubota, R. and Lin, A. (2009b) Preface. In R. Kubota and A. Lin (eds) *Race, Culture,
and Identities in Second Language Education: Exploring Critically Engaged Practice*
(pp. VIII–X). New York: Routledge.

Kubota, R. and Lin, A. (2009c) Race, culture, and identities in second language education:
Introduction to research and practice. In R. Kubota and A. Lin (eds) *Race, Culture, and
Identities in Second Language Education: Exploring Critically Engaged Practice* (pp. 1–23).
New York: Routledge.

Kumaravadivelu, B. (2006) Dangerous liaison: Globalization, empire and TESOL.
In J. Edge (ed.) *(Re-)locating TESOL in an Age of Empire* (pp. 1–26). Basingstoke:
Palgrave.

Lankov, A. (2007) Original English boom. *The Korea Times,* 4 October. See www.
koreatimes.co.kr/www/news/opinon/2016/02/165_11302.html (accessed 10 March
2016).

Lee, C. (2014a) U.N. calls for Korean anti-discrimination act. *The Korea Herald,* 8 October.
See www.koreaherald.com/view.php?ud=20141006001064 (accessed 18 January
2015).

Lee, C. (2014b) Defining racism in Korea. *The Korea Herald*, 4 September. See http://www.koreaherald.com/view.php?ud=20140904001088 (accessed 16 November 2014).

Lee, C. (2015) Teacher fined for bullying mixed-race student. *The Korea Herald*, 13 February. See www.koreaherald.com/view.php?ud=20150213000954 (accessed 5 May 2015).

Lee, C.J., Kim, Y. and Byun, S. (2012) The rise of Korean education from the ashes of the Korean War. *Prospects* 42 (3), 303–318.

Lee, E. (2015) Doing culture, doing race: Everyday discourses of 'culture' and 'cultural difference' in the English as a second language classroom. *Journal of Multilingual and Multicultural Development* 36 (1), 80–93.

Lee, E. and Simon-Maeda, A. (2006) Racialized research identities in ESL/EFL research. *TESOL Quarterly* 40 (3), 573–594.

Lee, E. and Bhuyan, R. (2013) Negotiating within Whiteness in cross-cultural clinical encounters. *Social Service Review* 87 (1), 98–130.

Lee, H., Ha, Y. and Sorensen, C.W. (2013) *Colonial Rule and Social Change in Korea, 1910–1945*. Seattle, WA: University of Washington Press.

Lee, I. (2009) Situated globalization and racism: An analysis of Korean high school EFL textbooks. *Language & Literacy* 11 (1), 1–14.

Lee, J. (2015) Survey: Only 5.5% of foreigners in Seoul say they've never experienced discrimination. *The Hankyoreh*, 25 May. See http://english.hani.co.kr/arti/english_edition/e_international/692693.html (accessed 27 May 2015).

Lee, J., Han, M. and Mckerrow, R.E. (2010) English or perish: How contemporary South Korea received, accommodated, and internalized English and American modernity. *Language and Intercultural Communication* 10 (4), 337–357.

Lee, J.W. (2014) Legacies of Japanese colonialism in the rhetorical constitution of South Korean national identity. *National Identities* 16 (1), 1–13.

Lee, J.W. (2016) The politics of intentionality in Englishes: Provincializing capitalization. *Critical Inquiry in Language Studies* 13 (1), 46–71.

Lee, M. (2016) 'Gangnam style' English ideologies: Neoliberalism, class and the parents of early study-abroad students. *International Journal of Bilingual Education and Bilingualism* 19 (1), 35–50.

Lee, S.S. (2013) South Korea's dreaded college entrance exam is the stuff of high school nightmares, but is it producing 'robots'? *CBS News*, 7 November. See www.cbsnews.com/news/south-koreas-dreaded-college-entrance-exam-is-the-stuff-of-high-school-nightmares-but-is-it-producing-robots/ (accessed 10 March 2016).

Lee, T. (2010) Biracial male citizens subject to conion [military duty]. *The Korea Times*, 30 December. See www.koreatimes.co.kr/www/news/nation/2010/12/116_78908.html (accessed 15 November 2014).

Lee, T. (2014a) American rejected for job in Korea because of being black. *The Korea Observer*, 13 November. See www.koreaobserver.com/american-rejected-for-job-in-korea-because-of-being-black-24676 (accessed 21 January 2015).

Lee, T. (2014b) Korea cuts 2,500 native English teachers in public schools. *The Korea Observer*, 26 August. See www.koreaobserver.com/korea-cuts-2500-native-english-teachers-at-public-schools-23271/ (accessed 23 January 2016).

Leong, N. (2013) Racial capitalism. *Harvard Law Review* 126 (8), 2151–2226.

Leung, C., Harris, R. and Rampton, B. (1997) The idealised native speaker, reified ethnicities, and classroom realities. *TESOL Quarterly* 31 (3), 543–560.

Lewontin, R.C. (1972) The apportionment of human diversity. *Evolutionary Biology* 6, 381–398.

L.G. v. Republic of Korea (2015) CERD/C/86/D/51/2012 (Committee on the Elimination of Racial Discrimination, 1 May 2015).

Lie, J. (ed.) (2014) *Multiethnic Korea? Multiculturalism, Migration, and Peoplehood Diversity in Contemporary South Korea*. Berkeley, CA: Institute of East Asian Studies.

Liggett, T. (2008) Frames of reference: The impact of race on teaching strategy and classroom discussion. *The Urban Review* 40 (4), 386–402.

Liggett, T. (2009) Unpacking White racial identity in English language teacher education. In R. Kubota and A. Lin (eds) *Race, Culture, and Identities in Second Language Education: Exploring Critically Engaged Practice* (pp. 27–43). New York: Routledge.

Liggett, T. (2014) The mapping of a framework: Critical race theory and TESOL. *The Urban Review* 46 (1), 112–124.

Light, R.L. (1967) English for speakers of other languages: Programs administered by the U.S. Office of Education. *TESOL Quarterly* 1 (1), 55–61.

Lin, A., Grant, R., Kubota, R., Motha, S., Sachs, G.T., Vandrick, S. and Wong, S. (2004) Women faculty of color in TESOL: Theorizing our lived experiences. *TESOL Quarterly* 38 (3), 487–504.

Lindemann, S. (2002) Listening with an attitude: A model of native-speaker comprehension of non-native speakers in the United States. *Language in Society* 31 (3), 419–441.

Lipsitz, G. (1995) The possessive investment in Whiteness: Racialized social democracy and the 'White' problem in American Studies. *American Quarterly* 47 (3), 369–387.

Llurda, E. (ed.) (2006) *Non-Native Language Teachers: Perceptions, Challenges and Contributions to the Profession*. New York: Springer.

Lo, A. and Kim, J. (2011) Manufacturing citizenship: Metapragmatic language competencies in media images of mixed race men in South Korea. *Discourse & Society* 22 (4), 440–457.

Low, M. (1999) Exploring cross-cultural inscriptions and difference: The effects of researchers' positionalities on inquiry practices. *TESOL Quarterly* 33 (2), 292–298.

Luke, A. (2009) Race and language as capital in school. In R. Kubota and A. Lin (eds) *Race, Culture, and Identities in Second Language Education: Exploring Critically Engaged Practice* (pp. 286–308). New York: Routledge.

Mahboob, A. (2004) Native or non-native: What do the students think? In L.D. Kamhi-Stein (ed.) *Learning and Teaching from Experience: Perspectives on Nonnative English-Speaking Professionals* (pp. 121–147). Ann Arbor, MI: Michigan University Press.

Mahboob, A. (2009) Racism in the English language teaching industry. In A. Mahboob and C. Lipovsky (eds) *Studies in Applied Linguistics and Language Learning* (pp. 29–40). Newcastle upon Tyne: Cambridge Scholars Publishing.

Mahboob, A. and Szenes, E. (2010) Linguicism and racism in assessment practices in higher education. *Linguistics and the Human Sciences* 3 (3), 325–354.

Mahboob, A. and Golden, R. (2013) Looking for native speakers of English: Discrimination in English language teaching job advertisements. *Voices in Asia Journal* 1 (1), 72–81.

Mar, T.B. and Edmonds, P. (2010) Introduction: Making space in settler colonies. In T.B. Mar and P. Edmonds (eds) *Making Settler Colonial Space: Perspectives on Race, Place and Identity* (pp. 1–24). Basingstoke: Palgrave.

Marchetti, G. (1993) *Romance and the 'Yellow Peril': Race, Sex, and Discursive Strategies in Hollywood Fiction*. Berkeley, CA: University of California Press.

Marcuse, H. (1964) *One-Dimensional Man*. Boston, MA: Beacon Press.

Marx, K. (1976) *Capital: A Critique of Political Economy* (Vol. 1). London: Penguin.

Marx, K. and Engels, F. (1998) *The German Ideology*. Amherst, NY: Prometheus Books.

Marx, S. and Pray, L. (2011) Living and learning in Mexico: Developing empathy for English language learners through study abroad. *Race Ethnicity and Education* 14 (4), 507–535.

Mazrui, A.A. (2006) A sociolinguistics of 'double-consciousness': English and ethnicity in the Black experience. In J. Brutt-Griffler and C.E. Davies (eds) *English and Ethnicity* (pp. 49–74). New York: Palgrave.

McCann, M. (2012) A cultural sensitivity training for White ESL instructors. Unpublished MA thesis, Saint Mary's College of California.

McCauley, C. (2014) 'Irish alcoholism nature' reason for job rejection for Irish teacher in South Korea. *BBC News*, 6 November. See www.bbc.com/news/world-europe-29929333 (accessed 27 May 2015).

McClure, S.M. (2007) White matters: When, where, and how? *Symbolic Interaction* 30 (3), 395–408.

McKay, S.L. (1997) Multilingualism in the United States. *Annual Review of Applied Linguistics* 17, 242–262.

Michael-Luna, S. (2009) Narratives in the wild. In R. Kubota and A. Lin (eds) *Race, Culture, and Identities in Second Language Education: Exploring Critically Engaged Practice* (pp. 234–251). New York: Routledge.

Mignolo, W.D. (2009) Epistemic disobedience, independent thought and de-colonial freedom. *Theory, Culture & Society* 26 (7–8), 1–23.

Miles, R. and Brown, M. (2003) *Racism*. London: Routledge.

Milner, H.R. (2007) Race, culture, and researcher positionality: Working through dangers seen, unseen, and unforeseen. *Educational Researcher* 36 (7), 388–400.

Min, E. (2013) English speakers in Korea. In L. Wee, R.B. Goh and L. Lim (eds) *The Politics of English: South Asia, Southeast Asia and the Asia Pacific* (pp. 269–286). Amsterdam: John Benjamins.

Ministry of Culture, Sports and Tourism (n.d.) Romanization of Korean. See www.mcst.go.kr/english/koreaInfo/language/romanization.jsp (accessed 10 March 2016).

Ministry of Justice, Korea Immigration Service (2015a) *The Sojourn Guide for Foreigners*.

Ministry of Justice, Korea Immigration Service (2015b) *Visa Instruction Guide*.

Modiano, M. (2001a) Linguistic imperialism, cultural integrity, and EIL. *ELT Journal* 55 (4), 339–346.

Modiano, M. (2001b) Ideology and the ELT practitioner. *International Journal of Applied Linguistics* 11 (2), 159–173.

Moon, G. (2009) Statistics paint Korean picture. *Korea JoongAng Daily*, 15 December. See http://koreajoongangdaily.joins.com/news/article/article.aspx?aid=2913964 (accessed 5 May 2015).

Motha, S. (2006) Racializing ESOL teacher identities in U.S. K-12 public schools. *TESOL Quarterly* 40 (3), 495–518.

Motha, S. (2014) *Race, Empire, and English Language Teaching: Creating Responsible and Ethical Anti-racist Practice*. New York: Teachers College Press.

Mühlhäusler, P. (1996) *Linguistic Ecology: Language Change and Linguistic Imperialism in the Pacific Region*. London: Routledge.

Myers, B. (2016) Where are the minority professors? *The Chronicle of Higher Education*, 14 February. See http://chronicle.com/interactives/where-are-the-minority-professors (accessed 21 February 2016).

Nakayama, T.K. and Krizek, R.L. (1995) Whiteness: A strategic rhetoric. *Quarterly Journal of Speech* 81 (3), 291–309.

Norton, B. (2004) Introduction. In B. Norton and K. Toohey (eds) *Critical Pedagogies and Language Learning* (pp. 1–17). Cambridge: Cambridge University Press.

Oak, S. (2010) Healing and exorcism: Christian encounters with Shamanism in early modern Korea. *Asian Ethnology* 69 (1), 95–128.

OHCHR (2014) UN expert on racism urges the Republic of Korea to adopt a comprehensive anti-discrimination law. See www.ohchr.org/EN/NewsEvents/Pages/DisplayNews. aspx?NewsID=15147&La ngID=E (accessed 18 January 2015).

Okely, J. (1996) *Own or Other Culture*. London: Routledge.

Onishi, N. (2008) For English studies, Koreans say goodbye to dad. *The New York Times*, 8 June. See www.nytimes.com/2008/06/08/world/asia/08geese.html?_r=1& (accessed 28 April 2015).

Page, H. and Thomas, R.B. (1994) White public space and the construction of White privilege in U.S. health care: Fresh concepts and a new model of analysis. *Medical Anthropology Quarterly* 8(1), 109–116.

Paolucci, P. (2006) Race and racism in Marx's camera obscura. *Critical Sociology* 32 (4), 617–648.

Park, G. (2009) 'I listened to Korean society. I always heard that women should be this way ...': The negotiation and construction of gendered identities in claiming a dominant language and race in the United States. *Journal of Language, Identity, and Education* 8, 174–190.

Park, J.K. (2009) 'English fever' in South Korea: Its history and symptoms. *English Today* 25 (1), 50–57.

Park, J.S. (2009) *The Local Construction of a Global Language: Ideologies of English in South Korea*. Berlin: Mouton de Gruyter.

Park, J.S. (2011) The promise of English: Linguistic capital and the neoliberal worker in the South Korean job market. *International Journal of Bilingual Education and Bilingualism* 14 (4), 443–455.

Park, J.S. (2013) English, class and neoliberalism in South Korea. In L. Wee, R.B. Goh and L. Lim (eds) *The Politics of English: South Asia, Southeast Asia and the Asia Pacific* (pp. 287–302). Amsterdam: John Benjamins.

Park, J.S. (2014) Cartographies of language: Making sense of mobility among Korean transmigrants in Singapore. *Language & Communication* 39, 83–91.

Park, S. and Abelmann, N. (2004) Class and cosmopolitan striving: Mothers' management of English education in South Korea. *Anthropological Quarterly* 77 (4), 645–672.

Pennycook, A. (1994) *The Cultural Politics of English as an International Language*. London: Longman.

Pennycook, A. (1998) *English and the Discourses of Colonialism*. London: Routledge.

Pennycook, A. (1999) Introduction: Critical approaches to TESOL. *TESOL Quarterly* 33 (3), 329–348.

Pennycook, A. (2001) *Critical Applied Linguistics: A Critical Introduction*. Mahwah, NJ: Lawrence Erlbaum Associates.

Phan, L. (2008) *Teaching English as an International Language: Identity, Resistance and Negotiation*. Clevedon: Multilingual Matters.

Phillipson, R. (1992) *Linguistic Imperialism*. Oxford: Oxford University Press.

Phillipson, R. (1994) English language spread policy. *International Journal of the Sociology of Language* 107 (1), 7–24.

Phillipson, R. (2007) Linguistic imperialism: A conspiracy, or a conspiracy of silence? *Language Policy* 6 (3–4), 377–383.

Phillipson, R. (2008) The linguistic imperialism of neoliberal empire. *Critical Inquiry in Language Studies* 5 (1), 1–43.

Phillipson, R. (2009) *Linguistic Imperialism Continued*. Hyderabad: Orient Blackswan.

Piller, I. and Takahashi, K. (2006) A passion for English: Desire and the language market. In A. Pavlenko (ed.) *Bilingual Minds* (pp. 59–83). Clevedon: Multilingual Matters.

Piller, I. and Cho, J. (2013) Neoliberalism as language policy. *Language in Society* 42 (1), 23–44.

Quach, L., Jo, J. and Urrieta, L. (2009) Understanding the racialized identities of Asian students in predominantly White schools. In R. Kubota and A. Lin (eds) *Race, Culture, and Identities in Second Language Education: Exploring Critically Engaged Practice* (pp. 118–137). New York: Routledge.

Rampton, B. (1990) Displacing the 'native speaker': Expertise, affiliation, and inheritance. *ELT Journal* 44 (2), 97–101.

Rauhala, E. (2010) South Korea: Should foreign teachers be tested for HIV? *TIME*, 24 December. See http://content.time.com/time/world/article/0,8599,2039281,00.html (accessed 27 May 2015).

Rex, J. (1986) The role of class analysis in the study of race relations. In J. Rex and D. Mason (eds) *Theories of Race and Ethnic Relations* (pp. 64–83). Cambridge: Cambridge University Press.

Reyes, A. and Lo, A. (eds) (2009) *Beyond Yellow English: Toward a Linguistic Anthropology of Asian Pacific America*. Oxford: Oxford University Press.

Rivers, D.J. and Ross, A.S. (2013) Idealized English teachers: The implicit influence of race in Japan. *Journal of Language, Identity and Education* 12 (5), 321–339.

Robinson, M.E. (2007) *Korea's Twentieth-Century Odyssey: A Short History*. Honolulu, HI: University of Hawai'i Press.

Rothermund, D. (2006) *The Routledge Companion to Decolonization*. London: Routledge.

Rubin, D.L. (1992) Nonlanguage factors affecting undergraduates' judgments of nonnative English-speaking teaching assistants. *Research in Higher Education* 33 (4), 511–531.

Rubin, D.L. and Smith, K.A. (1990) Effects of accent, ethnicity, and lecture topic on undergraduates' perceptions of nonnative English-speaking teaching assistants. *International Journal of Intercultural Relations* 14 (3), 337–353.

Ruecker, T. (2011) Challenging the native and nonnative English speaker hierarchy in ELT: New directions from race theory. *Critical Inquiry in Language Studies* 8 (4), 400–422.

Ruecker, T. and Ives, L. (2015) White native English speakers needed: The rhetorical construction of privilege in online teacher recruitment spaces. *TESOL Quarterly* 49 (4), 733–756.

Saad-Filho, A. and Johnston, D. (2005) *Neoliberalism: A Critical Reader*. London: Pluto Press.

Said, E.W. (1979) *Orientalism*. New York: Vintage Books.

Said, E.W. (1985) Orientalism reconsidered. *Cultural Critique* 1, 89–107.

Schaefer, R.T. (2008) *Encyclopedia of Race, Ethnicity, and Society*. Los Angeles: Sage Publications.

Schroeder, L. (2011) Racial preference for white English teachers prevalent in Korea. *Yonhap News Agency*, 15 April. See http://english.yonhapnews.co.kr/n_feature/201 1/04/04/99/4901000000AEN20110404002300315F.HTML (accessed 23 December 2015).

Seo, D. (2011) The will to self-managing, the will to freedom: The self-managing ethic and the spirit of flexible capitalism in South Korea. In J. Song (ed.) *New Millennium South Korea: Neoliberal Capitalism and Transnational Movements* (pp. 84–100). London: Routledge.

Seth, M.J. (2002) *Education Fever: Society, Politics, and the Pursuit of Schooling in South Korea.* Honolulu, HI: University of Hawai'i Press and Center for Korean Studies, University of Hawai'i.

Seth, M.J. (2010) *A Concise History of Modern Korea: From the Late Nineteenth Century to the Present.* Lanham, MD: Rowman & Littlefield.

Seth, M.J. (2011) *A History of Korea: From Antiquity to the Present.* Lanham, MD: Rowman & Littlefield.

Shacklock, G. and Smyth, J. (eds) (1998) *Being Reflexive in Critical Educational and Social Research.* London: Falmer Press.

Shapiro, S. (2014) 'Words that you said got bigger': English language learners' lived experiences of deficit discourse. *Research in the Teaching of English* 48 (4), 386–406.

Sheffer, J.A. (2014) The optics of interracial sexuality in Adrian Tomine's *Shortcomings* and Sherman Alexie's *The Lone Ranger and Tonto Fistfight in Heaven. College Literature* 41 (1), 119–148.

Shin, C. and Stringer, J. (2005) *New Korean Cinema.* Edinburgh: Edinburgh University Press.

Shin, G. (2006a) Korea's ethnic nationalism is a source of both pride and prejudice. *Stanford: Asia-Pacific Research Center,* 2 August. See http://aparc.fsi.stanford.edu/news/koreas_ethnic_nationalism_is_a_source_of_both_pride_and_prejudice_according_to_giwook_shin_20060802 (accessed 5 May 2015).

Shin, G. (2006b) *Ethnic Nationalism in Korea: Genealogy, Politics, and Legacy.* Stanford, CA: Stanford University Press.

Shin, G. and Izatt, H.J. (2011) Anti-American and anti-alliance sentiments in South Korea. *Asian Survey* 51 (6), 1113–1133.

Shin, H. (2006) Rethinking TESOL from a SOL's perspective: Indigenous epistemology and decolonizing praxis in TESOL. *Critical Inquiry in Language Studies* 3 (2–3), 147–167.

Shin, H. (2007) English language teaching in Korea: Toward globalization and glocalization? In J. Cummins and C. Davidson (eds) *International Handbook of English Language Teaching* (pp. 75–86). New York: Springer.

Shin, H. (2015) Everyday racism in Canadian schools: Ideologies of language and culture among Korean transnational students in Toronto. *Journal of Multilingual and Multicultural Development* 36 (1), 67–79.

Shohamy, E. (2013) The discourse of language testing as a tool for shaping national, global, and transnational identities. *Language and Intercultural Communication* 13 (2), 225–236.

Shohamy, E. and Gorter, D. (2009) *Linguistic Landscape: Expanding the Scenery.* New York: Routledge.

Shuck, G. (2006) Racializing the nonnative English speaker. *Journal of Language, Identity, and Education* 5 (4), 259–276.

Skutnabb-Kangas, T. (1990) Legitimating or delegitimating new forms of racism – the role of researchers. *Journal of Multilingual and Multicultural Development* 11 (1–2), 77–100.

Smith, L.T. (2012) *Decolonizing Methodologies: Research and Indigenous Peoples.* London: Zed Books.

Song, H. (2013) Deconstruction of cultural dominance in Korean EFL textbooks. *Intercultural Education* 24 (4), 382–390.

Song, J. (2009) Between flexible life and flexible labor: The inadvertent convergence of socialism and neoliberalism in South Korea. *Critique of Anthropology* 29 (2), 139–159.

Song, J.Y. (2011) Globalization, children's study abroad, and transnationalism as an emerging context for language learning: A new task for language teacher education. *TESOL Quarterly* 45 (4), 749–758.

Song, J.Y. (2016) Emotions and language teacher identity: Conflicts, vulnerability, and transformation. *TESOL Quarterly* 50 (3), 631–654.

Spencer, S. (2006) *Race and Ethnicity: Culture, Identity and Representation*. London: Routledge.

Spiegel, M. (2011) The academic analysis of the 2008 financial crisis: Round 1. *Review of Financial Studies* 24 (6), 1773–1781.

Springer, S. (2012) Neoliberalism as discourse: Between Foucauldian political economy and Marxian poststructuralism. *Critical Discourse Studies* 9 (2), 1–15.

Stephan, M. (2006) Musings of a Black ESL instructor. In A. Curtis and M. Romney (eds) *Color, Race, and English Language Teaching: Shades of Meaning* (pp. 107–120). Mahwah, NJ: Lawrence Erlbaum Associates.

Sterzuk, A. (2015) 'The standard remains the same': Language standardisation, race and othering in higher education. *Journal of Multilingual and Multicultural Development* 36 (1), 53–66.

Strother, J. (2007, July 9) Ethnic bias seen in South Korea teacher hiring. See NPR website: http://www.npr.org/templates/story/story.php?storyId=11826937 (accessed 6 May 2015).

Stryker, S. (1968) Identity salience and role performance: The relevance of symbolic interaction theory for family research. *Journal of Marriage and the Family* 30 (4), 558–564.

Stryker, S. and Serpe, R.T. (1982) Commitment, identity salience and role behavior: Theory and research example. In W. Ickes and E.S. Knowles (eds) *Personality, Roles, and Social Behavior* (pp. 199–218). New York: Springer.

Sung, C.C. (2011) Race and native speakers in ELT: Parents' perspectives in Hong Kong. *English Today* 27 (3), 25–29.

Takahashi, K. (2013) *Language Learning, Gender and Desire: Japanese Women on the Move*. Bristol: Multilingual Matters.

Talmy, S. (2010) Becoming 'local' in ESL: Racism as resource in a Hawai'i public high school. *Journal of Language, Identity & Education* 9 (1), 36–57.

Tan, P.K. (2008) The English language as a commodity in Malaysia: The view through the medium-of-instruction debate. In P.K. Tan and R. Rubdy (eds) *Language as Commodity Global Structures, Local Marketplaces* (pp. 106–121). London: Continuum.

Tan, P.K. and Rubdy, R. (2008) *Language as Commodity: Global Structures, Local Marketplaces*. London: Continuum.

Tannen, D. and Wallat, C. (1987) Interactive frames and knowledge schemas in interaction: Examples from a medical examination/interview. *Social Psychology Quarterly* 50 (2), 205–216.

Tao, H. (2007) A corpus-based investigation of *absolutely* and related phenomena in spoken American English. *Journal of English Linguistics* 35(1), 5–29.

Taylor, E., Gillborn, D. and Ladson-Billings, G. (2009) *Foundations of Critical Race Theory in Education*. New York: Routledge.

Taylor, L. (2006) Wrestling with race: The implications of integrative antiracism education for immigrant ESL youth. *TESOL Quarterly* 40 (3), 519–544.

TESOL (2012) A principles-based approach for English language teaching policies and practices: A TESOL white paper March 2012, March 1. See http://www.tesol.org/docs/pdf/a-principles-based-approach-for-english-language-teaching-policies-and-practices-.pdf?sfvrsn=0 (accessed 5 May 2015).

Trofimovich, P. and Turuševa, L. (2015) Ethnic identity and second language learning. *Annual Review of Applied Linguistics* 35, 234–252.

Tupas, T.R. (2008) Anatomies of linguistic commodification: The case of English in the Philippines vis-à-vis other languages in the multilingual marketplace. In P.K. Tan and R. Rubdy (eds) *Language as Commodity Global Structures, Local Marketplaces* (pp. 89–105). London: Continuum.

Turnbull, S.R. (2008) *The Samurai Invasion of Korea, 1592–98*. Oxford: Osprey.

Turner, J.H. (2012) *Contemporary Sociological Theory*. London: Sage.

van Dijk, T.A. (1988) *News as Discourse*. Hillsdale, NJ: Lawrence Erlbaum Associates.

van Dijk, T.A. (1993) *Elite Discourse and Racism*. London: Sage Publications.

van Dijk, T.A. (1997) *Discourse as Structure and Process*. London: Sage.

van Dijk, T.A. (2007) *Discourse Studies* (Vol. 1). London: Sage.

van Dijk, T.A. (2008) *Elite Discourse and Racism*. London: Sage.

VanVolkenburg, M. (2010) Data says it all: E-2s are law abiding. *The Korea Herald*, 30 March. See www.koreaherald.com/view.php?ud=%2020091006000065&cpv=0 (accessed 10 March 2016).

VanVolkenburg, M. (2012) Three decades of black face in Korea [Web log post], March 5. See http://populargusts.blogspot.com/2012/03/three-decades-of-black-face-in-korea. html (accessed 5 May 2015).

Veracini, L. (2010) *Settler Colonialism: A Theoretical Overview*. Basingstoke: Palgrave.

Vološinov, V.N. (1973) *Marxism and the Philosophy of Language*. New York: Seminar Press.

Wa Thiong'o, N. (1981) *Decolonising the Mind: The Politics of Language in African Literature*. Harare: Zimbabwe Publishing House.

Wagner, B.K. and VanVolkenburg, M. (2012) HIV/AIDS tests as a proxy for racial discrimination? A preliminary investigation of South Korea's policy of mandatory in-country HIV/AIDS tests for its foreign English teachers. *Journal of Korean Law* 11, 179–245.

Waters, M.C. (1990) *Ethnic Options: Choosing Identities in America*. Berkeley, CA: University of California Press.

Watts, R.J. (2011) *Language Myths and the History of English*. Oxford: Oxford University Press.

Weber, M. (1968) *Economy and Society: An Outline of Interpretive Sociology*. Berkeley, CA: University of California Press.

Weems, C.N. (1962) *Hulbert's History of Korea* (Vol. 1). New York: Hillary House.

West, C. (1988) CLS and a liberal critic. *The Yale Law Journal* 97 (5), 757–771.

Williams, R.A. Jr (1985) Small steps on the long road to self-sufficiency for Indian Nations: The Indian Tribal Governmental Tax Status Act of 1982. *Harvard Journal on Legislation* 22, 335–397.

Woolgar, S. (ed.) (1988) *Knowledge and Reflexivity: New Frontiers in the Sociology of Knowledge*. London: Sage.

Wright, W.E. (2007) Heritage language programs in the era of English-only and No Child Left Behind. *Heritage Language Journal* 5 (1), 1–26.

Wu, F.H. (2002) *Yellow: Race in America beyond Black and White*. New York: Basic Books.

Yang, G. and Ryser, T.A. (2008) Whiting up and blacking out: White privilege, race, and *White Chicks*. *African American Review* 42 (3/4), 731–746.

Yook, C. and Lindemann, S. (2013) The role of speaker identification in Korean university students' attitudes towards five varieties of English. *Journal of Multilingual and Multicultural Development*, 34 (3), 279–296.

Zhang, H., Chan, P.W. and Kenway, J. (2015) *Asia as Method in Education Studies: A Defiant Research Imagination*. London: Routledge.

Index